P9-CKU-728

The Seasonal Cabin Cookbook

Photos by Teresa Marrone
Illustrations by Julie Martinez
Book and Cover Design by Jonathan Norberg

3rd Printing

Copyright 2001 by Teresa Marrone

All rights reserved. No part of this book may be reproduced in any manner whatsoever without written permission except in the case of brief quotations embodied in critical articles or reviews.

Published by Adventure Publications, Inc.
820 Cleveland St. S.
Cambridge, MN 55008
1-800-678-7006
ISBN: 1-885061-79-X
First printing March 2001

The Seasonal Cabin Cookbook

by Teresa Marrone

Adventure Publications, Inc.
Cambridge, MN

Table of Contents

Introduction

Cabin life runs on a different pace than everyday life. Because you're free of the 9-to-5 schedule of the workaday world, your routines are likely to be less structured. Breakfast doesn't have to be a bagel-and-coffee over the kitchen sink at 7:45 while waiting for the car pool. Lunch isn't just the event that occurs between 11:45 and 12:45. Dinner doesn't have to be orchestrated to sandwich precisely between the end of the kids' soccer practice and the start of the evening aerobics class at the gym. At the cabin, you can kick back and watch a loon dive for its breakfast, pack a picnic lunch to take on a hike, and enjoy a leisurely dinner while watching the sunset.

In the city, we tend to lose track of the rhythm of the seasons. We know that in December we should wear a coat and in July we probably shouldn't, but we are separated from the things that make the change of seasons so interesting. In the city, we can go to the supermarket and buy fat domesticated blueberries in December. In the woods, we have to wait until July to pick tiny wild blueberries. But our patience is rewarded, for the wild blueberries we pick have far more flavor than their domestic cousins. As a bonus, we've had the pleasure of hiking through the woods and up the ridgeline where the sun makes the berries plump and ripe, and of enjoying the view of the lake in the distance as we picked.

This book is written to celebrate the change of the seasons, and to help you enjoy foods that are perfect for a cabin setting. The recipes in the book generally use ingredients that are easy to find, even at a small-town grocery. With few exceptions, these recipes are designed to be prepared with minimal fuss, in a kitchen that may not include all the conveniences of home. Each season features a food highlight (or two) that is particular to that time of year. In the spring, you'll learn about foraging for—and cooking—that most elusive of wild edibles, the morel mushroom. Summer is perfect for big parties, and the pig-roasting information in this book will tell you everything you need to know, from cooking to carving to cleanup. There's also a section on that blueberry-picking trip mentioned above, with recipes for the harvest (and yes, you can use store-bought blueberries in these recipes). Autumn is hunting season, so you'll find recipes for venison and other game to help you enjoy the rewards of the chase. Finally, you'll read about the art of making maple syrup in late winter, along with some recipes featuring raw maple sap and finished maple syrup.

Each chapter also includes a host of recipes for breakfast, light meals, appetizers, main dishes, vegetables, side dishes and desserts. You'll learn how to make your own variations on basic dishes such as potato salad, cobblers and other baked-fruit desserts, wraps of all sorts, layered dips and other fare. There are recipes that kids will enjoy making as well, such as ice cream churned in a coffee can, homemade play-dough, cinnamon ornaments and easy-to-make frozen pops.

Whether you're headed for the family cabin on a lake, a rental unit in a resort complex, or a primitive hunting shack, you'll find something in this book that will enhance your mealtimes away from home. It's also perfect for RVers living on the grid. You may even find yourself reaching for this book when you want to prepare simple, tasty food in your home kitchen. When did you say that aerobics class starts?

Advice on Equipment and Provisions

If you own your cabin (or RV), you have the luxury of furnishing it with some basic equipment and a simple pantry of staples. Rental cabins are a bit of a gamble. More than once, I've been unable to find some basic piece of equipment such as a can opener, a pot with a lid—any lid—or a sharp knife at a rental cabin. I've learned to carry along some basic kitchen necessities in a wooden "kitchen box," which I will detail below.

For those lucky enough to have their own place, here are some basics you may want to include in your cabin kitchen. If you keep an eye out at tag sales and secondhand stores, you can pick up most of these items for very little money.

Cookware

- 10-inch cast-iron or other heavy-bottomed skillet
- Dutch oven or large pot; a lid is essential
- Small, medium and large saucepans (at least one of each; lids are highly recommended)
- If your cabin has an oven: cookie sheet, muffin pan, 9x13x2-inch baking dish, 8- or 9-inch-square baking dish, optional broiling pan
- Griddle (optional, but very nice for pancakes, French toast, etc.)

Utensils and gadgets

- Large sharp knife such as a 10-inch chef's knife
- Small, sharp paring knife
- Stiff boning knife
- Bread knife or serrated knife (for slicing bread or tomatoes)
- Flexible fillet knife, especially if you fish
- Two or three large spoons for stirring and serving
- Potato masher
- Vegetable peeler

continued

- Whisk
- Pastry brush and/or basting brush
- Two metal spatulas
- Large slotted spoon
- Tongs (I like to have one long tongs and one short tongs)
- Garlic press (optional, but very handy)
- Instant-read thermometer (also optional, but very handy)
- Grating box or board
- Skewers for grilling
- Meat mallet/tenderizer
- Rotary-type eggbeater (unless you have an electric hand mixer)
- Wire-mesh strainer
- Large colander (optional, but a very good item to have)
- Corkscrew
- Can opener and church key (the opener that pokes triangular holes in a can)
- Grapefruit spoons (useful for coring fruit as well as eating grapefruits)
- Forks, spoons and table knives for 6 or more people
- Serving plates and bowls, both small and large if possible
- Small, medium and large mixing bowls (these can double as serving bowls also)
- Cutting board
- Measuring cup and measuring spoons

Optional equipment if your cabin has electricity

- Electric hand mixer
- Blender or food processor
- Deep fryer (the small Fry-Daddy units work very well at the cabin)
- Crock pot
- Electric skillet
- Waffle iron
- Drip coffee maker

Miscellaneous supplies

- Kitchen string
- Toothpicks
- Freezer tape
- Dish soap
- Towels, sponges and washing cloths
- Foil, plastic wrap, plastic bags, garbage bags

A basic pantry, all stored in insect-proof containers

These can be kept year-round even in an unheated cabin:

- Salt
- Pepper (in a peppermill, if possible; fresh-ground pepper is far superior to pre-ground)
- Seasoned salt, celery salt, onion salt, garlic salt (any or all)
- Spice blends such as blackening spices
- Flour
- Pancake mix (I particularly like the ones made by Sturdiwheat Company out of Red Wing, Minnesota; they have some great "just add water" mixes that are perfect for cabin life)
- Sugar (brown and white for sure, and possibly powdered)
- Oatmeal
- Baking soda
- Baking powder
- Sweet spices: cinnamon and nutmeg are the most common, but others such as allspice are nice if you have room
- Dried herbs: thyme, oregano and marjoram are the most common, but others such as rosemary, tarragon and basil are nice if you have room
- Dry mustard powder
- Crushed dried hot red pepper flakes and/or dried hot peppers
- Granulated bouillon or soup bases (although I don't like to use bouillon because it is so salty, it makes an acceptable broth substitute in a pinch; bases have a better flavor, but are more perishable and some need refrigeration)

continued

These should be removed if it gets below freezing in your area:

- Honey
- Maple syrup (real maple syrup needs to be refrigerated once opened)
- Soy sauce, teriyaki sauce (these keep indefinitely)
- Vegetable oil, olive oil
- Vinegar (white vinegar is the most basic, but wine vinegars are essential in my opinion; I also use cider vinegar and rice vinegar frequently)
- Tabasco sauce
- Worcestershire sauce
- Peanut butter
- Canned pineapple and/or other fruit
- Canned tomatoes and tomato sauce
- Canned broth: chicken, beef and/or vegetable
- Canned concentrated soup such as cream of mushroom
- Canned sliced olives
- Canned tuna and/or salmon
- Tinned anchovies
- Canned or bottled tomato juice
- Vacuum-packed smoked salmon (a luxury item that is very useful)

Refrigerator staples

- Mustard, including yellow and Dijon; grainy mustard is good if you have room
- Ketchup
- Pickles, both sweet and dill
- Mayonnaise or salad dressing
- Horseradish, if you like it
- Butter or margarine
- Real maple syrup
- Jams, jellies and preserves

Essentials for rental cabins

If you are traveling to rental cabins or resorts, I advise you—strongly—to bring a few essentials. I have a wooden box that contains a few food staples, as well as small essential kitchen implements. Here are the contents of my box; I replenish supplies after each trip as needed.

- Quart jar of flour
- Small jar of white sugar
- Strong plastic zip-top bag of brown sugar
- Small jar of instant coffee (I hate this stuff, but it has saved my sanity a few times)
- Small jar of powdered coffee creamer
- Tabasco sauce
- Small bottle of soy sauce
- Small bottle of olive oil
- Small bottle of vegetable oil
- Small bottle of white wine vinegar
- Small bottle of dish soap
- Small bottle of hand lotion
- Can of cinnamon
- Salt and pepper
- Several spice and herb blends, including seasoned salt
- Can of salmon (used as a threat: "If we don't catch any fish, we'll have to eat salmon patties")
- Can of baked beans
- Large serving/stirring spoon
- Small wooden spatula
- Carving fork (comes in handy for all sorts of things)
- Two small, sharp knives in sturdy sheaths (very important, for safety and also to keep the knives sharp as they kick around in the box)
- Sharp 10-inch-long knife in sturdy sheath
- Grater board
- Long-handled tongs

continued

- Miscellaneous silverware, contained in a sturdy plastic bag
- Another sturdy plastic bag with the following: folding waiter-style corkscrew, vegetable peeler, church key, small rotary can opener, grapefruit spoon, small serrated knife, a few twist-ties, a hunk of kitchen string, a cork in case one breaks
- Paper plates
- Paper coffee filters
- An assortment of plastic zip-top bags
- Large plastic garbage bags
- Several large pieces of foil, folded into smaller squares
- Two small plastic containers with lids (for leftovers)
- Two café-style wine glasses (no stems, short and chunky so they're less likely to break)
- Two large plastic glasses
- Small roll of freezer tape
- Old prescription bottle filled with toothpicks

As you can see, this is a lot of stuff to fit into a relatively small box (mine is just 18x12x10 inches). I've rigged it with corrugated-cardboard dividers to organize the space. This also makes it easier to get at things, because I don't have to remove everything to get to something that is at the bottom of the box. My wooden box also has holes in the side that act as carrying handles. If you can't find a wooden box, you can rig up a similar system with the plastic tote boxes that are sold at office-supply stores and home-supply stores; these boxes also have the advantage of sealing tightly with a plastic lid, discouraging mice.

Substitutions and Measurements

Most recipes aren't really as rigid as they might seem. If a recipe calls for walnuts but you have none, or if you don't like them, it's probably OK to leave them out (unless the title of the recipe is something like Walnut Cake). Amounts for ingredients such as garlic and other spices can be changed to suit your preference. And if you want to use more cheese to top a baked dish, or use pears instead of apples in a salad, who's to stop you? The Culinary Police aren't out patrolling to make sure you adhere strictly to a recipe. In fact, the only recipes for which I routinely measure are baked goods such as cakes or quick breads; with most other recipes, I admit that I belong to the dump-and-pour school. Once you become comfortable in the kitchen, you can get away with this, too.

However, the essence of cabin cooking is making do with what's on hand, or what is readily available. On the facing page are some easy substitutions for a few common items.

Missing ingredient	Substitution
1 cup milk	1 cup water mixed with 4 tablespoons powdered milk
1 cup milk	½ cup water mixed with ½ cup canned evaporated milk
1 cup buttermilk	1 cup regular milk mixed with 1 tablespoon vinegar; let stand 5 minutes
1 cup heavy cream	¾ cup whole milk mixed with ⅓ cup melted butter
1 cup sour cream	⅞ cup yogurt mixed with 3 tablespoons melted butter
1 teaspoon baking powder	¼ teaspoon baking soda and ½ teaspoon cream of tartar
1 tablespoon cornstarch	2 tablespoons flour
1 teaspoon fresh herb	Generous ¼ teaspoon dried herb
1 cup beef or chicken broth	1 cup water mixed with 1 teaspoon liquid or dry bouillon
1 cup honey	1¼ cups white sugar mixed with ⅓ cup water
¼ cup bread crumbs	1 slice stale bread, torn or chopped

There are also a few basic measurements that every cook needs to know. Here is a simple list for reference.

1 tablespoon	3 teaspoons; ½ fluid ounce
⅛ cup	2 tablespoons; 1 fluid ounce
¼ cup	4 tablespoons
⅓ cup	5 tablespoons plus 1 teaspoon
½ cup	8 tablespoons
¾ cup	12 tablespoons
1 cup	16 tablespoons; 8 fluid ounces
1 pint	16 fluid ounces; 2 cups
1 quart	32 fluid ounces; 2 pints; 4 cups
1 gallon	128 fluid ounces; 4 quarts; 8 pints; 16 cups

Spring

Table of Contents

Vegetables, Starches and Side Dishes

Desserts and Sweets

Beverages and Miscellaneous

The Rites of Spring: Morel Mushroom Season

My love affair with morels and morel-mushroom picking goes back about 15 years. Each spring, as the snows recede in my home state of Minnesota, I begin to get a special flutter when I look outside. How soon will it be before the ground is open, and the fiddlehead ferns start poking their heads out of the warming earth? Is that a leaf I see on the neighbor's oak tree? Are the lilac buds starting to swell? All of these things are natural indicators of morel growth.

Generally, my first foray into the woods is in mid-April. It's said that hope springs eternal in the human breast, and although I know odds are good that the mushrooms won't be up for at least two weeks, I still enjoy these first springtime treks. And there is always the possibility of an early season. Typically, the forest floor looks undressed. The lack of leaves on the scrubby trees, as well as scant undergrowth, makes it easy to see through the forest and easy to walk (a distinct difference from the conditions during the height of the morel season). I enjoy watching migrating spring warblers and other seldom-seen songbirds, and often catch a glimpse of a deer nosing among the underbrush for tender twigs.

I also become a dedicated weather-watcher during this time. Overnight temperatures need to be generally above 40°F, with daytime highs in the sixties, before morels appear. Rain is a major factor, too; even if all other conditions are right, the morels won't grow if the woods are bone-dry. The best weather is a combination of warm days, mild evenings and gently soaking springtime rains several times each week.

Suddenly, it happens. Overnight, I notice that the lilac buds are beginning to show color. The ferns are uncurling. And a quick check of the neighbor's oak tree reveals leaves the size of a squirrel's ear. As I enter the woods, I note that the prickly ash are leafing out nicely, especially on south-facing slopes. It's time to get serious about my pursuit.

Morel picking is a pleasant but serious hobby. Proper apparel makes the difference between an enjoyable jaunt in the woods and a nightmare of scratches, insect bites and turned ankles. My standard outfit starts with jeans or other sturdy long pants; I tuck the cuffs into thick socks to prevent unwanted insect intrusion up my leg (unfortunately, wood tick season coincides with morel season). Beat-up tennis shoes provide flexibility and grip on slopes. Sometimes I wear high-top hiking boots or unlined rubber-and-leather pac boots, which provide better ankle support in rough terrain. I usually wear a T-shirt and a corduroy jacket. Later in the season as the weather warms, I trade the jacket for a long-sleeved canvas shirt. Bug spray is de rigueur, and a baseball cap with a wide bill keeps the sun out of my eyes as I am climbing or looking up slopes.

Where, exactly, does one find wild morels? Sadly, the available picking grounds diminish every year in most areas. Urban sprawl is gobbling up the old woodlots, small rough-and-tumble green-spaces, and farm shelterbelts that make up so much of the good morel habitat around larger cities. From my first trip into the morel woods 15 years ago, to this year's expeditions, I have watched as over 50 percent of the areas I used to pick were bulldozed and paved over to become home to shopping strips, condos and endless highways.

I vividly remember a small woodlot in one of Minneapolis' second-tier suburbs, where I had enjoyed several years of morel bounty. This was the sort of place where kids built treehouses and buried messages in bottles as time "capsules." It was on the edge of a developed area containing single- and multiple-family homes, and afforded a pleasant greenspace as well as habitat for thrushes, wrens, bluebirds and all sorts of butterflies. One year I headed for this "honey hole" only to find that the trees had been replaced by a large, upscale grocery store and parking lot. I was hot and thirsty from my previous stop, so went into the store for a bottle of water. I could scarcely believe my eyes when I saw morel mushrooms in the produce department, selling for $25 per pound. I felt like flagging down the produce manager, grabbing him by the apron and informing him that, the previous year, I had picked several pounds of morels from the exact spot where the meat counter now sat. And just last year, a friend and I went to one of my secret spots only to find the bulldozers at work, tearing out the mushroom host trees as we watched. Last fall, I drove by the spot and noticed that it now holds the usual strip-mall accoutrements: a video-rental store, a tanning parlor, a convenience grocery and a mostly empty parking lot. None of the trees were left standing.

However, the good news is that there are still many places to find morels, even around big cities. I have the best luck around recently dead elm trees. The most productive trees seem to be those that are about as big around as a man's thigh, and still have most of their bark intact. That's not to say that you won't find morels around a dead matriarch elm tree that has lost all its bark, or in the middle of a grassy field. In many places, morel hunters favor old oak trees, abandoned apple

orchards, or areas of the boreal forest that have been burned by a forest fire the previous year.

I focus on dead elm (left). Since Dutch elm disease is still making its rounds, there are more dead elm trees each year, creating new morel hunting grounds. Dead elms are easy to identify from a distance. Their spiky branches stick out of the surrounding green trees in a very distinctive way. I admit to being a menace on the roadways at this time of year, as I drive along with one eye on the road and one eye on the groves ahead. I prefer to let a friend do the driving, so I can keep both eyes peeled for a possible morel site.

In urban areas, older industrial parks that are surrounded by tree belts make good starting points, and generally, no one cares if you walk in the woods in such places. Corridors along rivers are another good spot to investigate. At the edges of the city, shelterbelts on farms are often productive, but it's wise to ask permission before entering private woods. But I will pick them where I see them, even if it is in the middle of a city park or on a freeway greensward.

In rural or undeveloped areas where cabins and resorts are likely to be, it's easier to find spots to pick. Find a forested area with the proper sort of trees. You may want to ask a local resident for help in finding areas with dead elm, old orchards, or burned-over pine woods. An island in the middle of a lake can be a secret spot that doesn't get any picking traffic. Also, you'll usually have better luck if you get off the beaten path. Try walking down a hiking trail to get away from areas that are easy to drive to. I've even stumbled across morels in the middle of a sandy resort compound in Wisconsin. I wouldn't recommend searching out such places, however, because the likelihood of success is remote. Also, the sand is really hard to get out of the morel folds!

When I'm looking for morels, I take an approach akin to divination. I let my mind go blank. Then I begin scanning the ground, keeping a mental picture of the morel's distinctive honeycomb cap. I'll also frequently scan the forest ahead, looking for that unique dead elm silhouette. Elm trees are easy to identify. Break off a chunk of bark from the dead tree, then look at the cross section of the bark. Elm bark is layered with white and dark striations, as though the bark was light one year, dark the next.

Once you've found a likely-looking tree, begin scanning the ground near the base, working outward in a circle. Morels can grow as far as 10 feet from the base of a good tree. If you find one mushroom, stop and work the area thoroughly. Use a stick to bend small plants and to push aside dead leaves; morels are often hidden by such ground detritus. If searching in a hilly area, work your way uphill rather than downhill. The mushrooms are easier to spot when you're looking uphill, because you get a better view underneath ground-hugging plants.

Fresh morels have a unique smell that is at once earthy, woodsy and sweet. Several times, I have found a patch of morels by following my nose. This is more likely to happen in the warmer days toward the end of the season, when the mushrooms are large and the earth is warm. When considering size, be aware that there are a number of different morel subspecies, which can vary in size from an inch high to almost a foot tall. Also, color ranges from creamy white, to golden yellow, to tan, to dusky gray. The first morels to appear are usually the smaller, darker-colored variety, which are hard to spot. As the season progresses, you'll start finding the white, tan and yellow varieties. Usually these are an inch and a half to 3 inches tall. If you see the giant "bigfoots" that are as high as a foot, you'll know that the season is almost over. This usually coincides with the last bloom of the lilacs.

Morels are easy to identify—once you find them, that is! True morels are completely hollow and don't have any sort of gill structure at all; the cap flows smoothly into the stem. This can be clearly seen when the mushroom is cut in half from top to bottom. This smooth attachment of the cap to the stem is the key to identifying the true morel. The stems of "half-free" morels are attached to the cap midway or all the way to the top of the stem, exhibiting an arrowhead or skirt-like shape when halved. There is some debate as to the edibility of the half-free morel, so I avoid them. The huge, dark-colored false morel is not likely to be confused with the true morel. The interior is not hollow; rather it is filled with pockets of soft tissue, giving a multi-chambered impression, and the stems appear nearly solid (like ordinary button mushrooms). Some people react violently to false morels, while others experience no ill effects. The best advice is to leave them in the ground.

Keep in mind that this book is a cookbook, not a guidebook. Therefore, you should always rely on the guidance of an expert morel picker until you're certain that what you're picking is a true morel. I've taught 8-year-old kids to pick morels and they do quite well at it. However, I always examine their baskets afterward to be sure they haven't stumbled across something that is not a true morel. There are many excellent guidebooks available, and these can be quite helpful to the novice picker.

All morels need to be cleaned before cooking. I always cut them in half from top to bottom, which serves to confirm the identity of the mushroom as well as to dislodge any insect or slug inhabitants. Although many morel fanciers would be horrified to hear this, I put the mushrooms in a sinkful of cold water, then scrub each one very gently with a soft mushroom brush. Some people believe the morels will soak up water and become bland if you wash them, but this has not been my experience. When the mushrooms are clean, I rinse them and place them on a towel or cake-cooling rack to dry a bit before refrigerating. Fresh morels can be stored in a vented plastic bag in the refrigerator for a week or longer. If I'll be taking them to the cabin, I arrange a row of mushrooms on a paper towel so they don't touch one another, then roll the paper towel to enclose the mushrooms. Then I add another row, roll that, and repeat these steps until the paper towel is full. I place the rolls in a zip-top plastic bag, and keep them refrigerated.

For longer storage, or if you've really hit the jackpot, dry or freeze some of your morels. I routinely used to dry all my extra morels, but I have since given this up. Although they taste fine, reconstituted dried morels don't have a very pleasing texture. Nowadays, I dry only the mushrooms I need to make dried-food mixes for camping, and I freeze the rest. To freeze, simply sauté cleaned mushrooms, halved or chopped coarsely, as you prefer, in a generous amount of butter until they are barely tender. Cool the mixture, then transfer to small freezer containers with the butter and all juices. To use, simply thaw and treat as though they have been freshly fried. I think you'll be amazed the first time you pull a batch of morels from the freezer in January; the flavor and aroma will instantly transport you back to the freshness of the springtime morel woods.

MOREL CREAM SAUCE

4 servings

This is the absolute best way to fix fresh morels and is heavenly on freshly caught walleye or other fish. It also makes a tasty sauce for rice or mashed potatoes.

2 cups fresh morels, halved, quartered or coarsely chopped (about ¾ pound)
1 tablespoon plus 1 teaspoon butter or margarine
2 teaspoons flour
1 cup cream or half-and-half
1 tablespoon snipped fresh chives, optional

In large skillet, sauté the morels in the butter over medium heat, stirring occasionally, until mushrooms are just tender. Push the mushrooms, which will have reduced considerably in volume, to the side of the skillet, then sprinkle the flour over the butter in the center of the skillet, stirring constantly to prevent lumps. Cook, stirring constantly, for about a minute, then swirl the pan so all the butter and mushroom juices are incorporated into the flour. When the flour thickens and bubbles, stir the mushrooms back into the mixture and add the cream, stirring constantly; cook until sauce thickens and bubbles. Stir in chives, and salt and pepper to taste.

MOREL, SPRING ONION, ASPARAGUS AND BRIE PIZZA

4 servings

Morels, asparagus and spring onions all appear at about the same time and pair up nicely in this elegant pizza.

1 tablespoon butter or margarine
1 tablespoon olive oil or vegetable oil
¼ pound morels (about 10-12 medium), halved or quartered
2 teaspoons finely minced garlic
1 pre-baked focaccia-style crust, about 9 inches across and ½ inch thick
4 green onions, thinly sliced
¼ cup cooked asparagus tips
3 ounces Brie cheese with the rind

Heat oven to 425°F. In large skillet, melt the butter in the oil over medium-low heat. Add the morels and garlic. Cook, stirring occasionally, until mushrooms have softened and released their juices. Increase heat to medium and cook for about a minute; most of the mushroom liquid will be absorbed. Remove from heat.

Place the focaccia on a round baking sheet. Use a pastry brush to gather the oil and garlic from the bottom of the skillet, then brush it over the top and edges of the focaccia. Sprinkle the green onions evenly over the focaccia. Arrange the mushrooms, cut-side down, over the onions. Nestle the asparagus tips between the mushrooms. Sprinkle generously with salt and pepper. Slice the Brie, including the rind, thinly and arrange over the mushrooms and asparagus, covering as completely as possible. Place in oven, then reduce heat to 400°F and bake until cheese is bubbly and the edge of the crust is browned, 10 to 12 minutes.

Morel Soup

6 to 8 servings

If you've got a really big haul of mushrooms, splurge and make a batch of this creamy, delicious soup. If your harvest is not that great but you still want soup, add sliced white button mushrooms to fill out the amount; the soup will not be as flavorful, but it will still be good.

½ cup minced onion
½ cup thinly sliced celery
¼ cup butter or margarine (half of a stick)
4 cups coarsely chopped fresh morels (about 1½ pounds)
3 tablespoons flour
3 cups chicken broth
4 cups whole milk, or a combination of milk and half-and-half
½ teaspoon salt
¼ teaspoon nutmeg

In very large saucepan or Dutch oven, sauté onion and celery in butter over medium heat until vegetables are tender. Add morels and cook, stirring occasionally, until mushrooms have softened and released their juices. Sprinkle the flour over the vegetables, stirring constantly, and cook until the juices thicken. Add chicken broth slowly, stirring constantly. Heat to boiling; reduce heat and simmer about 10 minutes. Stir in milk, salt and nutmeg; cook about 5 minutes longer. Taste for seasoning and adjust as necessary.

Breakfast and Brunch Dishes

ALMOND-RHUBARB COFFEE CAKE

9 servings

Here's a recipe that's perfect for springtime. I've had it in my file for years and don't know where the original came from, but I have altered it over time to suit my tastes. I've pencilled "excellent!" in the corner, and I hope you enjoy it as much as I do.

1¼ cups buttermilk baking mix such as Bisquick
½ cup packed brown sugar
½ cup milk (2% milk works fine)
1 egg
½ teaspoon vanilla extract
¾ cup finely diced rhubarb
½ cup sliced almonds, divided
¼ cup white sugar
1 tablespoon flour
1 tablespoon cold butter or stick margarine, cut into small pieces

Heat oven to 350°F. Spray a 9-inch-square baking dish with nonstick spray, or butter lightly. In mixing bowl, combine baking mix, brown sugar, milk, egg and vanilla; beat well with a mixer or whisk. Stir in the rhubarb and ¼ cup of the almonds. Spread the mixture evenly in the prepared baking dish; it will be a thin layer, and this is normal.

In a small mixing bowl, combine the remaining ¼ cup almonds with the white sugar, flour and butter. Rub together with your fingers, or cut together with two forks, until the mixture is crumbly. Sprinkle evenly over the rhubarb mixture. Bake until a toothpick inserted in the center comes out clean, 25 to 35 minutes. Best served warm.

Pull-Apart Raisin-Cinnamon Loaf

10 servings

Refrigerated biscuits make this breakfast treat easy; raisins and cinnamon make it tasty. This needs to be baked in a small loaf pan; you can often find disposable foil loaf pans that are just right.

¼ cup packed brown sugar
¼ cup white sugar
½ teaspoon cinnamon
3 tablespoons butter or margarine
1 tube (10 ounces/10 biscuits) refrigerated flaky buttermilk biscuits
About ½ cup raisins

Heat oven to 350°F. Spray a small loaf pan (7¼ x 3½ x 2 inches) with nonstick spray, or butter lightly. Combine sugars and cinnamon in a small bowl. Place the butter in a small microwave-safe bowl and melt on LOW power; or, melt in a saucepan and pour into a small bowl. Separate biscuits. Dip the top of a biscuit into the melted butter, then into the sugar, pressing down gently. Put the biscuit, sugar-side up, on your work surface and top with a few raisins. Butter and sugar the top of another biscuit, then put it on top of the raisin-topped biscuit and add a few raisins to the second biscuit. Continue until you've used all the biscuits; if the "tower of biscuits" threatens to fall over near the end, simply lay it on its side, keeping the biscuits pressed together, and continue; or, enlist the aid of a helper to keep the stack upright. When adding the last biscuit to the stack, don't add any raisins. Carefully transfer the assembled loaf to the prepared loaf pan; drizzle the remaining butter over the top, and sprinkle with the remaining sugar mixture. Bake until loaf is light golden brown, 30 to 40 minutes. Cool loaf slightly before removing from pan. Serve warm.

Egg-in-a-Basket

Per serving

This classic recipe is a great weekend breakfast that kids particularly love.

1 slice bread
1½ to 2 teaspoons butter or margarine, divided
1 egg

Use a small glass or cookie cutter (or paring knife) to cut a 1½- to 2-inch-diameter hole in the bread. In small skillet,* melt 1½ teaspoons butter over medium heat. Add the bread and the circle and coat quickly with melted butter. Turn the bread and the circle to coat the second side with butter. Cook until the bread is nicely golden brown on the side that's down. Turn the bread and the circle, and add the remaining ½ teaspoon butter to the hole inside the bread if the skillet seems dry. Break the egg into the hole, taking care not to break the yolk. Salt and pepper to taste (seasoned salt is very good). Cook until the bottom of the egg is set and the bread is golden brown. Flip the slice and put the circle on the egg in the hole; cook until the egg is desired doneness.

*If you're making more than one of these at a time, use a skillet that is just large enough to hold the number of bread slices you'll be making; otherwise, the butter on the edges of the pan will burn.

Baked Egg Nests

Per serving

Similar to the Egg-in-a-Basket recipe on the previous page, this recipe uses a thick slice of French bread and tops it off with a little cheese.

1 inch-thick slice French bread, at least 3 inches across
2 teaspoons butter or margarine, softened
1 egg
A few drops of Tabasco sauce, optional
2 tablespoons shredded cheddar or other cheese

Heat oven to 375°F. Use nonstick spray to lightly coat a baking sheet or dish that is just large enough to hold all the egg nests you'll be cooking. Pull out some bread from the center of each bread slice to form a cup, being careful not to tear the edges and leaving a small amount of bread at the bottom (if you accidentally break through the bottom, the recipe will still work but it may not look as nice). Butter the top and bottom of the bread, and place in the prepared baking dish. When all pieces of bread you are fixing are in the baking dish, carefully break 1 egg into each cup. Sprinkle with salt and pepper and add a drop or two of Tabasco sauce to each egg. Top each with shredded cheese. Bake until egg whites are just set but yolks are still runny (8 to 10 minutes), or until eggs are completely hard if you prefer (12 to 15 minutes).

FRENCH TOAST

4 servings (2 slices each); easily adjusted to make more or less

Use any bread you have on hand to make French toast; traditionally, it is made with bread that is a bit too stale to enjoy in sandwiches. I particularly like thick-sliced French bread, or raisin-cinnamon bread.

1 cup milk, or slightly more as needed
3 eggs; have another ready in case you need it during cooking
1 teaspoon vanilla extract, optional
A pinch of salt
Butter or margarine for frying; you'll need 2 to 4 tablespoons
8 slices bread
Syrup, butter or margarine, powdered sugar, jam, etc., for serving

You may want to heat the oven to 250°F to keep the first pieces of French toast warm while you make the rest of it, but this is optional; you can also serve it as you cook it.

Use a pint measuring cup for the milk, then beat in the eggs, vanilla and salt; pour mixture into a wide bowl or 8-inch-square baking dish (alternately, combine ingredients in the wide bowl or baking dish and beat). Add about 2 teaspoons butter to a large skillet or griddle and melt over medium heat; in the meantime, place 3 or 4 slices bread into the egg mixture, turning to coat. When the butter stops sizzling, lift the bread from the egg mixture, allowing excess mixture to drip back into the bowl, and add to the skillet in a single layer. Cook, turning once, until the bread is golden with brown spots on both sides. Transfer to a plate and keep warm while you prepare the remaining bread, using additional butter for each batch; if the egg-milk mixture starts to run out, simply beat in another egg and a little more milk. Serve with syrup and butter, or other toppings as you prefer.

Variations:

French Toast with a Kick: Substitute 1 tablespoon Drambuie, Cointreau (orange-flavored liqueur), Kahlua, Irish Cream or other cordial or liqueur for the vanilla; you may want to heat the liquor for a minute or two to cook off some of the alcohol. Proceed as directed.

Cinnamon-Roll French Toast: Substitute 4 wide, flat cinnamon rolls (the kind that are made by coiling dough into a circle) for the bread. Cut each roll in half horizontally, so you end up with two thinner circles. Add 1 additional egg and ½ cup milk (for a total of 1½ cups milk) to the batter. Soak the rolls in the egg batter 5 to 10 minutes, turning once or twice, before frying.

BAKED DENVER FRENCH TOAST SANDWICHES

4 servings; easily adjusted to make more or less

Serve this easy dish with some fresh fruit salad for a wonderful brunch.

1 cup diced onion
1 cup diced red or green bell pepper, or a mix of the two
1 tablespoon butter or stick margarine, plus additional for greasing baking dish
1½ cups diced ham (about ½ pound)
4 large eggs, or 5 medium eggs
½ cup whole milk or half-and-half
½ teaspoon salt
8 slices white or soft whole-wheat bread (slightly stale bread is OK)
4 thin slices American or other cheese (slices should be about the same size as the bread, or slightly smaller; pre-sliced cheeses found in the dairy case work well)

In medium skillet, sauté the onion and pepper in the butter over medium heat, stirring frequently, until vegetables are tender-crisp. Add ham and cook, stirring frequently, for about 5 minutes; if the ham releases a lot of liquid, cook a bit longer until the liquid has cooked away. This may be done the night before you plan to serve the French toast sandwiches; place the vegetable/ham mixture in a dish, cover and refrigerate.

When ready to assemble the French toast sandwiches, heat oven to 375°F. Generously grease a 9-inch-square baking dish* with butter or nonstick spray. Combine eggs, milk and salt in a wide bowl; beat well with a fork. Dip a slice of bread into the egg mixture, coating both sides well; transfer to the prepared dish and repeat with 3 more slices of bread, arranging the bread in a single layer. Top each slice of bread with ¼ of the vegetable/ham mixture, spreading it almost to the edges of the bread. Top with the cheese slices. Dip remaining 4 slices bread into the egg mixture and place over the cheese. Pour any remaining egg mixture evenly over the sandwiches. Let the sandwiches stand about 10 minutes. Cover dish with foil and bake 15 minutes; remove foil and bake 5 minutes longer. Turn on the broiler and place the sandwiches under the broiler for about a minute, until golden brown (if you don't have a broiler, continue baking sandwiches a few minutes longer, until they are just firm when pressed lightly with your finger). Use edge of spatula to cut between each sandwich, then carefully remove each sandwich with the spatula.

*The sandwiches must fit snugly in the pan in a single layer; if the pan is too large, the extra egg mixture will burn. A 9-inch-square pan is perfect for 4 sandwiches; a 9x13-inch pan works great if you increase the recipe by half to make 6 sandwiches. If your pan is larger than it should be for the number of sandwiches you are preparing, make an insert that is the proper size using heavy-duty foil. Grease the foil very well, as the bread will stick to it; remove the cooked sandwiches carefully with a spatula.

SWEET FLAVORED BUTTERS

These take just minutes to make (except for the Honey Butter, which is easy but a little more involved), and keep for weeks in the refrigerator. Use them to top pancakes or waffles; to spread on warm biscuits or toast; or, to garnish a bowl of hot cereal.

Maple Butter: In mixing bowl, cream 1 stick softened butter until fluffy. With mixer running, slowly pour 1 cup maple syrup into the butter; beat until smooth and light. Makes about 1¼ cups.

Orange Spice Butter: In mixing bowl, cream 1 stick softened butter until fluffy. Add 3 tablespoons honey, 1½ teaspoons grated orange rind, ½ teaspoon cinnamon and ¼ teaspoon nutmeg; beat until smooth and light. Makes about ⅔ cup.

Cranberry Butter: In small saucepan, melt 1 stick butter over low heat. Add ¼ cup cranberry relish and stir well to blend. Remove from heat and stir until cooled. Makes about ⅔ cup.

Piña Colada Butter: In small saucepan, melt 1 stick butter over low heat. Add ¼ cup thawed piña colada concentrate (found with the frozen juices); remove from heat and stir until cooled. Makes about ⅔ cup.

Honey Butter: In medium saucepan, melt 1 stick butter over low heat. Stir in ¼ cup honey; remove from heat and cool to room temperature, whisking or beating with a fork occasionally. Place the saucepan in the refrigerator; as the mixture starts to cool, remove the saucepan from the refrigerator and whisk the mixture every few minutes to blend in the honey, then return the saucepan to the refrigerator. Continue whisking every few minutes until the mixture is chilled and light in color. Makes about ⅔ cup.

Light Meals, Lunch Dishes and Soup

Chicken Salad with Variations

A mix of dark and light meat produces the most flavorful chicken salad; however, all-white-meat chicken salad looks more elegant, so feel free to use what you like. For ease of preparation, buy already-cooked chicken from the deli or takeout restaurant; one average roasted chicken will provide 3 to 4 cups boneless meat. You can also find cooked boneless chicken chunks in the freezer case at the grocery; one 9-ounce package contains about 2 cups, perfect for these recipes. But for the best flavor of all, nothing beats a home-roasted or grilled chicken; try to save some leftovers next time you cook a whole chicken, so you can make delicious chicken salad the next day.

The chicken should be cut or shredded into pieces that are ¼ to ½ inch in size before measuring; 7 to 9 ounces of boneless, skinless chicken meat should equal 1½ to 2 cups. Although the recipes on pages 34-37 call for chicken, you can freely substitute turkey for the chicken. Each recipe makes 4 to 6 servings; the recipes with more ingredients beyond the basics make the higher number of servings. Serve chicken salad on bread, croissants or lettuce leaves. All recipes are easily doubled.

BARE-BONES CHICKEN SALAD

1½ to 2 cups cooked, diced boneless chicken meat
¾ cup diced celery
½ to ¾ cup mayonnaise or salad dressing (reduced-fat works fine)

In mixing bowl, combine chicken and celery. Sprinkle generously with salt and pepper; use onion salt or seasoned salt for more flavor if you like. Toss gently to combine the seasonings with the chicken. Add ½ cup of the mayonnaise and toss gently to coat; add additional mayonnaise if needed for desired texture.

Variations:

Lighter-Tasting Chicken Salad: Substitute up to ¼ cup sour cream for an equal amount of mayonnaise in the main recipe.

Herbed Chicken Salad: Add 1 to 2 tablespoons chopped fresh herbs (tarragon is particularly good). For more color, also add a tablespoon or two of minced fresh parsley.

Chicken salad add-ins: Add **one or two** of the following:

- 2 green onions, minced
- 2 tablespoons sweet or dill pickle relish, or finely chopped pickles
- ¼ cup chopped nuts (cashews are very good) or roasted, salted sunflower nuts
- ½ teaspoon dry mustard powder, or 1 teaspoon prepared Dijon or other mustard
- ¼ teaspoon Tabasco sauce

CHICKEN SALAD WITH CURRY DRESSING

Dressing:
⅓ cup mayonnaise (reduced-fat works fine)
⅓ cup sour cream (reduced-fat works fine)
2 tablespoons lime juice
1 tablespoon honey
½ teaspoon curry powder blend
¼ teaspoon salt, or to taste

1½ to 2 cups cooked, diced boneless chicken meat (7 to 9 ounces)
¾ cup seedless red grape halves
½ cup sliced celery (⅛-inch slices; if stalks are wide, cut lengthwise before slicing)
¼ cup slivered blanched almonds
½ cup diced red onion

Combine dressing ingredients in large mixing bowl; stir well to blend. If you have time, cover and refrigerate 1 to 2 hours to allow flavors to blend; if not, proceed as directed below.

Add remaining ingredients, stirring gently to coat; taste for seasoning and adjust as necessary. Serve on lettuce leaves or use as sandwich filling; croissants or pita breads are particularly good with this salad.

Variation:

Substitute cubed cantaloupe (seeds and rind removed before cutting into ½-inch cubes) for the grapes, increasing quantity to 1 cup. Substitute 3 green onions, thinly sliced, for the red onion. Proceed as directed.

WALDORF CHICKEN SALAD

½ cup mayonnaise (reduced-fat works fine)
¼ cup sour cream (reduced-fat works fine)
½ teaspoon salt
1½ to 2 cups cooked, diced boneless chicken meat (7 to 9 ounces)
1 cup diced apple
1 cup diced celery
½ cup coarsely chopped walnuts

In mixing bowl, stir together mayonnaise, sour cream and salt. Add remaining ingredients; taste for seasoning and add additional salt if necessary.

TEX-MEX CHICKEN SALAD

Dressing:
⅓ cup vegetable oil
¼ cup red wine vinegar
2 tablespoons lime juice, preferably freshly squeezed (from about 1 lime)
½ teaspoon chili powder blend
¼ teaspoon salt
A pinch of sugar

1½ to 2 cups cooked, diced boneless chicken meat (7 to 9 ounces)
¼ cup diced red onion
3 tablespoons chopped fresh cilantro leaves
3 tablespoons chopped pimientos or roasted red bell peppers
1 avocado, diced, optional
1 can (2¼ ounces) sliced ripe olives, drained

Combine all dressing ingredients in a mixing bowl; whisk until very well blended (alternately, you could put the ingredients in a small glass jar, cover tightly and shake to blend). Add remaining ingredients; taste for seasoning and add additional salt if necessary.

CHUTNEY CHICKEN SALAD

3 tablespoons mango chutney or other chutney
½ cup mayonnaise (reduced-fat works fine)
¼ cup sour cream (reduced-fat works fine)
1½ to 2 cups cooked, diced boneless chicken meat (7 to 9 ounces)
3 green onions, sliced ⅛ inch thick
1 stalk celery, diced
¼ cup slivered blanched almonds, or coarsely chopped cashews

Chop chutney into smaller pieces if necessary. Combine in mixing bowl with mayonnaise and sour cream; stir well. Add remaining ingredients; taste for seasoning and add a sprinkle of salt if necessary.

TORTELLINI SALAD

8 cups; 4 main-course or 8 side-dish servings

This makes a wonderful luncheon or light supper dish. It travels well and is great to take to a picnic or potluck dinner.

1 package (9 ounces) refrigerated or frozen cheese-stuffed tortellini
¼ cup fresh basil leaves, optional
¼ cup slivered blanched almonds
2 cups coarsely shredded cooked chicken meat (remove skin and bones before shredding and measuring)
1 roasted red bell pepper (page 299), cut into ½-inch pieces
8 ounces mozzarella cheese, cut into ½-inch cubes
1 jar (6 ounces) marinated artichoke hearts, drained and cut into 1-inch pieces
16 pitted ripe olives, cut into halves
10 cherry tomatoes, quartered
Half of a small red onion, cut into thin wedges from top to bottom and separated
½ to ¾ cup bottled Italian dressing or Hearty Italian Vinaigrette (page 99)

Cook tortellini in boiling water according to package directions. Drain and rinse; set aside until cool. Roll basil leaves up and slice into thin strips; set aside. In small cast-iron or heavy-bottomed skillet, toast almonds over medium heat, stirring constantly, until they begin to color. Transfer immediately to a large mixing bowl. Add remaining ingredients except dressing. Add basil strips and cooled tortellini to bowl. Add ½ cup dressing and toss gently to coat; add additional dressing until desired consistency.

Even easier: Substitute one 7.25-ounce jar roasted red bell peppers for the homemade roasted pepper. Drain and pat dry before cutting into ½-inch pieces.

TOSSED TACO SALAD

4 to 6 servings

Some people like to eat this salad immediately after it's tossed, so the chips are still quite crunchy. I prefer to let it mellow in the refrigerator for an hour or two first, so the chips become pleasantly chewy rather than crunchy.

1 pound ground beef*
1 envelope (1.25 ounces) taco seasoning mix*
1 can (8 ounces) kidney beans, drained
1 can (4 ounces) diced green chiles, drained, optional
½ cup Catalina or Thousand Island dressing
¼ cup taco sauce
Half of a small head lettuce, cut into 1-inch pieces
1 large or 2 medium tomatoes, cut into ¾-inch chunks
½ cup diced onion
1 cup shredded cheddar or colby-Jack cheese
1 can (2¼ ounces) sliced ripe olives, drained, optional
Half of a 15-ounce bag salted but not flavored tortilla snack chips, crushed lightly into 1-inch pieces

In medium skillet, brown ground beef over medium heat, stirring to break up. Drain excess grease. In measuring cup, stir taco seasoning mix into ¾ cup water; add to skillet. Simmer, stirring occasionally, until thickened, about 10 minutes. Remove half of the meat and save for another use if desired.* Add beans and diced chiles to meat remaining in skillet.

While meat is cooking, combine dressing and taco sauce in measuring cup or small bowl; stir to blend. Combine remaining ingredients in a very large bowl. Add meat-bean mixture and dressing mixture; toss well. Serve immediately, or cover and refrigerate an hour or two before serving.

*When I make this salad, I cook a pound of ground beef with the envelope of taco seasoning mix and water as described, then save half of the meat mixture to use for spur-of-the-moment burritos, tacos or other uses. If you like a really meaty salad, you may use the entire pound of beef in the salad; or, fry up just ½ pound of ground beef, using half of the taco seasoning mix and ½ cup water.

TABBOULEH SALAD

4 to 6 servings

Plan ahead to make this delicious Mideastern salad because bulgur can be hard to find (look in the ethnic foods aisle of a large city supermarket, or in a health food store or ethnic grocery). Stuff this into a pita bread for a delicious sandwich, or serve as a side dish with grilled meats.

1 cup medium bulgur
2 cups boiling water
¼ cup freshly squeezed lemon juice (from about 1 lemon)
¼ cup olive oil
½ teaspoon minced fresh oregano leaves, or scant ¼ teaspoon dried
½ teaspoon salt
¼ teaspoon ground allspice, optional
¼ teaspoon pepper
3 tomatoes, cored and seeded, cut into ¼-inch dice
1 bunch green onions, minced
1 cup chopped fresh parsley (do not substitute dried parsley)
3 tablespoons chopped fresh mint leaves, optional

Combine bulgur and boiling water; soak 30 to 45 minutes. Meanwhile, in large bowl, combine lemon juice, oil, oregano, salt, allspice and pepper; whisk or beat well with a fork to blend. Add tomatoes and green onions; stir to combine. Set aside. When the bulgur is tender, drain in a fine-mesh colander, pressing on the bulgur with your hands to squeeze out excess moisture. Add to the bowl with the tomatoes; add parsley and mint, and stir well. This can be served immediately, or allowed to mellow awhile before serving; cover and refrigerate if not serving within the hour.

HEARTY CAESAR PASTA SALAD

3 or 4 main-dish lunch servings

This pasta salad has a twist: lettuce adds crisp texture, and chunks of seafood or chicken make it a satisfying lunch. Serve with breadsticks and a pitcher of iced tea, or some light white wine.

4 ounces (about 1 cup) macaroni or other small pasta shape such as shells or rotini (uncooked)
1 package (8 ounces) imitation crab sticks or chunks, or 8 ounces boneless, skinless cooked chicken
2 cups romaine or crisp lettuce pieces (cut or torn into 1-inch pieces before measuring)
2 green onions, thinly sliced
¼ cup shredded Parmesan cheese
3 tablespoons finely diced celery
⅓ cup bottled Caesar salad dressing*

In a large pot of boiling salted water, cook macaroni until just tender; drain and rinse well with cold water. While macaroni is cooking, cut or shred crab or chicken into bite-sized chunks and place in a large mixing bowl. Add lettuce, green onions, Parmesan cheese and celery to mixing bowl. When macaroni is cool and excess water has drained off, add to mixing bowl and stir gently to combine all ingredients. Add salad dressing, stirring gently to coat.

*If your Caesar salad dressing is very spicy or strong (as some bottled dressings are), replace a tablespoon or so of the dressing with mayonnaise.

BUFFALO CHICKEN WITH VARIATIONS

Servings depend on variation used

Here's a versatile recipe that can be used to make appetizers, main-dish kabobs, sandwiches or a tasty main-dish salad. If you like really spicy Buffalo Chicken, substitute habañero sauce for part—or all—of the Louisiana hot sauce.

The basic Buffalo marinade:

¼ cup butter or margarine (half of a stick)
5 tablespoons Louisiana hot sauce (I prefer Crystal, but Tabasco will work also)
1 teaspoon white vinegar
1 packet (.65 ounce) dry Italian salad dressing mix

1 pound boneless, skinless chicken breasts or thighs, trimmed of excess fat and cut as directed in specific variations below

In saucepan, melt butter over low heat (or place in microwave-safe baking dish and melt at MEDIUM/50% power). Blend in hot sauce, vinegar and salad dressing mix. Marinate the chicken in the sauce 45 minutes at room temperature, or up to 4 hours refrigerated, turning chicken occasionally in the marinade. Continue as directed in specific variations below.

BUFFALO BOBS (APPETIZER OR MAIN DISH)

6 to 8 appetizer servings, or 4 main-dish servings

In addition to the basic ingredients, you will also need:

1 medium white or yellow onion
Blue cheese dressing (purchased, or made from recipe on page 98)

Cut chicken into 1-inch cubes; marinate as directed. While chicken marinates, cut onion into 1-inch chunks, then separate the chunks so each piece is about ½ inch thick. When ready to cook, prepare medium-hot grill. Thread chicken cubes onto metal skewers, alternating with onion pieces. Arrange kabobs on grill, then cover grill immediately to prevent flare-ups. Grill until chicken is cooked through, about 15 minutes, turning several times; onions will be slightly crunchy. Serve with blue cheese dressing.

BUFFALO CHICKEN STRIPS OR NUGGETS (APPETIZER)

6 to 8 appetizer servings

In addition to the basic ingredients, you will also need:
1 cup flour
Oil for pan-frying (about ¾ cup)
Celery sticks, optional
Blue cheese dressing (purchased, or made from recipe on page 98)
Sweet-and-sour sauce, optional

Cut chicken into 1-inch-wide strips or 1½-inch cubes, as you prefer; marinate chicken as directed. Place flour in a medium-sized paper bag. When ready to cook, heat oven to 300°F. Drain chicken pieces slightly and drop a few at a time into the bag with the flour; shake well to coat. Place coated pieces in a single layer on a plate or baking sheet; repeat until all pieces have been coated. Heat about ⅛ inch oil in a skillet over medium-high heat. When oil is hot, add a single layer of chicken pieces and cook until crispy and browned on all sides, turning as necessary with tongs. Transfer cooked chicken to paper-towl-lined baking sheet and keep warm in the oven while you fry the remaining chicken (add more oil to the skillet if necessary). Serve chicken with celery sticks, and bowls of blue cheese dressing and sweet-and-sour sauce for dipping.

Variation:

Cook in a deep fryer rather than in a skillet.

BUFFALO CHICKEN SANDWICHES

4 servings

In addition to the basic ingredients, you will also need:
¾ cup flour
Oil for pan-frying (you will need about ½ cup)
4 sandwich buns or English muffins, or 8 slices bread
Lettuce leaves for garnish
Blue cheese dressing (purchased, or made from recipe on page 98)

Note: For this recipe, it's more important to have the correct number of chicken pieces than the exact total weight. For chicken breasts: use 2 boneless, skinless breast half portions; cut each portion in half so you have a total of 4 pieces. For chicken thighs: use 4 boneless, skinless thighs. Pound each breast portion or thigh lightly with a meat mallet or the edge of a heavy plate so pieces are approximately equal in thickness. Marinate chicken pieces as directed.

When ready to cook, drain chicken slightly and dip in flour; shake off excess. Heat about ⅛ inch oil in a large skillet over medium-high heat. When oil is hot, add chicken and cook until crispy and browned, 4 to 5 minutes per side (if your skillet isn't large enough to hold all 4 pieces comfortably, cook 2 pieces at a time, then transfer the cooked chicken to a warm oven while you cook the remaining pieces). While chicken cooks, toast the bread or English muffins if using; buns are also good toasted, but this is not necessary. Drain chicken briefly on paper towels. Place on buns; top with lettuce. Serve blue cheese dressing on the side as a dip. This also makes an excellent cold sandwich.

BUFFALO CHICKEN SALAD

4 servings

In addition to the basic ingredients, you will also need:
8 cups torn mixed salad greens
1 cup shredded carrot
¾ cup thinly sliced celery (2 or 3 stalks)
¾ cup flour
Oil for pan-frying (about ½ cup)
½ cup hulled roasted, salted sunflower nuts or broken cashew pieces
2 cups croutons, optional
1 cup alfalfa sprouts, optional
Blue cheese dressing (purchased, or made from recipe on page 98)

Follow portioning, pounding and marinating instructions for Buffalo Chicken Sandwiches, facing page. While chicken marinates, distribute lettuce evenly among 4 dinner plates or wide, shallow bowls. Divide carrot and celery evenly among plates. Cover plates and refrigerate until serving time if this is done in advance.

When ready to cook, drain chicken slightly and dip in flour; shake off excess. Heat about ⅛ inch oil in a large skillet over medium-high heat. When oil is hot, add chicken and cook until crispy and browned, 4 to 5 minutes per side (if your skillet isn't large enough to hold all 4 pieces comfortably, cook 2 pieces at a time, then transfer the cooked chicken to a warm oven while you cook the remaining pieces). Slice each chicken portion into strips, and arrange on top of individual salad. Sprinkle each serving with 2 tablespoons sunflower nuts and ½ cup croutons. Top each with ¼ cup alfalfa sprouts. Serve blue cheese dressing on the side, allowing each person to add as much as desired (it's nice to serve each person a small bowl of dressing on the side).

VEGETARIAN BUFFALO TOFU SANDWICHES OR SALAD

4 servings

No kidding! Firm tofu makes an excellent substitute for chicken in this delicious vegetarian option.

Follow the recipe above for either Buffalo Chicken Sandwiches or Buffalo Chicken Salad, substituting a 1-pound block of firm tofu for the chicken. Slice the tofu into 4 equal portions. Proceed as directed, handling tofu as gently as possible during marinating, flouring and frying.

Sloppy Joe Variations

I'll let you in on a secret of cookbook authors: often, our concoctions are based simply on what we have on hand. Looking in the fridge, we figure, "That half-can of tomato paste could be used to make … and how about if I added some … a dash of this ought to help …" and suddenly, we have a recipe! To the reader, it seems carved in stone; but in reality, most recipes are fluid and can adapt to a variety of ingredients. Here are some examples featuring the humble Sloppy Joe. By all means, feel free to vary these based on the ingredients you have on hand; simply pay attention to the total amount of liquid and seasonings that you're altering, and it will work out fine. All recipes make 5 or 6 servings.

STANDARD SLOPPY JOES

1 pound lean ground beef
¾ cup diced onion
¾ cup barbecue sauce or 1 can (10½ ounces) condensed tomato soup
2 teaspoons sugar, optional
1 teaspoon prepared mustard
1 teaspoon celery salt or plain salt
Hamburger buns

In medium skillet, brown ground beef over medium heat, stirring to break up. Add onion and cook, stirring frequently, until onion is tender. Drain excess grease if necessary; if there is less than a tablespoon, leave the drippings in for flavor. Add barbecue sauce, sugar, mustard and salt. Cook over medium-low heat for 10 minutes, stirring occasionally. Serve in hamburger buns.

SLOPPY MARYS

One time after a Bloody Mary party, I had extra Bloody Mary mix left over, and needed to clean out the refrigerator. A Sloppy Joe-type mix seemed like a good solution.

¾ cup diced onion
½ cup diced celery, or a mix of celery and green bell pepper
2 teaspoons vegetable oil
1 pound lean ground beef
¾ cup flat beer, beef or chicken broth, or water
½ cup Bloody Mary mix or tomato juice
¼ cup tomato paste (you may substitute ½ cup ketchup; reduce beer to ½ cup)
2 tablespoons packed brown sugar
1 tablespoon chili powder blend
1 tablespoon Worcestershire sauce
1 or 2 teaspoons Tabasco sauce, optional
Hamburger buns

In medium skillet, sauté onion and celery in oil over medium heat, stirring occasionally, until just tender. Add ground beef and cook, stirring to break up, until meat is no longer pink. Drain excess drippings if necessary. Add beer, Bloody Mary mix, tomato paste, brown sugar, chili powder and Worcestershire sauce. Heat until bubbling, then reduce heat and simmer, stirring occasionally, 20 minutes or until thickened. Taste for seasoning and stir in Tabasco sauce if desired, and salt and pepper to taste. Heat an additional 5 minutes. Serve in hamburger buns.

SLOPPY JOSÉS

1 pound lean ground beef
½ cup prepared thick-and-chunky salsa
½ cup bottled taco or enchilada sauce
Cornbread, corn muffins or hamburger buns
Shredded Monterey Jack or colby-Jack cheese for garnish, optional

In medium skillet, brown ground beef over medium heat, stirring to break up. Drain excess grease. Add salsa and enchilada sauce. Cook over medium heat 10 minutes, stirring occasionally; if mixture is too juicy, cook a bit longer until excess liquid cooks away. Serve open-faced over cornbread or split corn muffins, or in hamburger buns; sprinkle with shredded cheese.

SLOPPY JOSEFS

4 slices thick-cut bacon
8 ounces fresh mushrooms, chopped
½ cup diced onion
1 pound lean ground beef
1 can (8 ounces) sauerkraut, drained and rinsed
2 tablespoons packed brown sugar
½ cup sour cream (reduced-fat works fine)
Hamburger buns

In large skillet, cook bacon over medium-low heat until crisp. Transfer bacon to paper towels. Add mushrooms and onion to skillet with drippings; cook over medium heat, stirring frequently, until vegetables are tender and any liquid from the vegetables has cooked away. Add ground beef and cook, stirring to break up, until meat is no longer pink. Drain excess grease from skillet. Crumble bacon and add to skillet. Add sauerkraut and brown sugar; cook until sauerkraut is hot, stirring occasionally. Blend sour cream into skillet and cook until mixture is bubbly, stirring frequently. Serve in hamburger buns.

SLOPPY TOMS

Here's an alternative that's lower in fat, but just as good as the traditional Sloppy Joe.

1 pound ground turkey
½ cup diced onion
1 stalk celery, diced
1 can (10½ ounces) condensed light cream of mushroom soup
2 tablespoons pickle relish with juice
1 tablespoon honey
2 teaspoons Dijon mustard
½ cup warm water
Hamburger buns

In medium skillet, cook ground turkey over medium heat, stirring frequently to break up, until meat is no longer pink; if meat is sticking, add a little vegetable oil. Add onion and celery. Cook, stirring frequently, until vegetables are tender. Add condensed soup, pickle relish, honey, mustard and the warm water. Cook over medium heat 15 minutes or until mixture is thickened, stirring occasionally. Serve in hamburger buns.

EASY CLAM CHOWDER

6 servings

¼ pound bacon (about 6 slices), cut into ½-inch pieces
1 medium onion, diced
½ cup diced celery
¼ cup flour
2 cups heavy cream
2 cups whole milk or canned evaporated skim milk
2 cans (7½ ounces each) minced clams with juice
½ teaspoon salt
¼ teaspoon white pepper (preferably) or regular black pepper
2 cups frozen "southern-style" hashbrowns (cubed, not shredded), thawed
Tabasco sauce for serving

In Dutch oven or large saucepan, cook bacon over medium-low heat until crisp, stirring occasionally. Add onion and celery; increase heat to medium and continue cooking until vegetables are tender. Sprinkle the flour over the vegetables, stirring constantly to prevent lumps; cook, stirring constantly, until mixture thickens and bubbles. Add first the cream, then the milk, slowly to the vegetable mixture, stirring constantly to prevent lumps. Cook about 2 minutes longer, stirring occasionally. Add the clams with their juices, and the salt and pepper. Heat just to boiling, then reduce heat and simmer about 15 minutes, stirring occasionally. Add cubed hashbrowns and cook about 15 minutes longer. Have a bottle of Tabasco sauce on the table so people can add it to taste.

Variation:

Easy Clam-Corn Chowder: Follow recipe above, reducing hashbrowns to 1½ cups. Add ¾ cup thawed frozen corn to the soup along with the potatoes. Proceed as directed.

Beer-Cheese Soup

6 to 8 servings

½ cup finely chopped onion
¼ cup butter (half of a stick)
6 cups whole milk
½ cup flour
1½ pounds pasteurized process cheese sauce such as Cheez Whiz
½ teaspoon onion salt, celery salt or garlic salt
½ teaspoon Worcestershire sauce
¼ teaspoon Tabasco sauce
1 bottle or can (12 ounces) beer
Popped popcorn or snipped fresh chives for garnish, optional

In large saucepan, sauté the onion in the butter over medium heat until the onion is tender. Meanwhile, heat the milk until just warm in another saucepan; cover and remove from heat. When the onion is tender, sprinkle the flour over the onion, stirring constantly to prevent lumps; cook, stirring constantly, until mixture thickens and bubbles. Add the warm milk slowly to the onion mixture, stirring constantly to prevent lumps. Cook about 2 minutes longer, stirring occasionally. Reduce heat to medium-low and gradually stir in the cheese sauce, stirring constantly until the cheese melts. Add the onion salt, Worcestershire sauce and Tabasco sauce; heat a minute longer, then taste for seasoning and adjust as necessary. Just before serving, add the beer and cook over medium-low heat, stirring frequently, until the mixture is hot. Garnish individual servings with popcorn or chives.

Appetizers and Snacks

SMOKED SALMON PÂTÉ

6 to 8 appetizer servings

Keep a vacuum-packed box of salmon in the cupboard so when unexpected company drops in, you can wow them with this quick-and-easy spread. Chilled champagne makes a wonderful beverage with this elegant appetizer.

½ pound smoked salmon, skin and bones removed before weighing
½ cup butter (1 stick), softened
¼ cup freshly squeezed lemon juice (from about 1 lemon)
2 tablespoons snipped fresh chives, optional
⅛ teaspoon black pepper
A good pinch of cayenne pepper, or ⅛ teaspoon Tabasco sauce
Crackers or hot buttered toast points for serving

In food processor work bowl, combine all ingredients except accompaniments. Pulse on-and-off until salmon is finely chopped and everything is well mixed. Mound into a pretty serving bowl and serve with crackers or toast.

Gyros Meatballs

About 35 1-inch meatballs

True gyros are roasted in large cakes on vertical spits. The cook slices off slivers of crusty meat for a sandwich, exposing additional meat to the heat so it, too, becomes deliciously crisp. These meatballs capture the flavor of gyros, without special equipment. If you wish, make larger meatballs and serve as a main course, perhaps accompanied by Tabbouleh Salad (page 40) or a salad tossed with Greek Vinaigrette (page 98).

1 pound ground lamb
2 tablespoons dry white wine
2 teaspoons finely minced fresh oregano leaves, or ¾ teaspoon dried
2 teaspoons finely minced fresh basil leaves, or ¾ teaspoon dried
1 teaspoon finely minced fresh mint leaves, or ½ teaspoon dried
1 teaspoon minced or pressed garlic
¾ teaspoon salt
½ teaspoon paprika
¼ teaspoon ground allspice
¼ teaspoon pepper
1 tablespoon olive oil or vegetable oil
Half of a small red onion, thinly sliced into quarter-rings
2 teaspoons flour
1 cup plain yogurt
Pita breads for accompaniment

In a mixing bowl, combine the lamb, wine, oregano, basil, mint, garlic, salt, paprika, allspice and pepper. Mix very well with your hands for about 2 minutes. Cover and refrigerate at least 2 hours, or as long as overnight.

When you're ready to cook, shape the meat into 1-inch meatballs. Heat the oil in a large skillet over medium heat. Add the meatballs and brown well on all sides. Use a slotted spoon to transfer the meatballs to a dish and set aside. Add the onions to the drippings in the skillet and cook, stirring occasionally, until the onions are just tender. Transfer the onions to the dish with the meatballs. Discard excess grease from the skillet. Add ½ cup water to the skillet, stirring to loosen any browned bits; cook until the liquid has reduced to about half volume. Mix the flour with about a tablespoon of cold water and add to skillet; cook for about a minute, stirring constantly. Stir in the yogurt and heat until small bubbles appear around the sides. Return the meatballs and onions to the skillet. Reduce heat and simmer, stirring occasionally, for about 10 minutes, or until meatballs are cooked through. Serve with a basket of pita quarters.

GYROS BURGERS

3 servings

Follow recipe on facing page for mixing the meat with the spices; cover and refrigerate as directed. When ready to cook, divide the meat into 3 equal portions and shape into 3½-inch-wide patties. Grill or broil to desired doneness. Serve in pita bread halves (or on hamburger buns) with raw sliced onions and plain yogurt for garnish.

BACON-HORSERADISH CREAM CHEESE LOG

8 to 10 appetizer servings

For an even easier appetizer, simply spoon the mixture into a pretty bowl rather than rolling into a log. Sprinkle parsley on top just before serving.

2 packages (8 ounces each) cream cheese, softened
4 green onions, thinly sliced
1 tablespoon prepared horseradish
1½ teaspoons garlic salt
¼ pound bacon (about 6 slices), cooked crisp, drained and crumbled
About ½ cup chopped fresh parsley, or finely chopped walnuts or pecans
Crackers for serving (hearty crackers, such as pumpernickel and wheat, work best)

Combine cream cheese, green onions, horseradish and garlic salt in large mixing bowl; stir well to blend. Add crumbled bacon and stir gently until just combined. Transfer cheese mixture to a sheet of waxed paper, then roll into a log, using the waxed paper to help shape the cheese. Wrap tightly and refrigerate at least 1 hour; this can be done a day in advance. When ready to serve, unwrap the log and roll in parsley. Place on a platter and surround with crackers.

Chutney-Cheese Ball

6 to 8 appetizer servings

I've had a hand-written copy of this recipe in my file for years and no longer remember where I got it. It's delicious, and I hope it becomes part of your recipe file, too!

⅓ cup chutney and liquid
1 teaspoon lemon juice
½ teaspoon curry powder blend
1 clove garlic, pressed or very finely minced
1 package (8 ounces) cream cheese, softened
½ cup chopped pecans
Crackers, carrot sticks, celery sticks, etc., as accompaniments

Chop chutney into small pieces. In medium mixing bowl, combine chopped chutney and liquid with lemon juice, curry powder and garlic; stir to mix well. Add cream cheese and stir until well blended. Shape into a ball, then roll in chopped pecans. Wrap and refrigerate at least 1 hour before serving with crackers or vegetables.

THE ORIGINAL PARTY MIX (CHEX MIX)

About 6¾ cups

This old favorite was developed by Ralston-Purina for its Chex-brand cereal back in the early '50s. Many variations have been made since that time, but the original is still the best, in my opinion.

6 tablespoons butter or stick margarine (three-quarters of a stick)
1 teaspoon seasoned salt
4 teaspoons Worcestershire sauce (this is 1 tablespoon plus 1 teaspoon)
2 cups Corn Chex cereal
2 cups Rice Chex cereal
2 cups Wheat Chex cereal
¾ cup salted mixed nuts

Heat oven to 250°F. Add butter to 13x9x2-inch baking dish, and place in oven until butter melts. Remove dish from oven; add seasoned salt and Worcestershire sauce, stirring to mix well. Add cereal and nuts; stir to coat all pieces with the butter mixture. Bake 45 minutes, stirring every 15 minutes. Cool before serving, and store in airtight containers.

RANCH SNACK MIX

About 10 cups

Not to be outdone, Kellogg's home economists came up with this recipe in the late '90s to take advantage of their cereal and Hidden Valley Original Ranch dressing mix. This is a non-baked snack mix, so is great for hot summer days, or if your cabin doesn't have an oven.

8 cups Kellogg's Crispix cereal
2½ cups small pretzels
2½ cups bite-sized cheddar cheese crackers
3 tablespoons vegetable oil
1 packet (1 ounce) Hidden Valley Original Ranch dressing mix

Combine cereal, pretzels and cheese crackers in a large plastic bag. Add the oil; close the bag and toss gently to coat. Sprinkle the dressing mix over everything; close the bag and toss again until well mixed.

Main Dishes

GREEK CHICKEN KABOBS

4 or 5 servings

Simple ingredients combine in this marinade to give chicken a flavor boost. The marinade also helps keep the chicken meat moist during grilling.

Marinade:
½ cup olive oil
¼ cup freshly squeezed lemon juice (from about 1 lemon)
¼ cup dry white wine
2 teaspoons minced garlic
1 teaspoon chopped fresh mint leaves, or ½ teaspoon crumbled dried
1 teaspoon crumbled dried oregano leaves
¼ teaspoon pepper

12 ounces boneless, skinless chicken breast meat, cut into 1-inch chunks
1 green bell pepper, cored and cut into 1-inch chunks
1 red bell pepper, cored and cut into 1-inch chunks
1 red onion, cut into eighths from top to bottom, then cut into 1-inch chunks

Combine marinade ingredients in a glass jar. Cover tightly and shake well to blend. Reserve and refrigerate ⅓ cup marinade. Place chicken chunks in nonaluminum bowl; pour remaining marinade over, stirring to coat. Cover and refrigerate 2 to 4 hours, stirring occasionally.

Prepare medium-hot grill, or the broiler; meanwhile, assemble kabobs. Thread chicken, pepper and onion pieces on skewers, alternating in a pretty arrangement; you will have 4 or 5 skewers. Grill or broil skewers until chicken and vegetables are just cooked, turning and brushing with reserved marinade every few minutes. Total cooking time will be about 15 minutes.

Chicken-Asparagus Rarebit

2 or 3 servings; easily increased

Use leftover or ready-cooked chicken for this easy dish. If you like, double the recipe for the sauce and keep the leftovers refrigerated; it will keep for up to a week. You can use it to make a quick rarebit-type meal or vegetable sauce; it's also great used as a cold spread for sandwiches.

6 to 9 asparagus spears, tough ends snapped off
2 or 3 large slices bread, or double the amount of regular-sized bread or English muffins
Rarebit Sauce (recipe below)
2 cups coarsely shredded cooked chicken meat (8 to 9 ounces; skin and bones removed before shredding and measuring)
1 tomato, sliced thinly (remove skin if you like; it's better if it's skinless)

Rarebit Sauce:

2 tablespoons butter or margarine
2 tablespoons flour
1 cup flat beer
½ teaspoon salt
¼ teaspoon Tabasco sauce
2 cups (8 ounces) grated sharp cheddar cheese

Cook the asparagus spears until just tender-crisp by steaming, microwaving, or simmering in a wide pot or skillet of gently boiling water. Drain and refresh immediately with cold water; set aside. Toast the bread and keep it warm.

Make the sauce: In a heavy-bottomed saucepan, melt the butter over medium heat until foamy. Whisk in the flour and cook, whisking constantly, for about 2 minutes; the mixture should be rich golden brown and have a nutty smell. Whisk in the beer, salt and Tabasco sauce, and cook, whisking frequently, until the mixture thickens and bubbles. Reduce heat to low and add the cheese. Cook, stirring constantly, until cheese melts and sauce is smooth. Add the shredded chicken and cook, stirring a few times, until chicken is heated through (if you are making extra sauce, remove it before adding the chicken).

Working quickly, place the toast on serving plates and top with the tomato slices. Top the tomato with the cooked asparagus. Spoon the cheese sauce evenly over the asparagus, and serve immediately.

CAJUN LINGUINI WITH CHICKEN AND SHRIMP

4 to 6 servings

Don't let the fancy name scare you off—this restaurant-style dish takes only about 30 minutes to make, and you can adjust the spice level to suit your preference.

1 pound boneless, skinless chicken breasts or thighs, or a combination
½ pound peeled, deveined raw shrimp* (frozen shrimp work fine; thaw them first)
1 to 3 tablespoons Cajun spice blend, such as Paul Prudhomme's Poultry Magic, or the homemade blend on page 300
1 tablespoon olive oil or vegetable oil
3 cups frozen pepper stir-fry blend (red, yellow and green bell peppers with onions), thawed; or, 2 cups fresh bell pepper strips and 1 cup thinly sliced onion wedges
¼ cup white wine, chicken broth or apple juice
1 can (14½ ounces) diced tomatoes with juice
1 pound linguini or other pasta (uncooked)
½ cup cream

Put a very large pot of salted water on high heat so it will come to a boil while you are making the sauce. Cut the chicken into bite-sized pieces. Keeping the chicken and shrimp separate, sprinkle each with 1½ to 3 teaspoons Cajun spice blend (1 to 2 tablespoons total), depending on how hot you want the dish; 1 tablespoon is mildly spicy, while 2 tablespoons will have a fair amount of heat. In a large heavy-bottomed skillet, heat the oil over medium-high heat. Add the chicken and cook, stirring occasionally, until lightly browned on all sides. Add the shrimp and cook, stirring frequently, until shrimp turns pink and opaque.* Use a slotted spoon to transfer chicken and shrimp to a large bowl; cover to keep warm. In the same skillet, cook pepper blend over medium heat, stirring frequently, until just tender. Transfer the vegetables to the bowl with the chicken and shrimp.

Add the wine to the skillet, stirring to loosen any browned bits, and raise heat to high. Cook, stirring frequently, until liquid has almost cooked away. Add tomatoes with their juice to the skillet; if you like really spicy food, add up to a tablespoon of additional Cajun spice blend. Cook over medium-high heat until liquid has almost cooked away, leaving just chunky tomato pulp, about 10 minutes; stir frequently near the end to prevent scorching.

When the sauce is almost reduced as described, add the pasta to the boiling water; stir pasta frequently while finishing the sauce. To finish the sauce, add the cream to the skillet with the reduced tomatoes and cook about 5 minutes longer, stirring frequently; sauce should be slightly thickened. Return the meats and vegetables to the skillet, along with any juices that have accumulated. Reduce heat to medium-low and cook until chicken and shrimp are heated through, 2 or 3 minutes; check the pasta at this point and drain when it is cooked through but still has a little firmness in the center. Serve the chicken and shrimp mixture over the pasta.

*If using pre-cooked shrimp, cook chicken alone for a total of about 5 minutes, then add shrimp and cook about 1 minute longer. Proceed as directed.

JUICY TURKEY BURGERS

4 servings; easily increased

If you've ever been disappointed by a dry, tough turkey burger, try this easy recipe.

⅓ cup small-curd cottage cheese
¼ cup finely minced onion
½ teaspoon mixed dried herb blend, such as Fines Herbes or Herbes de Provence
½ teaspoon salt
1 pound lean ground turkey (7% fat)
About 1 teaspoon vegetable oil
Hamburger buns and condiments as desired

In a mixing bowl, combine the cottage cheese, onion, herbs and salt, and mix well with a fork. Add turkey and mix gently with your hands. Divide into 4 equal portions and shape into ½-inch-thick patties. Place on a plate; cover and refrigerate about 30 minutes.

Prepare medium-hot grill, or the broiler. Brush turkey patties lightly on both sides with oil. Grill or broil 5 minutes, then turn and cook 5 minutes on the second side. Turn burgers and continue cooking until just done, usually 4 to 6 minutes longer, turning one more time. Serve with buns and condiments.

UPSIDE-DOWN CHICKEN À LA KING

4 servings

This is especially easy because it uses ready-to-eat cooked chicken that's now available from many delis, supermarkets and convenience stores.

3 cups cut-up cooked chicken (about 1 chicken; remove bones and skin before cutting or tearing into small bite-sized pieces)
⅔ cup frozen green peas
1 jar (2 ounces) sliced pimientos, drained, optional but very colorful
1 can (10¾ ounces) condensed golden mushroom soup or other mushroom soup
⅔ cup milk
1 tube (10.8 ounces/5 biscuits) refrigerated flaky buttermilk biscuits

Heat oven to 350°F. Spray an 8-inch-square baking dish or a 2-quart casserole with nonstick spray, or butter lightly. Combine chicken, peas and pimientos in the prepared baking dish; stir gently to mix. Blend together soup and milk with fork in a mixing bowl; pour over chicken mixture, stirring gently to combine. Cover the dish with foil; bake 30 minutes. Uncover dish and arrange biscuits evenly over chicken mixture (one in each corner and one in the center). Return uncovered dish to oven for 15 to 18 minutes, or until biscuits are golden brown.

Variations and improvisations:

- If you can't get a tube of refrigerated biscuits, make a batch of biscuits from a biscuit mix (such as Bisquick). Simply spoon them on top of the hot chicken mixture and proceed as directed; they'll cook in about the same amount of time.
- If you are starting with raw chicken pieces rather than a cooked chicken, you may simmer them in a little chicken broth or water until cooked (about 15 minutes for boneless pieces, or 20 minutes for bone-in). Cool the chicken pieces in the broth, then pull the meat from the bones and skin.
- Make your own white sauce to substitute for the condensed mushroom soup. Melt 2 tablespoons butter or margarine over medium-low heat and blend in 2 tablespoons flour. Cook, stirring constantly, for about 2 minutes. Blend in 1¾ cups milk and cook, stirring constantly, until thickened. Add salt and pepper to taste; a little nutmeg is good also. You may stir in a can of sliced mushrooms (drained) if you like, or some sliced fresh mushrooms that have been sautéed in butter.
- You could also substitute condensed cream of chicken or celery soup, or even cheese soup, for the mushroom soup. It won't exactly be Chicken à la King, but it will still be tasty.

- Can't get frozen peas at the local convenience store? Personally, I detest canned peas and would simply eliminate the peas from the recipe. For color, you could add a little diced green bell pepper or some chopped parsley, if you like.
- If your cabin doesn't have an oven, simmer the chicken mixture on the stovetop until hot, then spoon it over purchased biscuits. It's not quite the same, but it fills that hungry spot, especially on a cold, grey day.

POACHED PHEASANT OR CHICKEN SALAD

4 servings

Poaching is great for cooking light poultry, because it keeps it moist and tender. This method also produces a nice stock, which is not used in this recipe but is great for another meal.

1 carrot, cut up
1 stalk celery, cut up
1 small onion, quartered
1 bay leaf
1 teaspoon dried mixed herbs
1 pheasant, cut up, or 2 bone-in chicken breast halves
6 cups mixed salad greens
Half of a medium red onion, thinly sliced into quarter-rings
1 cup fresh raspberries
¼ cup toasted slivered almonds
Raspberry Vinaigrette (facing page)

In large saucepan or small Dutch oven, combine carrot, celery, onion, bay leaf and herbs. Add 6 cups cold water. Heat to boiling over high heat. Cover; reduce heat to a gentle boil and cook 30 minutes. Add pheasant pieces and heat just to simmering. Simmer, covered, until pheasant is tender, about 45 minutes; do not boil, or the meat will be tough. Remove pheasant from broth and allow to cool slightly. Pull meat from bones. To finish the pheasant stock, return bones and any skin to the saucepan and continue cooking 30 minutes longer. Strain and discard solids; save stock for another use (freeze if you won't be using it within 2 days).

Shred pheasant meat into bite-sized pieces. Combine with greens, red onion, raspberries and almonds. Add dressing and toss just before serving.

RASPBERRY VINAIGRETTE

About 1 cup

½ cup olive oil or peanut oil
¼ cup honey
3 tablespoons raspberry vinegar
2 teaspoons grated onion
1 teaspoon poppy seeds
½ teaspoon dry mustard powder
½ teaspoon salt

Combine all ingredients in a jar. Cover tightly and shake well. Refrigerate unused portions for up to a week.

ISLAND-FLAVOR STEAKS

Per 2 servings; easily increased

You could also use this technique with thick pork chops or boneless chicken breasts.

3 cloves garlic
2 tablespoons olive oil or peanut oil
2 tablespoons freshly squeezed lime juice (from about 1 lime)
1 tablespoon packed brown sugar
1 tablespoon soy sauce
2 choice New York strip or other tender steaks, 6 to 8 ounces each
⅓ cup dark rum

If you have a mini food chopper or blender, process the garlic, olive oil, lime juice, brown sugar and soy sauce until smooth; otherwise, mince the garlic as fine as you can, then use a fork or whisk to blend it with the other ingredients in a small bowl. Place the steaks in a nonaluminum casserole or small baking dish and pour the marinade over; turn the steaks to coat both sides. Let stand at room temperature 1 hour, or up to 2 hours refrigerated.

Prepare medium-hot grill. Allow excess marinade to drip from steaks, then place on grate and cover grill immediately to prevent flare-ups. Cook until done to your preference,* turning once; well-done steaks may be tough, and have a greater risk of charring. Just before the steaks are ready, heat the rum very gently in a medium skillet over medium-low heat. Transfer the steaks to the skillet, then place the skillet on a flameproof surface away from curtains, long hair or anything flammable. Carefully ignite the rum with a long-handled match, and allow to burn until the flames die down. Pour a little of the rum left in the skillet over each steak when serving.

*To test a steak for doneness, poke it with your thumb. A rare steak will feel soft; medium will feel tender but not mushy; well done will feel firm and relatively unyielding.

EASY CHILI WITH GROUND BEEF

5 or 6 servings

For a more complex chili that has no beans, *see page 348.*

1 pound lean ground beef
1 small onion, diced
1 green or red bell pepper, diced
2 cloves garlic, pressed or minced, or 1 teaspoon bottled chopped garlic
3 tablespoons chili powder blend
1 teaspoon sugar
¼ to 1 teaspoon crushed dried hot red pepper flakes, optional
2 cans (14½ ounces each) diced tomatoes, undrained (seasoned tomatoes are good)
1 can (6 ounces) tomato paste
1 can (15 ounces) kidney beans, drained but not rinsed, or 1½ cups cooked beans
Garnishes: shredded cheese, crackers, sliced jalapeños, sour cream, chopped onions

In nonaluminum Dutch oven or large pot, brown ground beef over medium heat, stirring to break up. Drain all but 2 teaspoons drippings. Add onion and bell pepper to the Dutch oven; cook, stirring occasionally, until vegetables are tender-crisp. Stir in garlic, chili powder, sugar and hot pepper flakes; cook, stirring occasionally, about 3 minutes. Add tomatoes and ½ can water and cook until mixture just comes to a gentle boil. Reduce heat and simmer 30 minutes, stirring occasionally. Stir in tomato paste and beans; fill tomato paste can halfway with water, swish around to rinse can and add to chili. Cook about 15 minutes longer. Taste and add salt if necessary (depending on the chili powder you use, additional salt may not be necessary). Serve with garnishes as desired.

Add-in ingredients: Customize your chili with **one or more** of these optional ingredients:

- Add at same time as other vegetables:
  - ½ cup chopped carrot (medium-fine chop; adds a sweet, rich flavor)
  - ½ cup sliced celery
- Add at same time as garlic and chili powder:
  - 2 teaspoons cocoa powder (adds deep, interesting flavor; a secret ingredient in many prize-winning chilis!)
  - ½ teaspoon crumbled dried oregano leaves, or 2 teaspoons fresh
  - ⅛ teaspoon cinnamon (another secret ingredient that adds unusual spice)
- Add at same time as canned tomatoes:
  - 1 can (4 ounces) diced green chiles, undrained
  - Substitute beer or beef broth for the half-can of water

Lemonade-Barbecued Pork

Servings depend on size of roast

This is one of the best things I've ever made on the grill—and I use the grill a lot! The pork turns out juicy and tender, with a beautiful, shiny golden-brown exterior.

Lemonade Marinade:
¼ cup frozen lemonade concentrate, thawed
¼ cup soy sauce
3 tablespoons vegetable oil
2 tablespoons honey
2 teaspoons Dijon mustard
½ teaspoon finely minced garlic
½ teaspoon chopped fresh thyme leaves or ¼ teaspoon crumbled dried, optional

1 boneless pork loin roast

Combine marinade ingredients in small saucepan (or microwave-safe bowl). Heat just to boiling over medium heat (or microwave at REHEAT/80% power until mixture just starts bubbling), stirring occasionally. Let mixture cool completely.

Prick pork roast all over with a fork. Place in a nonaluminum dish; pour half the marinade over the pork, turning to coat. Cover and refrigerate 3 to 5 hours, turning occasionally; refrigerate remaining marinade separately.

Prepare grill for indirect heat (page 154), and place a water pan under the grate in the area away from the coals. Place pork on oiled grate over the water pan. Cover grill and cook until pork is just done, turning and basting with the reserved marinade every 15 to 20 minutes. Pork should read 160°F on an instant-read thermometer when done, and juices should run clear when the meat is pricked in the thickest part; a 3-pound roast will take 1¼ to 1¾ hours. Remove meat from the grill and let stand 10 minutes before slicing.

LEMONADE CHICKEN WINGS

8 appetizer servings; 4 main-dish servings

For easy packing, combine the wings and marinade at home before your trip. Place the wings into a freezer-weight plastic zipper bag, then add the marinade and seal, pressing out all air. Freeze for at least a day (but no longer than a week), and carry to the cabin in a cooler while still frozen. Thaw in the refrigerator the day you plan to cook the wings; the marinating is already done!

Lemonade Marinade (page 66)
2 to 3 pounds chicken wings

Place wings in a large nonaluminum baking dish, or in a large plastic zipper bag. Add all but ½ cup marinade; turn to coat. Cover dish or seal bag and refrigerate 3 to 5 hours, turning wings occasionally; refrigerate remaining marinade separately.

To cook in the oven: Heat oven to 375°F. Transfer wings to rack of broiler pan. Bake 25 to 30 minutes, turning wings and brushing with the reserved marinade every 5 or 10 minutes. Wings should be golden brown and cooked through. For browner, crispier wings, turn on the broiler and broil wings for about 10 minutes after the main baking time, turning and brushing frequently with marinade.

To cook on the grill: Prepare medium-hot grill. Place wings on grate. Cover grill and cook 20 to 25 minutes, turning wings and brushing with the reserved marinade every 5 or 10 minutes. Wings should be nicely browned and cooked through. If wings are getting too browned before they are cooked through, move to cooler area of grill and continue cooking.

SHREDDED PORK TACOS (CARNITAS)

4 to 6 servings

If the only tacos you're familiar with are hard-shell tacos stuffed with ground beef, this dish will be a revelation. It's much closer to the type of taco actually eaten in Mexico.

1½ pounds boneless pork butt or other cut that has a bit of fat
1 dried ancho chile, optional
Half of an onion, cut into 1-inch chunks
2 or 3 cloves garlic, cut in half
2 dried red hot peppers (each about 1¼ inches long), or ¼ teaspoon crushed dried hot red pepper flakes
¼ cup chicken broth, beer or water
Soft flour tortillas
For garnish, any or all of the following: shredded cheese, prepared salsa,* guacamole (see Chunky Guacamole, page 138), chopped tomatoes, chopped onions

Trim excess fat from pork; you want some fat, and if the meat is well marbled you don't need much external fat. If the meat is not marbled, then keep a fair amount of the external fat. Cut pork into 1-inch cubes and place in a crock pot (or, see page 69 for stovetop instructions). Remove and discard the stem from the ancho chile, then break the chile open so you can shake out and discard the seeds (if you are sensitive to chile pepper oil, wear rubber gloves when handling the chile). You may have to break the chile into several pieces to get all the seeds out, and that's OK, since the chile will get broken up during the cooking anyway. Add the chile pepper, broken into several pieces, to the crock pot along with the onion, garlic, hot peppers and chicken broth. Cover the crock pot and cook on HIGH 1 hour, then reduce heat to LOW and cook 6 to 7 hours longer. By this time, the meat should be tender enough that it will shred apart when poked with a wooden spatula (or, you can pull it apart with two forks). If you're not ready for dinner yet, you can leave the meat in the crock pot on LOW for another hour or two; you can also prepare the meat up to this point, then refrigerate up to 2 days until you're ready for the final step.

When it's close to dinnertime, shred the meat coarsely with a wooden spatula or two forks. Transfer the meat mixture and all juices to a skillet; salt generously. Cook over medium heat, stirring occasionally, until the juices have cooked away and the meat is nicely browned; this should take about 20 minutes total. Serve the shredded meat with warmed flour tortillas and garnishes of your choice.

*For variety, try one of the salsas on page 217.

SHREDDED PORK TACOS ON THE STOVETOP

Follow the ingredients list on the facing page, adding a tablespoon of lard or vegetable oil and increasing the chicken broth to 1 cup; trim the pork of all external fat for this cooking method. Slice or chop the garlic cloves. Heat the lard in a heavy-bottomed Dutch oven over medium heat. Add the pork and cook, stirring occasionally, until browned on all sides; near the end of the browning time, add the onion and garlic. Crumble the seeded ancho chile into the pot with the browned meat, and add the onion, garlic, hot peppers and the cup of chicken broth. Reduce heat to medium-low and cook, stirring occasionally, until the pork is quite tender and the liquid has cooked away, about 2 hours; if the pot becomes dry before the meat is tender, add a little additional chicken broth or water. When the meat is tender, shred it with a wooden spatula or two forks, then raise the heat to medium and continue cooking until the meat shreds are browned, about 15 minutes longer, stirring occasionally. Serve the shredded meat with warmed flour tortillas and garnishes of your choice.

STUFFED PORK CHOPS WITH APPLE GLAZE

2 servings; easily increased

A tasty apple glaze caramelizes during cooking for beautiful appearance; the saltwater soak makes these chops incredibly juicy. Buy extra-thick bone-in chops; most butchers will be happy to cut these for you.

Brine:
2 cups cold water
3 tablespoons salt*
2 tablespoons packed brown sugar

2 center-cut bone-in pork chops, 1 inch thick (11 to 12 ounces each)
¾ cup coarse bread crumbs
⅓ cup chopped apple
¼ cup chopped celery
¼ cup minced onion
2 tablespoons butter or margarine, melted
About ¼ cup chicken broth, vegetable broth or white wine
¼ cup frozen apple juice concentrate, thawed

In nonaluminum mixing bowl, combine brine ingredients and stir until salt and sugar dissolve. Use a paring knife to cut a wide pocket in each pork chop, cutting from the meat side to the bone but leaving the meat connected at the sides. Place the chops in the brine; refrigerate 1 to 2 hours. Remove chops from brine; rinse briefly and pat dry. Discard brine. Combine bread crumbs, apple, celery and onion in mixing bowl; toss to combine. Drizzle melted butter over apple mixture, tossing to coat evenly. Add broth until the stuffing is just moist, stirring to mix well. Stuff each chop firmly with half the stuffing mixture.

To cook on grill: Prepare grill for indirect heat (page 154). Place stuffed chops on grate away from heat. Cover grill and cook until chops are cooked through and center of stuffing is hot (it should read 160°F on an instant-read thermometer), basting chops with apple juice concentrate and gently turning every 10 minutes; total cooking time will be 40 to 50 minutes.

To bake: Heat oven to 350°F. Place chops in baking dish. Bake, uncovered, until chops are cooked through and center of stuffing is hot (it should read 160°F on an instant-read thermometer), basting chops with apple juice concentrate every 10 minutes; total cooking time will be 35 to 45 minutes.

*Canning/pickling salt is best, but regular table salt works for this brine because the meat doesn't soak too long; for longer-brined items, the iodine in table salt has unwanted side effects.

Pork and Mushroom Noodle Bowl

2 large servings, or 3 medium servings

Shopping alert: This recipe contains an ingredient (or two) that you won't be able to pick up at the small-town grocer! But it's so easy to make, and so delicious, that it's worth picking up these items in a larger city and carrying them with you. Most supermarkets in large cities carry dried black mushrooms these days, and the ramen noodle soup is even easier to find.

6 dried Chinese black mushrooms, or 3 tablespoons sliced, dried Chinese mushrooms
8 ounces pork tenderloin
2 packages (3 ounces each) mushroom or pork-flavored ramen noodle soup mix
2 teaspoons peanut oil or vegetable oil, divided
¼ cup julienned carrot (⅛ x ⅛ x 2-inch strips) or thickly shredded carrot
3 green onions, thinly sliced on a diagonal to make wider slices
1½ cups thinly sliced cabbage
½ teaspoon minced gingerroot, optional

Soak mushrooms in warm water to cover until tender; this usually takes 20 to 30 minutes, and can be done in advance. When mushrooms are tender, remove and discard stems; slice caps ⅛ inch thick and set aside. Strain soaking liquid through a coffee filter. Add water to equal 2¼ cups; set aside.

Slice pork ⅛ inch thick across the grain and lay out in a single layer on work surface. Sprinkle with the seasoning packet from one package of ramen, reserving the noodles and the other package. Pound the seasoning lightly into the meat, using a meat mallet or the bottom of a sturdy coffee cup.

In a saucepan, heat mushroom soaking liquid to boiling. Add the ramen noodles from both packages, and the remaining seasoning mix packet. Stir to break up the noodles, and cook 2½ minutes, stirring frequently, until noodles are separated and almost tender. Remove from heat; cover and set aside.

In wok or large skillet, heat 1 teaspoon oil over high heat. Add pork and mushroom slices and stir constantly until pork is just barely cooked. Transfer the pork mixture to the saucepan with the noodles; re-cover. Add the remaining teaspoon oil to the wok and reduce heat to medium. Add carrot, onions, cabbage and gingerroot; stir-fry until vegetables are just tender-crisp, about 3 minutes. Divide noodle mixture and broth evenly between 2 or 3 large, wide bowls; distribute vegetables evenly between bowls.

Even easier: Substitute 1¾ cups packaged coleslaw vegetables for the cabbage and carrot.

LAZY LASAGNA

6 servings

This simple recipe eliminates the chore of pre-cooking the lasagna noodles ... a real time-saver! You can vary the flavor by choosing different prepared pasta sauces.

1 pound bulk Italian sausage (if you buy uncooked sausages, remove the casings)
1 jar (26 ounces) prepared tomato-based pasta sauce
6 lasagna noodles (uncooked)
10 ounces ricotta cheese (dry or small-curd cottage cheese may be substituted)
6 to 8 ounces shredded mozzarella cheese (1½ to 2 cups)
¾ cup shredded Romano or Parmesan cheese

Heat oven to 350°F. Cook sausage in a skillet over medium heat, stirring to break up, until no longer pink; drain and discard grease. Pour ¾ cup sauce into 8-inch-square baking dish, spreading evenly on bottom. Carefully break off a 3-inch length from each lasagna noodle; save the shorter pieces. Arrange 3 of the longer pieces of lasagna side-by-side on the sauce; press gently into the sauce. Spoon dollops of sauce over each lasagna noodle, spreading with the back of a spoon. Distribute one-third of the cooked sausage over the sauce. Spoon one-third of the ricotta over the sausage. Sprinkle with one-third of the mozzarella, then with ¼ cup Romano. Spread a few dollops of sauce over the Romano. Arrange the 6 shorter pieces of lasagna noodles over the sauce, pressing gently. Repeat layers using half of the remaining sauce, sausage, ricotta, mozzarella and Romano cheeses (don't forget the layer of sauce on top of the Romano cheese). Arrange remaining 3 longer pieces of lasagna over the sauce, pressing gently. Add ½ cup water to the sauce jar and shake to loosen sauce clinging to the inside of the jar, then pour over the top layer of noodles. Top with remaining sausage, ricotta, mozzarella and Romano. Bake until golden brown and bubbly, 45 to 50 minutes. Remove from oven and let stand 15 minutes before cutting.

To help you remember the layers, here is a summary:

(Base layer of sauce)
Uncooked lasagna noodles
Dollops of sauce, spread over noodles
Sausage (or olives and mushrooms for Lazy Vegetarian Lasagna, see below)
Spoonfuls of ricotta cheese
Mozzarella cheese
Romano cheese
Dollops of sauce (this layer of sauce is not used in top layer)

Variation:

Lazy Vegetarian Lasagna: Follow recipe for Lazy Lasagna on the facing page, omitting the sausage. It its place, use 1 drained can (2¼ ounces) sliced ripe olives and 1 drained can (15 ounces) sliced mushrooms. Proceed as directed, using one-third of the olives and mushrooms for each layer.

Crab-Stick Cobbler

6 servings

An easy-to-make dish that makes an ordinary meal seem like a party!

½ cup chopped onion
½ cup chopped red or green bell pepper
1 teaspoon chopped garlic, optional
1 tablespoon butter or margarine
2 tablespoons sherry or water
1 package (8 ounces) imitation crab sticks or crab bits
¼ cup flour
1 can (12 ounces) condensed skim milk, divided
2 teaspoons Dijon mustard
1½ cups (6 ounces) shredded cheddar cheese, divided
1 can (14½ ounces) diced tomatoes, drained
2 cups buttermilk baking mix such as Bisquick

Spray an 8-inch-square baking dish with nonstick cooking spray, or butter lightly; set aside. Heat oven to 425°F. In large skillet, cook onion, pepper and garlic in butter over medium heat about 3 minutes, stirring occasionally. Add sherry and cook, stirring frequently, until sherry is almost cooked away and vegetables are tender. Meanwhile, cut crab sticks into 1- to 1½-inch pieces and shred coarsely with your fingers. When vegetables are tender, sprinkle the flour over the vegetables in the skillet, stirring constantly. Cook and stir for about 45 seconds. Blend in 1 cup of the condensed milk and the mustard; cook, stirring constantly, until thickened and bubbly. Add 1 cup of the cheese and cook, stirring frequently, until cheese melts. Remove from heat; stir in drained tomatoes and shredded crab sticks. Pour the mixture into the prepared baking dish, spreading evenly.

In a medium bowl, combine the baking mix and remaining ½ cup cheese; stir to coat cheese with the baking mix. Add water to remaining ½ cup condensed milk to equal ⅔ cup; add to the baking mix and stir until dry ingredients are just moist. Drop in 9 equal rounded portions onto crab mixture. Bake 15 to 20 minutes, or until biscuits are golden brown.

Fish cakes

10 cakes; 5 or 6 servings

Most fish-cake recipes you'll see require several cups of leftover cooked fish. I never have that amount of cooked fish left over, and I don't usually feel like taking the time to cook and cool fish just so I have it available. This recipe uses fresh, uncooked fish; I got the inspiration for the technique from Chef Ron Berg's wonderful Gunflint Lodge Cookbook.

1 pound boneless, skinless walleye or other firm white fish fillets
2 eggs
2 teaspoons salt
½ teaspoon dry mustard powder, optional
1 cup cream
½ cup instant mashed potato flakes
2 tablespoons finely minced onion
2 tablespoons finely minced celery
Vegetable oil for frying

Cut fish into 1-inch chunks and place in food processor or blender container with eggs, salt and mustard powder. Pulse a few seconds at a time until mixture is coarsely chopped; then, with the motor running, add the cream and process until smooth. Add potato flakes, onion and celery, and pulse a few times until mixture is blended.

In large skillet, heat ¼ inch oil over medium heat. Spoon about ⅓ cup of the ground fish mixture into the skillet, forming into a round cake; add as many cakes as the skillet will hold comfortably. Fry until golden brown on the bottom. Flip carefully and cook until golden brown on the second side. Transfer to paper-towl-lined plate; cover and keep warm while you fry remaining fish cakes, adding additional oil if necessary.

Vegetables, Starches and Side Dishes

GRILLED FRESH ASPARAGUS

2 servings per packet

For additional servings, make additional packets. Each packet comfortably holds about ½ pound of fresh spears; if you overload the packet, the asparagus will not cook properly.

8 ounces ready-to-cook* fresh asparagus spears (weight after snapping off tough ends)
2 teaspoons butter or margarine
A wedge of fresh lemon, optional

Prepare grill for medium heat. Rinse asparagus spears well and let drain briefly. Place on the shiny side of a sheet of heavy-duty foil (or a doubled-over sheet of regular-weight foil); the asparagus should be parallel to the long sides and there should be 3 inches of extra foil at each end. Add butter; sprinkle generously with salt and pepper. Bring the long edges of the foil together and roll-fold at least twice to seal. Roll up the ends, making sure each end has at least 3 roll-folds. Grill, turning packet frequently, 10 to 12 minutes. Open packet carefully to allow steam to escape; spritz with fresh lemon juice if desired.

*To prepare asparagus for cooking, bend the asparagus until the tough, woody end snaps off. Discard woody ends, or use when making vegetable stock.

COLORFUL MARINATED SALAD

4 to 6 servings

This make-ahead salad is perfect for a picnic, or just to have in the refrigerator. It keeps well for several days.

¾ cup wine vinegar
½ cup vegetable oil or olive oil
½ cup cold water
Half of a packet (.65 ounce) dry Italian salad dressing mix
Half of a head of cauliflower, cut into small flowerets
2 carrots, peeled and cut on the diagonal into ⅛-inch wide slices
2 stalks celery, cut on the diagonal into ⅛-inch wide slices
1 green bell pepper, cored, cut into ½ x 2-inch strips
¾ cup pitted black olives

In large nonaluminum saucepan, combine the vinegar, oil, water and salad dressing mix; stir until well blended. Add remaining ingredients except olives. Heat just to boiling. Cover and reduce heat; simmer 5 minutes, stirring once or twice. Remove from heat and stir in olives. Transfer to nonaluminum bowl and cool completely. Cover and refrigerate overnight, or as long as 3 days.

WILTED SPINACH SALAD

4 side-dish servings; 2 light main-dish servings

This makes a nice side dish with chicken or steak; I also like to serve it for lunch or as a light supper, accompanied by hot breadsticks or a crusty loaf of bread.

1 pound fresh tender spinach
¼ pound bacon, cut into ½-inch pieces
8 ounces sliced fresh mushrooms
¼ cup diced red onion
1 egg
3 tablespoons red wine vinegar or cider vinegar
2 tablespoons sugar
¼ teaspoon dry mustard powder, optional
¼ teaspoon salt
A few grindings of black pepper
1 or 2 hard-cooked eggs, cooled and sliced or quartered

Wash spinach well in several changes of cold water; spin or pat dry. Discard tough stems; tear larger leaves into bite-sized pieces and put all in a large bowl. Cover with a clean towel and set aside.

In large nonaluminum skillet, cook bacon over medium heat until crisp. Use a slotted spoon to transfer the bacon to a dish; set aside. Sauté the mushrooms and onion in the bacon drippings until just tender; transfer to the dish with the bacon. In a small bowl, combine the egg, vinegar, sugar, mustard powder, salt and pepper; beat with a fork. Pour into the warm bacon drippings, stirring constantly. Cook, stirring constantly, until thickened and glossy. Return bacon and mushrooms to the skillet; heat through. Pour the entire mixture over the spinach, tossing lightly until well coated. Arrange egg(s) attractively over the top.

WILTED LETTUCE SALAD

Follow recipe above, substituting 1 pound Boston, bibb or tender leaf lettuce for the spinach. Omit the mushrooms; substitute ½ cup thinly sliced onion half-rings for the diced onion. Proceed as directed.

JAPANESE CUCUMBER SALAD

4 to 6 servings

Rice vinegar and fresh gingerroot are the ingredients that make this salad special. Look in the Asian foods section of a large supermarket for rice vinegar. A substitution is given below, but the flavor is not the same.

2 cucumbers, thinly sliced
2 teaspoons salt
1 tablespoon sesame seeds
¼ cup finely shredded carrot
2 tablespoons finely minced onion
½ cup rice vinegar*
½ cup sugar
1 teaspoon minced fresh gingerroot

Place cucumbers in a large nonaluminum bowl and sprinkle with the salt; let stand 30 minutes. Meanwhile, place sesame seeds in small heavy-bottomed skillet; cook over medium heat, stirring constantly, until the seeds begin to color lightly. Transfer immediately to a medium bowl and set aside to cool.

When the cucumbers have been salted for 30 minutes, rinse in cold water and drain well. Return the cucumbers to the large bowl; add the carrot and onion. Add rice vinegar, sugar and gingerroot to the bowl with the toasted sesame seeds; stir to combine. Pour the vinegar mixture over the cucumbers, stirring to coat. Cover and refrigerate 1 hour or longer.

*If you can't find rice vinegar, substitute 1 tablespoon plus 1 teaspoon white vinegar, mixed with 2 teaspoons water.

SECRET INGREDIENT COLESLAW

7 to 10 servings

Pineapple is the secret ingredient that gives this coleslaw its tangy taste.

1 can (8 ounces) crushed pineapple packed in juice
¼ cup cider vinegar
2 tablespoons packed brown sugar
1 tablespoon cornstarch
1 tablespoon soy sauce or teriyaki sauce
¼ teaspoon dry mustard powder, or ½ teaspoon Dijon mustard
4 to 5 cups finely shredded cabbage (a mix of green and red is nice)
½ cup roasted, salted sunflower nuts, optional
3 tablespoons grated onion
1 large carrot, shredded
¼ cup mayonnaise (low-fat works fine)

Drain pineapple juice into small nonaluminum saucepan; transfer drained pineapple to a large bowl and set aside. Add vinegar, brown sugar, cornstarch, soy sauce and mustard to saucepan with the pineapple juice, stirring well to blend. Cook over medium heat, stirring constantly, until sauce thickens, bubbles, and becomes translucent, about 2 minutes. Remove from heat and set aside to cool completely.

Add cabbage, sunflower nuts, onion and carrot to bowl with pineapple; mix well. When vinegar mixture has cooled completely, blend in mayonnaise with a fork. Add dressing to cabbage mixture; stir gently but thoroughly to combine.

Even easier: Substitute pre-packaged coleslaw mix for the cabbage, onion and carrot. Proceed as directed.

CUCUMBER-YOGURT SALAD

4 servings

Serve this cool and refreshing salad with curry or other spicy foods; it also goes well with Gyros Burgers (page 53).

1 cup plain yogurt (reduced-fat works fine)
3 tablespoons chopped fresh mint leaves
1 tablespoon olive oil or vegetable oil, optional
2 teaspoons freshly squeezed lemon juice
½ teaspoon salt
2 cups thinly sliced cucumber

In medium bowl, stir together yogurt, mint, olive oil, lemon juice and salt. Add cucumbers and stir gently to coat. Cover and refrigerate 30 minutes or longer; stir before serving.

WARM POTATO SALAD WITH CAESAR DRESSING

4 to 6 servings as a side dish; 3 or 4 servings as a vegetarian main dish

1 pound potatoes (about 2 medium Idaho potatoes)
6 tablespoons olive oil (no substitutes)
2 cloves garlic, pressed or minced
3 tablespoons freshly squeezed lemon juice (from about three-quarters of a lemon)
1 tablespoon Worcestershire sauce
2 teaspoons Dijon mustard
1 mashed anchovy fillet, or ½ teaspoon anchovy paste, optional but recommended
½ teaspoon salt
A few good grindings of black pepper
4 cups romaine lettuce, torn into bite-sized pieces
⅓ cup grated Parmesan cheese

Scrub potatoes and add to a large pot of boiling water. Cook until just tender when pierced with a fork, about 15 minutes. Drain and refresh with cold running water; slip skins off and discard. (Potatoes may be prepared up to this point a day or two in advance, and kept refrigerated until needed; don't peel the potatoes until you are ready to use them, and return to room temperature before final cooking.) When you are ready for final preparation, dice the potatoes into ¾-inch chunks.

In a large skillet, heat the oil over medium heat. Add the garlic and cook about 2 minutes, stirring occasionally. Add lemon juice, Worcestershire sauce, mustard, mashed anchovy, salt and pepper. Whisk together, or blend well with fork; continue cooking until warm. Add potatoes and reduce heat to medium-low. Cook, gently stirring occasionally, until potatoes are warmed through.

Place the lettuce in a large salad bowl. Add warm potato mixture and Parmesan cheese. Toss gently, and serve immediately.

STRAW AND GRASS (TWO-COLOR PASTA WITH CREAMY SAUCE)

4 to 6 servings

Paglia e fieno, *as this dish is called in its native Italy, is so named because it resembles the straw and grass (or hay, as some translations have it) at harvest time. I've seen recipes for this which use mushrooms instead of the peas; but any time I've had this in Italy, peas are included, so that's the way I make it. If you want to impress your neighbors with the name of this dish, it is correctly pronounced "PAHL-ya eh fee-YAY-no" and if you say this very quickly (PAHLya-eh-feeYAYno), you will sound very Italian indeed.*

8 ounces spinach fettuccini (uncooked)
8 ounces egg fettuccini (uncooked)
1 tablespoon butter or margarine
⅔ cup frozen green peas, thawed, or fresh shelled peas
1 clove garlic, pressed or minced, optional
½ cup finely julienned ham (thinly sliced, then cut into ⅛ x 1-inch strips before measuring; about 2 ounces)
1 egg yolk
1 cup heavy cream
½ cup grated Parmesan cheese, plus additional for serving

Heat a very large pot of salted water to boiling. Add both batches of fettuccini slowly, stirring constantly to prevent sticking. Cook, stirring very frequently at first and less often after awhile, until the pasta is tender yet still has a firm bite. While the pasta is cooking, melt the butter in a large skillet over medium heat, and stir in the peas and garlic. Cook, stirring occasionally, until the peas are bright green and cooked through, which will take just a few minutes. Stir in the ham and cook about a minute longer. Remove from heat and set aside. Drop the egg yolk into the measuring cup with the cream, and beat gently; set aside.

When pasta is cooked, drain and return the pasta to the pot. Add the pea-ham mixture and the cream-egg mixture. Cook over medium heat, stirring frequently, until heated through and slightly thickened. Stir in the Parmesan cheese; cook a few minutes longer. Serve with additional grated Parmesan cheese.

Spaghetti with Browned Crumbs

4 to 6 servings; easily cut in half

This is a simple, home-style Italian dish that looks too simple to be good; but trust me, it is wonderful. It makes a nice, quick side dish to accompany grilled chicken or steak.

1 pound spaghetti (uncooked)
½ cup butter (1 stick)
⅔ cup Italian-flavored bread crumbs, or plain crumbs with a few mixed herbs added
½ cup chopped fresh parsley
½ cup grated Romano or Parmesan cheese
A few good grindings of black pepper

Heat a very large pot of salted water to boiling. Add spaghetti slowly, stirring constantly to prevent sticking. Cook, stirring very frequently at first and less often after a while, until the pasta is tender yet still has a firm bite. While the pasta is cooking, melt the butter in a large skillet over medium heat, and stir in the bread crumbs. Cook, stirring frequently, until the crumbs are rich golden brown and very fragrant. Remove from heat and set aside.

When pasta is cooked, carefully scoop out about ½ cup of the pasta cooking water and set aside. Drain the pasta and return to the pot. Add the buttered bread crumbs, along with the parsley and grated Romano cheese; grind a generous amount of black pepper over the pasta and stir again. Add a little of the pasta-cooking water (a tablespoon at a time), stirring gently, until the pasta is just moistened but not soggy. Serve immediately.

SALSA RICE

4 or 5 servings

½ cup diced onion
1 tablespoon vegetable oil
½ to ¾ cup prepared salsa, depending on how spicy you like your rice
1 teaspoon chicken bouillon granules*
1⅓ cups converted rice (uncooked)

In a heavy-bottomed saucepan that has a good lid, cook the onion in the oil over medium heat, stirring occasionally, until the onion is just tender. While onion is cooking, measure desired amount of salsa, then add water to equal 2½ cups. Stir in the chicken bouillon granules, then set aside. When onion is tender, add salsa-water mixture and the rice to the saucepan. Stir well and heat to boiling. Reduce heat to medium-low and cover the saucepan. Cook for 15 minutes (without stirring), or until the liquid is absorbed and the rice is just tender. If the liquid cooks away before the rice is tender, add a few tablespoons hot water and continue cooking, covered, until rice is tender. Remove from heat and let stand 5 to 15 minutes. Fluff rice gently with a fork before serving.

*You may substitute chicken broth for the water and chicken bouillon granules; add a little salt if the broth seems to need it.

Festive Rice Salad

4 servings

Tote a container of this salad in the cooler for a vegetarian picnic dish, or serve alongside grilled sausages or burgers. For extra flavor and nutrition, use brown rice; it takes longer to cook than white rice, but makes a very interesting salad.

3 cups vegetable broth or chicken broth
1½ cups uncooked rice (long grain or converted white rice, or Basmati or brown rice)
2 teaspoons butter or margarine
⅓ cup olive oil or peanut oil
3 tablespoons red wine vinegar
2 tablespoons snipped fresh chives
1 teaspoon Dijon mustard
½ teaspoon salt
½ cup currants or coarsely chopped raisins
½ cup diced celery
½ cup shredded carrot
½ cup coarsely chopped peanuts
¼ cup chopped fresh parsley

In medium saucepan, heat vegetable broth to boiling over medium heat. Add rice and butter, stirring well. Cover and cook over low heat until the broth is absorbed and the rice is tender; add a little additional broth or water if the rice is drying out before it is tender. White rice will take 15 to 20 minutes; brown rice will take 35 to 45 minutes, and is more likely to need additional liquid.

While the rice is cooking, combine olive oil, vinegar, chives, mustard and salt in a large mixing bowl; whisk or blend well with a fork. When rice is cooked, add it to the bowl with the dressing; stir well and set aside. When rice has cooled to room temperature, add the currants, celery and carrot; stir to combine. Cover and refrigerate at least 1 hour, and as long as overnight. Just before serving, stir in the peanuts and parsley.

Noodles with Thai Peanut Sauce

4 servings

Shopping alert: some of the ingredients for this dish will need to be purchased in advance; you won't be able to pull into most small-town grocers and find Asian sesame oil or rice vinegar. These ingredients are usually available at larger city supermarkets, and are becoming more common every day.

1 cup chicken broth
¼ teaspoon crushed dried hot red pepper flakes
⅔ cup chunky peanut butter
2 tablespoons packed brown sugar
2 tablespoons soy sauce
2 tablespoons seasoned rice vinegar*
1 large carrot, grated coarsely
3 green onions, sliced ¼ inch thick
1 tablespoon Asian sesame seasoning oil
12 ounces linguini or fettuccini (uncooked)
3 tablespoons chopped fresh cilantro leaves or parsley
3 tablespoons coarsely chopped peanuts, optional

Make the sauce: In medium saucepan, combine broth and hot pepper flakes. Heat to boiling over medium heat; reduce heat and simmer about 5 minutes. Strain out and discard the hot pepper flakes; a paper coffee filter works well for this. Add peanut butter, brown sugar, soy sauce and rice vinegar to broth, stirring to blend. Heat just to boiling; reduce heat and simmer until thick, about 1 minute, stirring frequently. Remove from heat and stir in the carrot, green onions and sesame oil; set aside.

Heat a very large pot of salted water to boiling. Add the linguini slowly, stirring constantly to prevent sticking. Cook, stirring very frequently at first and less often after a while, until the pasta is tender yet still has a firm bite. Drain and return the pasta to the pot. Add the peanut butter sauce, stirring gently to coat. Transfer to a serving dish; sprinkle cilantro and peanuts on top of the pasta. Serve warm or at room temperature.

*Rice vinegar is found with the Asian specialty foods at large supermarkets. If you can't find it, substitute 1 tablespoon plus 1 teaspoon white vinegar, 2 teaspoons water and ¼ teaspoon sugar.

Desserts and Sweets

"AS YOU LIKE IT" LAYER BARS (MAGIC BARS)

32 bars

Here's another example showing how to adapt a recipe for what you have on hand, or what you prefer. The basics, which you must include, are the buttered crumb base (layers one and two), the sweetened condensed milk (layer three), and some sort of chocolate or other melting candy such as butterscotch chips (layer four).

The basic ingredients:
Layer one: **½ cup butter or margarine (1 stick)**
Layer two: **1½ cups (about 4 ounces)** *of **one** of the following:*
- **graham cracker crumbs**
- **finely crushed buttery crackers such as Ritz**
- **finely crushed thin pretzels or pretzel sticks**
- **finely crushed cereal such as Golden Grahams, Chex, or Cheerios**
- **finely crushed saltine crackers**
- **finely crushed vanilla wafers**

Layer three: **1 can (14 ounces) Eagle Brand sweetened condensed milk**
Layer four: **12 ounces** *of **one** of the following, or* **6 ounces** *each of **two**:*
- **chocolate chips**
- **butterscotch chips**
- **broken-up chocolate bars such as Hersheys (chocolate with nuts is OK)**
- **small chunks of white chocolate or almond bark**
- **broken-up Chunky candy block (with raisins and nuts)**

Heat the oven to 350°F (325°F for glass dish). Place the butter in a 13x9x2-inch baking dish; heat in oven until the butter melts. Remove the dish from the oven and sprinkle the crackers, pretzels, cereal or wafers over the butter; stir gently and press evenly over bottom of baking dish with a spoon. Pour the sweetened condensed milk evenly over the crumb layer. Sprinkle chips or candy evenly over the milk.

*Final layers: **two or three** of the following:*
- **1 cup raisins or diced dried fruit such as apricots (these should go on first if using)**
- **1 cup sweetened coconut flakes**
- **1 cup coarsely chopped pecans, walnuts or other nuts**
- **1 cup chopped-up Mounds or Butterfingers candy bars**

- **1 cup M&M's or Reese's Pieces**
- **1 cup chocolate-covered raisins**
- **2 cups miniature marshmallows (these should go on last if using)**
- **Or use your imagination!**

Sprinkle chosen ingredients evenly over the chocolate chip layer; press down firmly. Bake until lightly browned, 25 to 30 minutes. If desired, top with Chocolate Drizzle Topping (below). Cool before cutting. If the bars are too crumbly to remove from the baking dish, refrigerate until hardened.

Chocolate Drizzle Topping

In microwave-safe dish at LOW power (or in small saucepan over very low heat), melt 4 ounces semi-sweet chocolate chips or candy bars with 1 tablespoon vegetable shortening, stirring frequently, until smooth. Drizzle over bars before cutting.

Two-Layer Rhubarb Pie

1 pie

I got this recipe years ago from a friend, who got it from another friend and so on, so I have no idea who first came up with this unusual technique that produces a pie with two layers: fruit and a sort of custard. It's delicious!

Pastry for single-crust pie (purchased or homemade; see page 198 for a low-fat crust you can use)
3 eggs
1 cup sugar
¼ cup butter (half of a stick), softened
¼ cup flour
2 tablespoons frozen orange juice concentrate, thawed
¼ teaspoon baking soda
¼ teaspoon salt
2½ cups cut-up rhubarb (¼-inch-thick slices)

Heat oven to 375°F. Roll pie crust out and fit into pie dish. Flute edges if desired (there is no top crust on this pie, so the edge will show). Refrigerate crust while you prepare the other ingredients.

Separate the eggs, putting the whites in a large mixing bowl and the yolks in another large mixing bowl. Add the sugar, butter, flour, orange juice concentrate, baking soda and salt to the yolks, and beat with an electric mixer or crank-style eggbeater until light in color. Stir in the rhubarb with a large spoon or rubber spatula.

Clean the beaters very well and dry them, or switch to a whisk. Beat the egg whites until they form soft peaks. Fold gently into the rhubarb mixture. Pour into the pie crust. Bake at 375°F for 15 minutes, then reduce heat to 325°F and bake 45 minutes longer; the filling will be puffy and deep golden brown. Cool before serving.

Double-Peanut Cookies

26 to 30 cookies

I based this recipe on one from a Betty Crocker booklet. They're the folks who make Bisquick baking mix, and they have come up with some wonderful ways to use this convenient product.

Half of a 14-ounce can sweetened condensed milk (⅔ cup)
1 egg
½ cup peanut butter
2 cups Bisquick Original baking mix
¾ cup honey-roasted peanuts, chopped coarsely (measure before chopping)
Sugar for tops of cookies (about 2 tablespoons)

Heat oven to 375°F. In large mixing bowl, combine condensed milk and egg; blend with a fork until smooth. Add peanut butter and blend until smooth. Add Bisquick and chopped nuts; mix with a large spoon until just incorporated. Pinch off walnut-sized balls, rolling until smooth between your palms; place on ungreased cookie sheet about 2 inches apart. Lightly grease the bottom of a drinking glass, then dip in sugar. Lightly press each cookie until it flattens to just over 2 inches in diameter, dipping glass in sugar for each cookie. Bake 10 minutes, or until cookies are just beginning to brown lightly on the edges; do not overbake. Cool on wire rack.

SIMPLE POUND CAKE WITH PINEAPPLES

Variable servings; 1 slice per serving

Frozen pound cake makes this dessert super-easy. It's pretty enough for company but easy enough for any day, and it tastes great!

Frozen pound cake loaf, thawed, or homemade pound cake loaf
2 teaspoons butter or margarine per serving
1 canned pineapple ring per serving, well drained
Powdered sugar for dusting (about 2 teaspoons per serving)
Half of a maraschino cherry per serving, optional

Cut off as many 1-inch-thick slices of pound cake as you need; a 10.75-ounce frozen pound cake yields about 8 slices. Melt 2 teaspoons butter per serving in a large skillet over medium heat. Add pound cake slices; when the first side is lightly coated with butter, turn them to coat the second side. Fry until lightly golden brown, then turn and fry the other side. Place a slice on an individual dessert plate. Top with a pineapple slice. Sprinkle powdered sugar over each serving (very easy to do if you place the powdered sugar in a small wire-mesh strainer; simply shake or tap the strainer to release an even dusting of powdered sugar). Place cherry, cut-side down, in center hole of pineapple. Serve immediately.

SWEET FRIED TORTILLA STRIPS

Variable servings

Try these for a light dessert, perhaps with a dish of ice cream, or as a sweet snack. Kids and adults alike love these, so make plenty.

Flour tortillas (one 8-inch tortilla makes 2 servings)
Vegetable oil for frying
Cinnamon-sugar (mix ½ cup sugar with a tablespoon of cinnamon; increase proportions as needed)
Honey for dipping, optional

Line a baking sheet with newspaper, then cover the newspaper with clean paper towels. Cut tortillas into 1-inch-wide strips; for a variation, cut them instead into quarters. Heat ¼ inch oil in a heavy-bottomed wide skillet until the oil is hot but not smoking (to test the oil, cut off a small square of tortilla and add it to the oil; it should turn golden brown in 25 to 30 seconds without burning). Add a few strips at a time and cook until golden brown, 25 to 30 seconds on each side. Transfer with tongs to the lined baking sheet and sprinkle generously with cinnamon-sugar (you may want to enlist the aid of a helper to do the sprinkling while you fry more strips). Serve with a bowl of honey for dipping if you've got a real sweet tooth.

HOBO ICE CREAM

4 to 6 servings

This recipe has been around forever, and appears in many community cookbooks. It's great for keeping the kids occupied, and it really works (although it makes a terrible racket). You'll need two different-sized coffee cans; you might be able to snare the larger one from the office or local church dining hall.

The Needed equipment:

13-ounce coffee can (if you find a 1-pound coffee can, that's fine, too) with snap-on lid
39-ounce or larger coffee can with snap-on lid
Several pounds of coarsely crushed ice
About 1½ cups salt, any type including kosher, table or rock salt

The ice cream:

1½ cups heavy cream
¾ cup whole milk
1 egg, or ¼ cup pasteurized egg substitute, such as Egg Beaters, if you're concerned about eating raw egg
⅓ cup sugar
1 teaspoon vanilla extract or other flavoring
Optional: about 1 cup of chocolate chips or chopped-up fruit

Wash the coffee cans well and dry them. Place the smaller one in the freezer while you prepare the ice cream. In a blender, combine the cream, milk, egg, sugar and vanilla; process for 2 minutes (alternately, you can whip this in a chilled bowl for 5 minutes with an electric mixer). Stir in the chips or fruit, and pour the mixture into the smaller coffee can. Seal the lid tightly; if the lid doesn't seal well, you have a big problem so make sure, in advance, that the lid and top rim of the can are in good shape.

Place an inch of crushed ice into the larger can; sprinkle with salt. Place the small can on the bed of ice, and fill the space between the two cans with layers of ice and salt. Seal the large can securely.

If you're doing the mixing indoors, put the cans into a large plastic bag and seal tightly before you start in case the lid pops off the larger can. Roll the can on the ground (or shake vigorously, but this is deafening) for about 5 minutes. Open the larger can and drain off any water, then add more salt and ice and roll about 10 minutes longer. Open and drain again, then check the ice cream inside. It may be done already, but will probably need another 10 or 15 minutes of rolling; if so, add more ice and salt and continue until the ice cream is ready. If it still isn't firm, put the small can in the freezer for 15 or 20 minutes until it hardens.

Beverages and Miscellaneous

HOMEMADE IRISH CREAM LIQUEUR

About 1 quart

You'll be surprised how good this easy-to-make liqueur is. Serve it over ice as an after-dinner drink, pour it over ice cream, or use it in place of cream to spike coffee. It keeps for up to a month in the refrigerator ... but it probably won't last that long!

2 cups (1 pint) half-and-half
1 can (14 ounces) Eagle Brand sweetened condensed milk
¾ cup bourbon
⅓ cup dark rum
¼ cup chocolate syrup
1 teaspoon vanilla extract

Combine all ingredients in a pitcher and stir well. Use a funnel to pour the mix into a quart bottle; replace the cap and refrigerate.

FRUIT SMOOTHIES

3 or 4 servings

Get the taste of summer all year long with these delicious drinks. Feel free to use any fresh, canned or frozen fruit you have on hand to make your own variations. Just remember to balance the amount of liquid with the amount of solid fruits; for example, if you use a very juicy fruit such as watermelon, decrease the liquid a bit.

Yogurt-based Smoothie

1 cup low-fat yogurt, plain or flavored as you prefer
1 cup chilled fruit juice
2 cups fresh, canned or thawed frozen fruit (a mix of 2 varieties is good)
1 small banana

Milk-based Smoothie

1 cup milk (reduced-fat works fine)
½ cup chilled fruit juice
2 cups fresh, canned or thawed frozen fruit (a mix of 2 varieties is good)
1 small banana
½ cup crushed ice

Juice-based Smoothie

1½ cups chilled fruit juice
2 cups fresh, canned or thawed frozen fruit (a mix of 2 varieties is good)
1 small banana
½ cup crushed ice
2 tablespoons malt powder or dry milk powder, optional

Sherbet- or ice cream-based Smoothie

1 cup slightly softened sherbet (or ice cream, if you don't mind the calories)
1 cup chilled fruit juice
2½ cups fresh, canned or thawed frozen fruit

Combine all ingredients in blender and purée until smooth. Taste, and add a teaspoon of sugar or honey if needed, blending for a few seconds. Serve immediately.

"What kind of dressing do you want with that?"

Salad dressings are useful for more than flavoring a bowl of greens. Vinaigrettes make excellent marinades for meat before grilling, and also are used to dress pasta and potato salads; blue cheese dressing is used as a dip for spicy chicken wings. Here are salad dressing recipes that appear on other pages of this book.

- Raspberry Vinaigrette, page 63
- Honey-Mustard Dressing, page 127 (great for salads that include fruit)
- Island Dressing, page 131 (for salads that go well with Hawaiian flavors)

On pages 98–101 are recipes for seven more dressings. Experiment until you find one that you like, and don't be afraid to adjust the recipes to suit your taste.

Vinaigrettes are the most basic of dressings, and are generally made with the proportions of 3 parts oil to 1 part vinegar (for example, ¾ cup oil and ¼ cup vinegar). If you use lemon juice in place of vinegar, you'll need a higher proportion, since lemon juice has less acid than vinegar. Also, the flavors of various oils vary tremendously. A rich green extra-virgin olive oil has a lot more flavor than commodity olive oil or vegetable oil; specialty oils, such as walnut and Asian sesame oil, have even more flavor, and should be used more sparingly. The flavor of the oil can really show in a vinaigrette, so if you want the taste of olive oil, get the best, most flavorful olive oil you can find. Walnut oil goes rancid in a short time, and should be kept refrigerated. Some cooks refrigerate olive oil as well. I don't, because I use it quickly enough that it doesn't have the chance to get rancid.

For the smoothest, creamiest texture, blend vinaigrettes in a blender or food processor; a hand mixer also does a good job at this. If you combine the ingredients in a bowl and beat them with a fork, the dressings will be more likely to separate. This is all right, as long as you use it right away, or mix it again just before using. You may also mix vinaigrettes in a jar. Combine all ingredients in a jar large enough to hold all ingredients comfortably with room to spare, cover very tightly and shake until well mixed. If you have a mortar and pestle, mash the herbs and garlic together before adding them to the rest of the ingredients. The addition of coarse salt also helps when mashing with a mortar and pestle.

Vinaigrettes have the best flavor if used the day they are made, but can be kept refrigerated for a few days before using. Thicker dressings, such as blue cheese or honey-mustard dressing keep, for a week or so in the refrigerator. If they separate during storage, simply stir with a fork before using.

SIMPLE VINAIGRETTE

¾ cup extra-virgin olive oil, or other oil of your choice
¼ cup wine vinegar, or other vinegar of your choice
½ teaspoon salt
½ teaspoon Dijon mustard, optional
¼ teaspoon finely minced garlic, optional
A few grindings of black pepper

Combine all ingredients and mix well as described on page 97. Taste, and adjust as necessary.

GREEK VINAIGRETTE

¾ cup extra-virgin olive oil
⅓ cup freshly squeezed lemon juice (from about 1½ lemons)
2 tablespoons grated red onion, optional
1 teaspoon chopped fresh parsley
¾ teaspoon Dijon mustard
¾ teaspoon minced fresh oregano leaves, or ¼ teaspoon dried
½ teaspoon finely minced garlic
½ teaspoon salt
A few grindings of black pepper

Combine all ingredients and mix well as described on page 97. Taste, and adjust as necessary.

BLUE CHEESE DRESSING

½ cup mayonnaise (reduced-fat works fine)
½ cup sour cream (reduced-fat works fine)
1 tablespoon freshly squeezed lemon juice
¼ teaspoon finely minced garlic
3 ounces blue cheese, crumbled (about ¾ cup crumbled cheese)

In mixing bowl, stir together the mayonnaise, sour cream, lemon juice and garlic. Add the blue cheese and mix well; if you prefer a smoother dressing, mash the cheese crumbles against the bowl with a fork, or process briefly in a blender or food processor. Taste, and add a little salt, or additional lemon juice, if necessary.

HEARTY ITALIAN VINAIGRETTE

The inspiration for this thick dressing came from Top Secret Restaurant Recipes, *by Todd Wilbur. His recipe is the first I've seen to use dry pectin as a thickener for dressing, and it works really well.*

⅔ cup extra-virgin olive oil
½ cup cold water
½ cup white wine vinegar
2 tablespoons dry pectin (available in the canning department at the supermarket)
2 tablespoons grated Parmesan or Romano cheese
1 tablespoon sugar
1 tablespoon chopped fresh parsley
1 teaspoon chopped fresh basil leaves, or ¼ teaspoon dried
¾ teaspoon salt
½ teaspoon finely minced garlic
A pinch of crushed dried hot red pepper flakes
A few grindings of black pepper

Combine all ingredients in mixing bowl, and beat with a hand mixer for about a minute. Taste, and adjust as necessary. Chill thoroughly before serving.

FRESH GREEN GODDESS DRESSING

½ cup mayonnaise (reduced-fat works fine)
½ cup plain yogurt (reduced-fat works fine)
2 green onions, finely chopped
2 tablespoons chopped fresh parsley
2 tablespoons snipped fresh chives
2 teaspoons finely chopped tarragon leaves, optional
1 teaspoon lemon juice
½ teaspoon finely minced garlic

Combine all ingredients in mixing bowl; stir well. Taste, and adjust as necessary. Chill thoroughly before serving.

Caesar Dressing

For the authentic Caesar salad, the dressing is made to order in the salad serving bowl, with fresh greens tossed in at the end. This Caesar dressing is made in advance. For safety, pasteurized egg substitute is used instead of the traditional raw egg.

½ cup pasteurized egg substitute such as Egg Beaters
2 tablespoons freshly squeezed lemon juice (from about half a lemon)
½ cup extra-virgin olive oil
1 or 2 anchovy fillets, mashed well with a fork
¼ to ½ teaspoon finely minced garlic
½ teaspoon Worcestershire sauce
¼ teaspoon salt
A few grindings of black pepper
2 tablespoons shredded Parmesan or Romano cheese

Using a whisk or mixer, beat the egg substitute for a few seconds. Continue beating while you add first the lemon juice, then the olive oil, in a thin stream. Beat until the mixture is smooth and creamy. Add remaining ingredients and beat well. Taste, and adjust as necessary.

POPPY SEED DRESSING

About 1 cup

Use this dressing on any green salad that features fruit. I like to combine spinach, sliced red onions and orange sections with a few toasted, roasted, salted sunflower nuts, then toss with this dressing.

½ cup vegetable oil
⅓ cup honey
3 tablespoons white wine vinegar
½ teaspoon salt
1 tablespoon grated onion
¾ teaspoon poppy seeds
½ teaspoon dry mustard powder

Combine all ingredients in a glass jar. Cover tightly and shake well to blend.

Fun with Flatbreads

Many cracker and bread products are called flatbreads. What I'm talking about here are pre-baked bread rounds similar to pizza crusts. Because they're already baked, they don't need any tedious rising and are ready for action at a moment's notice. If you have a freezer in the cabin, keep a package or two of these versatile breads on hand; they can be thawed very quickly when you need them. Otherwise, pack some with the groceries for your vacation.

Flatbreads help you make good use of leftover vegetables, cooked meats or other ingredients for easy appetizers, quick pizzas and unusual open-faced sandwiches. Here are a few quick-and-easy ideas to get you started:

- For a quick Italian-themed appetizer, sauté some chopped garlic and a few flakes of crushed dried hot red pepper flakes in a tablespoon of olive oil or butter, then brush on a flatbread. Sprinkle with Parmesan or Romano cheese. Bake at 375°F for about 10 minutes, then cut into wedges.
- Make quick-and-easy pizza by spreading a flatbread with tomato-based pasta sauce (from a jar, or leftover homemade). Sprinkle with anything you have on hand that sounds good: chopped bell peppers, onions, salami, cut-up leftover cooked sausage, diced ham, or sliced olives are good alone or in combination with one or two other items. Sprinkle with whatever type of shredded cheese you have on hand. Bake at 375°F until the cheese is bubbly, about 15 minutes.
- For an elegant white pizza, spread a flatbread with prepared Alfredo or other white sauce. Top with one or two of the following: sliced mushrooms, cooked broccoli cut into small flowerets, roasted red bell pepper chunks, thin slivers of red onion, cooked diced chicken, leftover cooked shrimp (cut into slices if the shrimp is large), or sliced canned artichoke hearts. Sprinkle with shredded mozzarella or Monterey Jack cheese, and a little Parmesan if you have it. Bake at 375°F until cheese is bubbly, about 15 minutes.
- How about open-faced peanut-butter-and-bacon sandwiches? Spread a flatbread liberally with peanut butter—chunky is particularly good. Top with crisp, crumbled bacon, and cut into quarters. For a sandwich with a bit more heft and nutrition, combine ¼ cup peanut butter, a few tablespoons shredded carrot and a tablespoon of honey; spread over flatbread and top with bacon if desired.

Here's a delicious flatbread-based breakfast pizza that uses up small amounts of leftovers or that chunk of green pepper that's too small to bother packing into the cooler for the trip home. Of course, there's no law that says it has to be made from leftovers; this is good enough that you may want to bring ingredients especially to make this easy meal. This recipe uses a small flatbread to serve two, but is easy to double or triple. If you're using a larger flatbread, increase the ingredients proportionally. Don't worry too much about exact quantities of the ingredients; part of the fun of cooking with flatbreads like this is that you can adapt almost anything and you don't have to measure precisely.

Breakfast Pizza

2 servings; easily doubled or tripled

1 pre-baked flatbread (about 6 inches in diameter)
3 tablespoons diced green or red bell pepper
A bit of chopped garlic, optional
1 teaspoon butter, margarine, bacon drippings* or vegetable oil
¼ cup diced ham or Canadian bacon; or 2 slices bacon, cooked* and crumbled
2 eggs, lightly beaten
½ cup shredded marble Jack or other cheese

Heat oven to 375°F. Place flatbread on a cookie sheet and cover with a large, domed pot lid (or a tent of foil). Place in oven while you prepare the topping. Sauté the pepper and garlic in the butter over medium heat until beginning to soften. Add the ham, and cook until vegetables are tender-crisp. Add the eggs and cook, stirring constantly, until just beginning to firm up; eggs should still be runny or they will not bond properly to the flatbread. Quickly spread the egg mixture over the flatbread. Sprinkle with the cheese. Re-cover the flatbread with the pot lid and return to the oven until the cheese is melted and the eggs are set, about 10 minutes. If you like, place the pizza under the broiler for a few minutes until the cheese is very bubbly. To serve, cut pizza into quarters.

*If you're using bacon instead of ham, fry it before the pepper, then use a teaspoon of the drippings to sauté the pepper and garlic.

Options: Add a bit of chopped onion or celery to the pepper, or use them in place of the pepper. In place of the ham, substitute a diced cooked sausage; crumble up a leftover hamburger or slice of meatloaf; or, for a vegetarian option, eliminate the meat entirely.

Summer

Table of Contents

Appetizers and Snacks

Main Dishes

Desserts and Sweets

Beverages and Miscellaneous

Pig Roast Party

Nothing beats an old-fashioned pig roast for a big summer get-together. Although I've roasted whole pigs as early as March, I prefer to wait until about August, when the local sweet corn in my area is ripe and plentiful, and the weather is warm enough to hang around outside from dawn till dusk—and beyond. If you can dig a large pit and cook the pig in the ground, by all means do so. Once the pit has been fired and the pig buried, you need do nothing further until you're ready to eat. The pit is also ideal for roasting fresh sweet corn, potatoes, even a chicken or turkey for those guests who don't care to eat pork.

Spit-roasting, on the other hand, is a more exciting experience for the guests, because they will be tantalized with the aroma and sight of the roasting pig for several hours before dinnertime. Spit-roasted pig finishes off with a crispy, glazed exterior, leaving lots of special crusty treats for the cook's helpers. Most spit roasters are portable. They are often on a trailer that can be pulled behind a vehicle, much like a boat trailer. And you don't end up with a huge hole in the lawn the next day! I'll give information on both methods below, and let you decide how you want to proceed.

For either technique, the ideal is a young, whole pig that dresses out at about 100 pounds. You can get whole pigs from a pig farmer (obviously), and many butchers and supermarkets also can special-order one. Tell them how you'll be cooking the pig so they know how to prepare it for you. Like most traditionalists, I prefer the pig with the head left on. However, if this is upsetting to you or your guests, you can have the head removed at the time of butchering. Be sure that the pig will be boiled and scraped to remove the hair from the skin, or skinned completely. You may also want the farmer or butcher to cut off the feet, and if you're spit-roasting, you will probably want the butcher to remove the skin and some of the fat.

The pig should be slaughtered at least a day in advance, and hung in a refrigerated meat locker to allow it to chill completely. Most pig farmers work with a butcher, processing plant or meat locker with this sort of facility, if they don't have a locker themselves. If you pick up the pig the night before your party, put it into an old bathtub filled with ice in the coolest place you can find.

Pit-roasting

Preparing the pit—Needed tools and supplies

Pit-roasting is often considered a Hawaiian or tropical technique, and indeed, traditional recipes call for the use of banana leaves to wrap the pig. I've never had access to banana leaves, however, so I've developed a technique using fresh cornstalks and leaves. The cornstalks lend a wonderful, rich taste to the pig (I imagine the banana leaves contribute a unique flavor as well), and during corn season, stalks and leaves are easy to come by, if you're near an agricultural area. In fact, you can probably get them from the same source as the ears of corn you'll want to roast with the pig. You'll need six to eight gunnysacks of cornstalks and leaves. The stalks should be pulled from the ground shortly before you get them so they are still fresh and green.

Dig the pit at least a day in advance, as you'll need to begin burning wood in the pit in the wee morning hours the day of the pig roast. The pit should be about 3 feet deep, and approximately 4 feet wide by 6 feet long. Heap the dirt off to the side of the pit as you dig; you'll need a good amount of it to bury the pig while it is cooking. Gather a dozen or more soccer-ball-sized rocks and a few dozen fist-sized rocks from the land surrounding the pit. Don't take them from a lake or stream, however, as these will explode in the heat of the fire. Lava rocks are used in Hawaii for pig roasts, because they retain the heat very well, but this is not practical for most of the country. You'll also need about a third of a cord of hardwood, cut to size for a fireplace. This amount is often called a fireplace cord or a face cord. Feel free to gather clean, non-rotten deadfall if you are in a wooded area, but make sure to choose only dry hardwoods; green wood will not burn properly, and wood from evergreen trees will give the meat an unpleasant flavor. Also, gather smaller sticks to use as kindling, or use an axe to split some of the fireplace wood into thinner strips.

You'll need two or three heavy-duty garden rakes or forked hoes to get the pig into and out of the pit. You could also improvise some sort of strong hook on a long handle for this job. Have enough chicken wire on hand to securely wrap the pig; you'll use this to move the pig in and out of the pit. Some sturdy wire will be needed to fasten the chicken wire, as well as a pair of wire snips to cut it. A half-dozen burlap or heavy canvas sacks will be used to cover everything before the dirt is shoveled back on. If you buy corn in burlap sacks, you've got it made. Finally, have a large tarp available to cover the pit after the pig is buried; it will help hold the heat in, and also keep light rainfall from turning the pit to mud. If you are unlucky enough to have a heavy rainfall on the day of the pig roast, you have a problem on your hands, and I don't know what to tell you. The items you should have for serving are listed below, in the carving and serving instructions.

Plan your timing backwards from the time you want to serve the pig. A whole pig will take about 8 hours in the pit. If you want to speed this up—and also make handling a bit easier—have the pig cut into quarters, then wrap the quarters individually and arrange them in the pit. Quarters will cook in about 5 hours. Whether you're cooking a whole pig or quarters, you'll need to begin firing the pit four hours in advance. If you want to serve a whole pig at 4 p.m., for instance, you'll need to start firing the pit at 4 a.m. Now don't those quarters sound like a better option? You won't need to start firing the pit until 7 a.m. if you're cooking quarters.

Firing the pit and cooking

Be sure to use safety precautions and common sense when working with fire, especially one of this magnitude. At the appropriate hour (as calculated in the preceding paragraph), start the fire in the pit. There are many ways to do this. One way is to lay a border of the large wood pieces and the rocks all around the edges of the pit, then heap the center with kindling and light it. Although many purists would frown, I believe it is OK to use charcoal-starting fluid, because by the time the pig is anywhere near the fire, the solution has long since burned off. When the kindling is burning merrily, start adding a few larger pieces of wood, gradually increasing the amount as the larger pieces catch fire. When the fire is going well, use your long-handled hoe to push the rocks closer to the hottest part of the fire, always respecting the fire and the sparks it will kick up. Continue adding more wood until the rocks are red- to white-hot and the pit is extremely hot. You really can't make it too hot.

Meanwhile, someone else needs to be dealing with the pig. Slash the pig on the outside, but not deeply into the meat, and rub salt into the slits. Or, as I prefer, chop up several heads of garlic with a cup of kosher salt and a few good handfuls of fresh herbs, then rub this mixture into the slits. Another nice flavoring option is to press whole stalks of fresh rosemary against the pig after salting the slits. Place the whole pig on a piece of chicken wire that is large enough to completely go around it. If using quarters, each quarter gets its own piece of chicken wire. If wrapping a whole pig, leave the chicken wire unfastened until the pit is ready. The wrapping for quarters can be fastened any time you like, even the night before.

Also wrap a few whole chickens, or a whole turkey if you like, in chicken wire. Foil-wrap a scrubbed baking potato for each guest, and soak the unhusked ears of corn in a large vat of cold water (unless the corn was picked just that morning). Some cooks like to throw a few whole pineapples in the pit along with everything else, and these need no advance preparation. Soak the burlap sacks in cold water also.

When the pit is hot and ready, carefully fish out a few of the hot rocks and place them in the cavity of the whole pig, especially between the hams. Fasten the chicken wire securely, using sturdy wire to tie the edges together. These wires will be under a lot of pressure as you lower and raise the pig, so the fastenings need to be secure. Pull out half of the remaining rocks, dragging them up onto the ground next to the pit. Now throw a full layer of cornstalks over the logs and the rocks that remain in the pit. Position the pig on its back (if possible) over the cornstalks. If cooking quarters, distribute them evenly, in a single layer, in the pit. Now push the hot rocks back into the pit, nudging them as close as you can to the pig. They can be used to help prop the pig up on its back. Arrange the wrapped poultry, potatoes and soaked corn around edges of the pit where the fire is cooler. Cover the entire shebang with another layer of cornstalks, then top with the wet burlap sacks, making a very solid layer with wide overlaps. Now, shovel dirt onto the burlap sacks, mounding it as necessary so the dirt is about a foot thick. Cover all with the tarp, and ignore it for the required amount of time: 8 hours for a whole pig, or 5 hours for quarters. Adjust the timing if your pig is smaller or larger than 100 pounds dressed weight.

Digging up the pit

Near the end of the cooking time, make sure all carving and serving items are at hand. (See pages 114-117, "Carving and serving the pig," for specifics.) When all is ready, pull off the tarp, setting it to one side, then carefully shovel away the dirt. Have a helper wipe the tarp clean with wet cloths, if necessary. Pull off the burlap sacks carefully to avoid getting dirt on the layers below. Use the rake to pull away the cornstalks, revealing the pig and surrounding vegetables and poultry. At this point, two strong people need to work together to raise the hot pig from the pit. The best way is to hook the tines of two spanking-clean forked hoes or strong garden rakes into the chicken wire, then lift in tandem and move the bundle to the tarp. Once the pig is on the tarp, unwrap the chicken wire at the front and cut off one front leg as described on page 114, then move it individually to the carving table. (If you've cooked the pig in quarters, lift one of the front quarters from the pit and transport it directly to the carving table.) Check the temperature of the pig with an instant-read thermometer; it should read 160°F to 165°F. The forequarters cook more quickly than the hindquarters. In the unlikely event that the hindquarters aren't yet done, you can put the rest of the pig back onto the fire (or leave it there, in the case of individually wrapped quarters) while you start working on the forequarter.

While the head cook starts carving the pig, another helper or two should remove the corn and potatoes from the fire, stacking them anywhere that makes sense (a big washtub works well for this). Pull the poultry out and transfer it to a separate carving table. A helper should carve the birds, while the head cook works on the pig.

Spit-roasting

Needed tools and supplies

Spit-roasting is a lot simpler than pit-roasting, provided you have a decent rotary pig roaster. Party rental outfits usually offer these for weekend rental. Look for a unit with a heavy-duty electric motor that turns the spit. Make sure the unit is clean when you pick it up from the rental place; I've heard stories of people who got one with the carcass of the previous meal still embedded on the spit! You'll need a long heavy-duty extension cord to plug the motor in. Also, buy about 100 pounds of charcoal, starter fluid for the charcoal, two boxes of heavy-duty aluminum foil, and two pair of long, heavy-duty barbecue or oven mitts, which will end up getting trashed. An instant-read thermometer is a necessity.

If possible, bring the spit along to the butcher when you pick up the pig, and ask them to help you secure the pig to the spit. Most spits have some sort of pronged unit at both ends to hold the pig, but take my word: these may not hold. Anything you can do to provide additional security for the pig is worth it, including wiring the feet and the head to the spit. It's a disaster if the pig "comes loose" from the spit halfway through the cooking time. The spit continues to turn, but the pig just hangs there, usually with the backside down, while the spit turns merrily inside the pig. Another catastrophe waiting to happen is an inadequate motor, which may conk out halfway through the roasting. Make sure that the roaster you rent has a motor that is adequate for the size pig you are roasting.

Most cooks prefer to have the skin removed for a spit-roasted pig; the butcher will do this for you. Make sure they leave a good amount of fat on the outside of the pig to baste the meat as it cooks. Skinned spit-roasted pigs are deliciously crispy on the outside. If the skin is still on during roasting, you will have less problem with flare-ups, but the skin will not be good to eat unless you like that sort of thing (and some people do). I like to get the skinned pig the night before, and rub it with some sort of soak or light marinade; a mix of pineapple juice, herbs and garlic works well. Of course, you'll have to keep the pig cold overnight as described on page 109, so you may want to forego the soaking and just pick up the pig in the morning.

Spit-roasting a whole pig usually takes about 5 hours, and it is easy to see how the cooking is going so you can remove it sooner, or cook it longer, if necessary. Plan on starting the charcoal 45 minutes before putting the pig on. However, before putting any charcoal in the roaster, line the entire bottom and up the sides of the roaster with heavy-duty foil with the shiny side up. Start with a sheet of foil at one end, then lay foil sheets along the bottom so that each sheet overlaps the previous sheet by at least 3 inches. This makes cleanup much easier (see page 119). Add a 4- to 5-inch layer of coals along the bottom, on top of the foil. Soak the coals generously with charcoal-starting fluid and light carefully. Allow the coals to burn until covered with gray ash before putting the pig into the roaster.

It will take two strong individuals to wrestle the spit into place, and this can be the most stressful moment of the entire day. The coals are very hot, the pig is heavy, and the spit doesn't always go into the motor sockets with great ease. Both individuals should be wearing long barbecue mitts on both arms. Asbestos fireplace mitts are even better, but may get ruined with pig grease and soot. Once the pig is in place and the spit is turning, drop the lid on the roaster, crack open a beer (you've earned it) and let the spit turn until the pig is done. You may baste the pig periodically with a light basting liquid if you like (the pineapple juice soak mentioned on the previous page works well), but don't use a heavy, sugar-based sauce, because it will burn badly before the pig is even half done. Toss a good amount of fresh charcoal into the fire every 45 minutes or so. If you want a smoky flavor, also add some soaked hardwood or fruitwood chunks to the coals periodically.

To check the temperature of the pig, temporarily stop the motor and insert an instant-read thermometer deeply into the meat. Don't let the thermometer touch bone; it needs to be solidly into the meat. Pig is done at 160°F to 165°F. If the cooking is going more quickly than you anticipated and you are in danger of getting done ahead of schedule, spread the coals out to the back of the roaster and leave the lid partially open. On the other hand, if the pig isn't cooking quickly enough, pile on more coals, close the lid and open a few more ventilation holes to increase the heat. Keep in mind that the forequarters will cook more quickly than the hindquarters, and with spit roasting it is relatively easy to cut away a forequarter and begin carving it while the rest of the pig cooks.

Carving and serving the pig

Needed tools and supplies

Carving a roasted pig is a messy job. Buy an oven mitt for your left hand (assuming you're right-handed). The mitt will get wrecked, so you may want to use an old one that you won't mind tossing out afterward. You'll also need a decent chef's knife (7- to 10-inch blade is best) and a stiff-backed boning knife (not a fillet knife). If you have a clean hacksaw or meat saw, you may find it helpful for the ribs. Assemble a bunch of turkey roasters or large disposable foil pans such as those used for cooking turkeys; you'll need two or three for the meat, and a separate one for the fat and other scrap. I keep a large stockpot or two on hand for bones that will become the basis for delicious stock (more on that later). Line a large sturdy table with a plastic picnic table cover for your work surface. Have lots of garbage bags and a big garbage can ready for disposal of the fat and other scrap. Use a double bag, because it will get heavy, and it's a disaster if this breaks. It's nice to have a pan of warm, sudsy water to occasionally dip your greasy hands in. Tie an apron around your waist, and hang a cotton towel or two from the apron; you'll be grateful for a clean place to wipe your hands.

First, remove one front leg (if you've pit-cooked quarters, you don't have to remove the front leg; just proceed to the actual carving stage). To remove the front leg, arrange the pig on its side with the cavity facing you and the head to your right (if you've used a spit, get the spit to stop so the quarter is toward you). Pull the right front leg up and away from the body, and slip the chef's knife between the pig's "armpit" and body. Begin cutting near the front shoulder and working your way back, continuing to pull the shoulder away (you may want a helper, also armed with an oven mitt, to help with the holding and pulling). Unlike a hip or knee, the shoulder has no ball-and-socket joint to cut around, so it is very easy to remove. When you get it free, set it on the table with the outside up, then carve off and discard any excess fat or burned stuff.

There is little meat on the inside of the front leg; most of it is on the outside and around the edge. The front leg has a large flat bone shaped like a fan that gives the upper part of the leg its shape. This fan has a ridge that runs at an angle, which you'll have to carve around. Locate the ridge by feeling with your hand. Use the boning knife to cut along one side of the ridge down to the fan-shaped bone (a depth of about 2 inches), then slip the boning knife sideways until you can continue cutting along the flat surface of the fan-shaped bone. Eventually, you'll free a piece of boneless meat. Carve this into slices across the grain and put them into one of your serving roasters. Remove the meat on the other side of the ridge in the same fashion and carve it, too. This isn't as complicated as it sounds! Now use your hands to pull away any large chunks of meat that remain, using the boning knife to free them as needed. Slice if necessary, but actually, a lot of the meat will come away in long shreds which simply need to be cut shorter. The meat on the shank (the lower part of the leg) has lots of tendons and may not be the best part. But you can cut it away from the bone, then separate it with your hands and boning knife to remove the tendons. Or, leave the meat on the shank and use it later to flavor a pot of beans. Separate the two parts of the front leg by cutting through the joint, and put the bones in the stockpot (unless you are saving the shank for beans, in which case you should wrap the shank separately and refrigerate it).

Now it's time to tackle the rear leg—the ham. This is where the majority of the meat is, and also takes the longest to cook. Take the meat's temperature; if it's below 160°F, you may want to carve off the hind leg and put it onto a kettle grill to complete the cooking, while the guests start eating the rest of the pig. Removing the hind leg is a bit tricky. There is a complicated ball-and-socket joint, like your hip bone, that is hard to separate. Grab the shank and pull the leg away from the body to locate its natural seams. Wiggle it around until you can see where it wants to come apart. Make a cut with the chef's knife at the "natural" hip line, and cut until you hit bone. Lift the leg and cut from underneath until you hit bone again. Make a cut at the natural seam along the top of the rump until you hit bone. At this point, you can pull the leg around and hopefully see the ball-and-socket joint. Use the tip of your boning knife to separate the ball from the socket. Have a helper hold the leg at this point, because the leg is heavy, and it's difficult—and dangerous—to both hold and cut by yourself. The helper should pull the leg away from the body to help you see what you're doing. When you get the hind leg off, lay it on the carving table. Remove excess fat and burned stuff, then carve just like a regular bone-in ham. To do this, cut slices across the grain down to the bone, then make a cut parallel to the bone to free the slices. Rotate the leg until you've carved all sides of it. The rear shank is the same story as the front leg; do what you like about that.

Now for the best part: the loin. There are two "sides" to the loin. Each loin is a long strip of muscle that runs parallel to the backbone, along its whole length, on top of the pig. Either spin the pig around so the back is facing you, or go to the other side of the table if possible. Use your boning knife to make a cut along the backbone, starting at the point where you removed the shoulder and running down to the area where the hind leg was removed. You'll be cutting along the sides of the thin "blades" that stick up along the back. (If you aren't sure about pig anatomy, go to the store a day in advance and look at a bone-in loin chop. There is a T- or wedge-shaped bone that is very flat on one end. The flat part is where the butcher has split the carcass through the middle of the backbone. If you place two of these together with the flat parts touching, you will see the shape of the backbone "blade" as well as the shape of the loin.) Once you've cut along the "blade," then cut along the tops of the ribs to free the loin. Lay the loin on the table and cut into slices across the grain. Save some for yourself, because this is the best part of a roast pig.

At this point, you may want to pull off any larger chunks of meat that are still attached to various areas of the side you've been carving. Save the fine picking for later. If there are any kids in the crowd, they will be pulling these tidbits off anyway, and eating it as you carve.

Now you can turn the pig over and do the other side in the same way. If you want to make use of the ribs, use the saw to cut the ribs away along the edge of the backbone. You can also do this with a knife, but it takes a lot of pressure. With your greasy hands, you could easily end up with a serious cut, so be very careful about this. I like to baste the ribs with barbecue sauce at this point and toss them on a kettle grill for a while. They are not very "crispy," since they've been largely covered up with fat and legs, and the additional barbecuing makes them delicious. Or, you can carve the meat from between the ribs if you prefer, in which case you don't have to tinker with cutting the rib bones away from the backbone.

Now that you have all the quarters removed, you can locate and carve the tenderloin. This consists of two strips of meat inside of the body cavity, along either side of the backbone, near what you'd call the lower back. You can free these with your boning knife and cut them up. They're not huge, but they are very tender and tasty. (More for the cook's personal supply of goodies!) Now take a break and eat, before you pass out from all this excitement.

After you've had something to eat, or whenever you like, pull off or cut off the small bits of meat that are all over the carcass, shredding the meat with your fingers. I like to sauté a few chopped onions, add the shredded meat and some barbecue sauce, and simmer for a while. This makes a delicious barbecue sandwich to serve later, after everyone has digested the first helping and is looking for a little snack. You can do this for a second service in the evening, or save it for the next day.

I always make stock from the bones, usually the next day. If the bones are too big for your stockpot, cut them in half with a meat saw or clean hacksaw. For the best stock, brown the bones by roasting in a large roasting pan at 400°F in the oven for about 45 minutes. This serves two purposes. One, the browning adds flavor to the stock; and two, it removes more of the fat, which you don't want in the stock anyway. Pour off the fat and discard, then put the browned bones in a stockpot. Pour some water into the roaster and scrape up any browned bits at the bottom; add the water and browned bits to the stockpot. Add a few quartered onions, a half-dozen carrots (depending on the size of your stockpot), some celery, a few bay leaves and some black peppercorns. Cover with cold water. Heat to boiling, then reduce to a simmer and cook for 6 hours or so. If you don't want to take the time to roast the bones, just proceed with the rest of the instructions.

When the stock is rich and fragrant, pull out the bones with a long tongs and discard; strain the stock through cheesecloth to remove the vegetables, etc. Cool immediately. After it is well chilled, scrape off the cake of fat that will be floating on the surface. This stock makes excellent soup, baked beans, cabbage, etc., and I highly recommend it. If you have a pressure canner, you can easily can the stock and keep it in the pantry. Otherwise, freeze it for future use. You can also reduce the strained, de-fatted stock so it takes up less room. Simply boil it until the volume is reduced by a third.

Go-along dishes and other necessary items

Certain things just seem to go well with a pig roast. Here is a list of items I like to have on hand.

Side dishes:

- Coleslaw (a necessity, because it helps cut the grease)
- Potato salad, pasta salad
- Baked beans
- Potato chips, corn chips
- Fresh fruit salad
- Corn on the cob (if you've pit-roasted the pig, this is already done; otherwise, you may need to cook this separately, although some spit-roasters feature shelves for cooking corn and potatoes)
- Baked potatoes, sweet potatoes (again, this is part of the method if you've pit-roasted the pig)

Bread:

- Small buns or hamburger buns for sandwiches or on the side
- Sliced bread
- Cornbread or corn muffins

Sauces and other accompaniments:

- Barbecue sauce
- Mustard (several kinds, preferably)
- Hot sauce
- Mayonnaise
- Butter, margarine (for the corn and also the bread)
- Pickles (sweet and dill)
- Olives
- Salt and pepper

Beverages:

- Beer (it's best to buy a keg, even a small one, if your crowd likes beer)
- Soft drinks, mineral water
- Iced tea
- Lots of ice
- Mixers and alcohol as desired

Service items:

- Paper plates, including smaller plates for serving sandwiches later in the party
- Plastic forks
- Lots and lots of napkins, rolls of paper towels
- Wet-naps for kid cleanup
- Plastic cups for beverages
- Big garbage cans lined with plastic bags

Cleanup

The natural result of a pit-roasted pig is an evening bonfire. This is a good opportunity to burn the paper plates and napkins (if permitted by local ordinances). The cornstalks can be burned also, and you may even be able to burn the discarded corncobs and the carved-off fat and burned pieces, if the fire is really hot.

If you've spit-roasted the pig, let the roaster and ashes cool down completely; this may take longer than overnight. I don't recommend dousing the coals with water unless you have to, as it makes a terrible mess in the roaster. However, if there's dry grass around and the fire is still very hot when you're ready to call it a night, you'll have to pour buckets of water over the coals until they are dead. If the coals are still warm but basically dead, simply cover the roaster and close the vents before you retire for the evening.

The next day, or whenever the roaster is completely cold, you can easily clean out the roaster by rolling up the ashes, fat and other junk in the foil. Start at the same end that you began laying down the foil; as you roll, the overlaps will enable you to roll up the foil as one continuous piece. Even if you have to break it into two sections, it will be much simpler than cleaning out an unlined roaster. Soak the spit in a large tub of hot, soapy water and scrub well. Lightly oil it to prevent rust, and return the clean spit to the clean roaster.

Breakfast and Brunch Dishes

WAFFLE SANDWICHES

Per serving; make as many as you wish

When the kids are in a hurry to get out and start their day, hand them one of these quick yet nutritious sandwiches and send them out the door.

2 frozen toaster waffles, or leftover homemade waffles cut into quarters
A tablespoon or so of peanut butter
One-third of a banana, peeled and sliced
A tablespoon or so of jam or preserves

Toast the waffles in a toaster. Spread one with peanut butter; top with bananas. Spread the other with jam, and put on top of the bananas, jam-side down; press gently together.

Variations:

- Substitute sliced fresh strawberries for the banana
- Drizzle a few teaspoons of honey on top of the banana, then sprinkle with a few teaspoons granola; omit the jam
- Use Honey Butter (page 33) in place of the peanut butter
- Sprinkle a few chocolate chips on top of the peanut butter before adding the banana

BREAKFAST SUNDAES

Per serving; make as many as you wish

This is my all-time-favorite cabin or camping breakfast. It's quick-and-easy, and I don't feel logged down all morning from a heavier breakfast such as bacon and eggs. Fresh wild blueberries or raspberries are a true breakfast feast when served like this.

¾ to 1 cup fresh fruit such as cut-up apples or pears, berries, or a mix
¼ cup plain or vanilla yogurt (reduced-fat works fine)
1 tablespoon packed brown sugar, optional
3 to 4 tablespoons granola, or to taste

Place the fruit in an individual bowl. Spoon the yogurt in a mound in the center. Sprinkle with brown sugar, then with granola. For a fancier presentation, layer half of the ingredients in a parfait glass, the repeat with remaining ingredients.

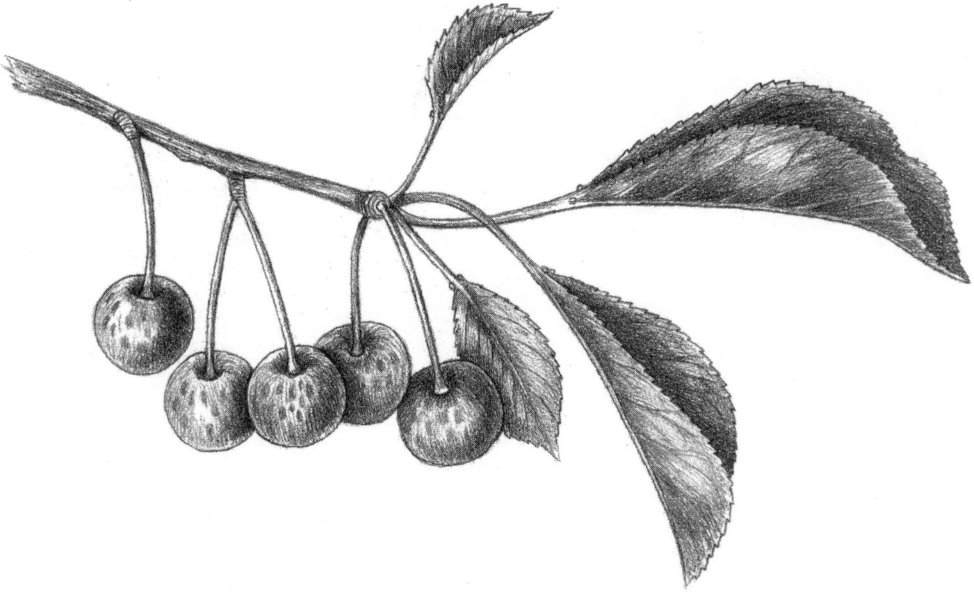

BANANA PANCAKES

4 to 6 servings

Mashed bananas provide taste and texture in these easy pancakes. Since the size of the bananas affects the consistency of the batter, you won't know exactly how much milk to use until you start mixing. Start with the lesser amount, then add more as needed until the batter is the consistency you like.

3 ripe bananas
1 egg
2 teaspoons vegetable oil
1½ cups regular pancake mix* or buttermilk baking mix such as Bisquick
2 tablespoons sugar if using baking mix (not needed with pancake mix)
¾ to 1½ cups milk
Nonstick spray or vegetable oil for frying
Maple syrup, and butter or margarine for serving

Peel the bananas and mash well with a fork or potato masher in a large mixing bowl. Add the egg and oil; stir to mix well. Add the pancake mix (or baking mix and sugar) and ¾ cup milk. Stir until just combined, then add additional milk as needed to bring the batter to the consistency you like. Set the batter aside while you heat the griddle.

Heat a griddle or heavy-bottomed large skillet until a drop of water dances on the surface (if you're using an electric, temperature-controlled griddle or skillet, heat to 375°F). When griddle is hot, grease lightly and ladle the batter onto the skillet to form pancakes; each pancake should use just under ¼ cup batter. Cook until the top side bubbles and the edges are firm, then flip and cook the second side until golden brown. Keep warm while you fry the remaining pancakes. Serve with maple syrup and butter.

*This recipe is not written for an "add water only" type of pancake mix. If this is what you have, omit the eggs and milk, and add water to the desired consistency. You will probably use less water than the instructions on the package indicate.

Variation:

Stir ½ cup chopped walnuts or pecans into the batter with the first amount of milk.

BREAKFAST TORTILLA ROLL-UPS

4 servings; quantity easily adjusted

If your refrigerator has suitable leftovers, feel free to substitute them for the fresh ingredients listed here. For example, leftover steak or chicken can be cut into strips and warmed up rather than using fresh-cooked sausage (cook the vegetables first in a little oil, then add the cooked meat strips and heat through just before serving).

8 ounces uncooked breakfast or Italian sausage ("lite" turkey-and-pork sausage works great), casing removed if you've bought links rather than bulk sausage
¾ cup red and/or green bell pepper pieces (½-inch pieces)
½ cup diced onion
1 stalk celery, optional
4 eggs
½ teaspoon chili powder blend, optional
¼ teaspoon salt
4 flour tortillas (preferably 10-inch diameter), warmed
½ to ¾ cup shredded colby-Jack or other cheese (finely shredded works best)
¼ to ½ cup salsa

In large skillet, brown sausage over medium heat, stirring to break up. Drain all but 1 tablespoon drippings. Add bell pepper, onion and celery. Cook, stirring frequently, until vegetables are just tender. Meanwhile, beat together eggs, chili powder and salt in a small bowl. When vegetables are just tender, add eggs to skillet and cook, stirring constantly, until set.

Let each person assemble his or her own tortilla roll-up by spooning some of the egg mixture into the center of a warmed tortilla, then topping it with shredded cheese and salsa. Fold one edge of the tortilla over the filling, then fold in the sides and roll completely up.

STOVETOP COFFEE CAKE WITH STREUSEL

6 servings

When you don't have an oven, or just don't want to heat the place up, try this stovetop coffee cake. I think you'll be surprised at how good it is! You could even cook this at a campsite on a propane stove.

Streusel topping:
⅓ cup packed brown sugar
⅓ cup chopped pecans or other nuts
3 tablespoons flour
2 tablespoons butter or margarine, cut into small pieces

1¼ cups buttermilk baking mix such as Bisquick
3 to 4 tablespoons sugar, depending on your sweet tooth
¼ teaspoon cinnamon, optional
1 can (5 ounces) evaporated milk, or ¼ cup plus 2 tablespoons whole milk
1 egg
1 tablespoons butter or margarine, melted

Make the streusel topping by mixing together all ingredients until crumbly.

You'll need a 10½-inch cast-iron skillet and a 9-inch-round metal baking pan, as well as 4 or 5 small pieces of foil. Crumple the pieces of foil into small balls about ½ inch in diameter, and position them evenly in the bottom of the skillet. Spray the baking pan with nonstick spray, or butter lightly.

In a mixing bowl, combine the baking mix, sugar and cinnamon; stir with a fork to mix well. Combine milk, egg and melted butter in small bowl or measuring cup and beat with a fork. Add to the baking mix, and stir until dry ingredients are just moistened. Spread evenly in the prepared baking pan. Top with streusel mixture. Place pan on foil balls in skillet (the foil balls create a heat trap that prevents the coffee cake from burning on the bottom). Cover the skillet with a domed lid and cook over medium heat 5 minutes. Reduce heat to low and cook 25 minutes without raising the lid; rotate the pan around occasionally on the heat. After 25 minutes on low, remove the lid and quickly check the coffee cake for doneness; it should be just firm to the touch. If it is not quite done, replace the lid and cook 5 to 10 minutes longer.

Variation:

Stovetop Coconut Coffee Cake: Follow recipe above, substituting canned coconut milk for the evaporated milk. Add ¼ cup sweetened coconut flakes to the streusel topping; reduce nuts to ¼ cup.

NUTTY STRAWBERRY BREAD

1 loaf

Serve this delicious bread for breakfast, brunch or snacks; it's particularly good with whipped cream cheese and a drizzle of honey, or one of the flavored butters on page 33.

1½ cups flour, plus a tablespoon for dusting the pan
2 eggs
¾ cup sugar
½ cup vegetable oil
1 teaspoon cinnamon
½ teaspoon vanilla extract
½ teaspoon baking soda
1 package (10 ounces) frozen sliced sweetened strawberries, thawed
¾ cup chopped walnuts or pecans

Heat oven to 350°F. Spray a standard loaf pan (8½ x 4½ x 2½ inches) with nonstick spray, or butter lightly; sprinkle with a tablespoon of the flour, then shake out the excess. In a medium mixing bowl, beat eggs until foamy with a hand mixer or whisk. Add sugar, oil, cinnamon, vanilla extract and baking soda; beat until smooth. Add strawberries with their juices, walnuts and the 1½ cups flour; stir until just moistened. Pour mixture into the prepared loaf pan. Bake until a toothpick inserted into the center comes out clean, about 1 hour or a little longer. Remove from oven and cool 10 minutes, then turn loaf out and set upright on a wire rack to cool completely. Cool to room temperature; serve at room temperature or chilled.

Light Meals, Lunch Dishes and Soup

NORTH SHORE SUMMER SALAD

Per serving; make as many as you wish

Wild blueberries ripen in northern Minnesota (my home away from home) around July 4, and usually go for 4 or 5 weeks. One summer day, I enjoyed a particularly bountiful harvest of wild blueberries, and also picked up some smoked Lake Superior fish; I made this delightful salad, and enjoyed it with some of the excellent Campagnola bread from The Coho Café and Bakery in Tofte, Minnesota … a true North Shore feast!

1½ to 2 cups mixed tender salad greens
3 ounces chunked smoked whitefish, herring, cisco or other light-colored fish (about 1 cup; skin and bones discarded, and fish broken into bite-sized pieces before measuring)
1 slice bacon, cooked crisp, drained and crumbled
⅓ cup fresh blueberries
1 thin slice red onion, quartered after slicing
2 tablespoons pecan pieces*
2 tablespoons blue cheese crumbles, optional
Honey-Mustard Dressing (facing page)

Place washed, dried salad greens on individual serving plates. Top with smoked fish, bacon and blueberries; scatter red onion, pecan pieces and blue cheese crumbles on top. Serve Honey-Mustard Dressing on the side.

*The pecan pieces are best if lightly toasted: Place the total amount you will need for all salads in a small cast-iron or other heavy-bottomed skillet, and toast over medium-high heat, stirring constantly, until fragrant and lightly browned. Transfer immediately to a cool dish after toasting, to prevent overcooking; let cool before scattering over salad.

HONEY-MUSTARD DRESSING

1½ cups

- ½ cup extra-virgin olive oil (no substitutes)
- ⅓ cup apple cider vinegar
- ¼ cup honey
- ¼ cup Dijon mustard
- 2 tablespoons dry white wine
- ¼ teaspoon salt
- ⅛ teaspoon white pepper

Combine all ingredients in 1-pint glass jar. Cover tightly and shake well to blend. Refrigerate up to 2 weeks.

MEDITERRANEAN PASTA SALAD

6 to 8 servings

This salad captures the sunny flavors of Greece and Italy, and makes a great lunch or light supper on a hot summer day. For a vegetarian version, omit the chicken; the garbanzo beans and cheese provide plenty of protein.

1 pound bowtie pasta or other small pasta shape (uncooked)
1 teaspoon olive oil or vegetable oil
1 jar (6 ounces) marinated artichoke hearts, drained and cut into 1-inch pieces
1 can (15 ounces) garbanzo beans, drained; or 1¼ cups cooked garbanzo beans
1 can (2¼ ounces) sliced ripe olives, drained
4 to 6 pepperoncini peppers,* seeds and stem removed and discarded, cut into rings
1 cup coarsely shredded cooked chicken (about 9 ounces; remove skin and bones before shredding and measuring)
½ cup diced red onion
½ cup diced roasted red bell pepper or uncooked red bell pepper**
1 cup cubed mozzarella cheese (cut into ½-inch cubes before measuring)
1 cup Greek Vinaigrette (page 98)

Cook pasta in a very large pot of boiling, salted water, stirring frequently to prevent sticking, until tender. Drain and refresh immediately with lots of cold water; shake colander after rinsing to get rid of excess water. Transfer pasta to a large mixing bowl and toss with the oil (this prevents the pasta from sticking together as it cools). Set aside to cool completely. When pasta is cool, add remaining ingredients; stir gently to mix and coat everything with the vinaigrette. This salad can be served immediately at room temperature, or can be refrigerated an hour or longer and served cold.

*Pepperoncini peppers are brined, light-green peppers, usually 2 inches long. They can be hard to find in smaller grocery stores, but the taste is wonderful so they are worth looking for. Try an ethnic grocery that specializes in Italian or Greek foods, or look near the olives in large city supermarkets.

**Roast your own peppers following the instructions on page 299; or buy the roasted red bell peppers in jars.

Salade Niçoise (French Composed Salad with Tuna)

Per serving; make as many as you wish

Don't let the name scare you from making this wonderful summer salad. It's one of the best of the "composed" or arranged salads, and perfect for a summer luncheon or light supper. Iced tea, or chilled white wine, would be wonderful with this salad. (In case you don't speak French but want to tell your luncheon guests what you're serving, the name is pronounced "salad nee-SWAHZ.")

1 or 1½ skin-on medium-sized red potatoes
2 or 3 ounces fresh green beans, stem ends snipped off
Lettuce or mixed salad greens (see note below)
One-third to one-half can of chunk tuna, drained (oil-packed tuna is traditionally used)
Half of a hard-cooked egg, cut into quarters
1 small tomato, or half of a medium tomato, cut into quarters or eighths
6 to 8 black olives, preferably imported oil-cured olives
2 anchovy fillets
Simple Vinaigrette (page 98) or purchased vinaigrette

Heat a large pot of salted water to boiling. Add the potatoes you'll be cooking for all the salads you are making and cook until just tender. Use a slotted spoon to transfer the potatoes to a bowl of cold water and set aside to cool. Add the beans to the still-boiling water and cook until bright green and just tender-crisp, about 2 minutes. Drain immediately in a colander and refresh with a large amount of cold water to stop the cooking and set the color; allow to drain thoroughly. Remove the cooled potatoes from the cold water and add to the colander to drain.

Line an individual salad plate with lettuce leaves. Cut the potatoes into quarters or eighths (depending on size) and arrange in the center of the plate, leaving a small space in the center of the potato wedges. Place the tuna in the center of the potatoes. Arrange the green beans, egg and tomato attractively around the potatoes. Scatter the olives over the salad; cross the 2 anchovies over the tuna. Drizzle the salad with a tablespoon or so of vinaigrette, and serve with additional vinaigrette on the side.

Note about the greens: I prefer softer lettuces such as bibb or Boston for this salad, but romaine can also be used and will wilt less quickly. The salad will be prettier if you use a mix of red-edged lettuces along with green lettuces, and best yet if you can include some "exotic" or wild greens such as dandelion, watercress, oak leaf lettuce or other fancy greens. If using bibb or Boston lettuce, you may use whole leaves to line the plate; or if you prefer, tear them into large bite-sized pieces.

CHILLED VEGGIE PIZZA

9 to 12 appetizer servings; 6 main-dish servings

Here's a great dish to have in the refrigerator for those busy weekends at the cabin. It's easy for hungry vacationers to cut off a piece of this tasty pizza; the rest will keep in the refrigerator for several days.

1 tube (10 ounces) refrigerated pizza crust dough
1 package (8 ounces) cream cheese, softened (light cream cheese works fine)
2/3 cup mayonnaise (light or fat-free mayonnaise works fine)
1 package (.4 ounces) dry ranch salad dressing mix
3/4 cup shredded carrot
3/4 cup very small cauliflower florets* (no bigger than 3/4 inch)
3/4 cup very small broccoli florets* (no bigger than 3/4 inch)
1/2 cup shredded broccoli stems, optional
1/4 cup very thinly sliced celery (about 1 stalk)
2 thinly sliced green onions
1/2 cup roasted, salted sunflower nuts, optional
1 1/2 cups shredded cheddar or other cheese of your choice

Heat oven to 425°F; spray a rimmed cookie sheet (15 1/4 x 10 1/2 inches) with nonstick spray, or butter lightly. Unroll pizza dough onto the sheet, stretching gently to fit; roll edges slightly to form a shallow rim. Bake until golden brown and completely cooked, 12 to 15 minutes. Allow to cool completely.

Meanwhile, beat together cream cheese, mayonnaise and ranch dressing mix. Spread over cooled crust. Arrange vegetables evenly over topping, pressing gently into topping. Sprinkle evenly with sunflower nuts, then with shredded cheese. Cover and refrigerate at least 2 hours before serving.

*Although it is not traditional, I personally prefer lightly blanched cauliflower and broccoli florets. Simply drop them into a pot of rapidly boiling salted water, return to boiling, then drain immediately and refresh with cold water. Drain very well and let dry on paper towels before using on the pizza. The blanched vegetables have a mellower flavor than raw vegetables.

Even easier: Substitute a purchased pre-baked pizza crust for the home-baked crust. Depending on the size of the purchased crust, you may need to cut down the amount of the vegetables, sunflower nuts and shredded cheese. If there is extra cream-cheese topping, use as a dip for vegetables or chips.

GRILLED CHICKEN SALAD WITH ISLAND DRESSING

4 servings

Some of these ingredients will be hard to find at the small-town grocer, so you need to plan ahead for this salad … but it's worth it! For make-ahead ease, prepare the dressing up to 4 days in advance and keep in a covered container in the refrigerator.

¼ cup teriyaki sauce, purchased or homemade (page 301)
2 tablespoons peanut oil or vegetable oil
2 tablespoons seasoned rice vinegar*
2 boneless, skinless chicken breast halves (about 12 ounces total)
6 cups mixed salad greens, torn into bite-sized pieces before measuring
2 cups fresh spinach leaves, torn into bite-sized pieces before measuring
1 can (8 ounces) pineapple chunks packed in their own juice, drained, juice reserved
1 orange, peeled, seeded, sectioned and cut into 1-inch chunks
Half of a small red onion, cut into thin wedges from top to bottom and separated
Fried wonton strips for garnish, optional

Island Dressing:

½ cup mayonnaise (reduced-calorie works fine)
2 tablespoons honey
3 tablespoons Asian sesame seasoning oil
2 tablespoons freshly squeezed lime juice (from about 1 lime)
2 tablespoons reserved pineapple juice (from the salad ingredients above)
2 tablespoons Dijon mustard
½ teaspoon minced fresh gingerroot
½ teaspoon salt

In nonaluminum dish, stir together teriyaki sauce, oil and rice vinegar. Add chicken breasts, turning to coat; cover and refrigerate 2 to 4 hours. Meanwhile, stir together all dressing ingredients in a small bowl; cover and refrigerate.

Prepare medium-hot grill. Meanwhile, toss salad greens and spinach together in a large salad bowl. Arrange pineapple, orange and onion on top of greens. Cover salad bowl with a clean towel and set aside. Grill chicken until nicely marked on both sides and just cooked through. Slice into thin strips and arrange on top of the salad. Garnish with the wonton strips; serve Island Dressing on the side.

*Rice vinegar is found with the Asian specialty foods at large supermarkets. If you can't find it, substitute 1 tablespoon plus 1 teaspoon white vinegar, 2 teaspoons water and ¼ teaspoon sugar.

MEDITERRANEAN VEGETABLE SANDWICH

4 to 6 servings

Called pan bagna *(literally, "bathed bread") in French, this elegant sandwich is great for lazy weekends at the cabin because it is prepared as much as a day in advance. For a quick-and-easy lunch—or a great picnic—just slice off what you need and enjoy with iced tea or chilled white wine. Some options for a few of the ingredients are given below, as well as two non-vegetarian versions.*

1 loaf French or Italian bread, about 3 inches in diameter
Half of a cucumber
10 or 12 pitted black olives, preferably oil-cured
1 or 2 cloves garlic
3 or 4 anchovy fillets, optional (omit for a totally vegetarian sandwich)
2 tablespoons olive oil
1 tablespoon lemon juice or white wine vinegar
½ teaspoon Dijon mustard, optional
4 or 5 very thin slices of red onion
4 or 5 thin slices of green or red bell pepper (remove seeds)
10 or 12 fresh whole basil leaves, optional
2 medium tomatoes, sliced ¼ inch thick

Cut the bread in half horizontally (so you have a top half and a bottom half). Scoop out about a third of the soft bread, being careful not to take enough to break the crust; set the scooped-out bread aside for other uses. Score the peel of the cucumber with a fork, then slice thinly and set aside.

In food processor, combine olives, garlic, anchovy fillets, olive oil, lemon juice and mustard; process until fine (alternately, chop the olives, garlic and anchovies finely by hand, then combine in a small bowl with the other ingredients). Spread half the olive mixture on each of the cut surfaces of the bread.

Arrange the remaining ingredients in layers, in the order given, on the bottom half of the loaf. Top with the cucumbers. Sprinkle generously with salt and pepper. Place the top half of the bread on the sandwich and press gently together. Wrap the whole loaf tightly in plastic wrap and place on a baking sheet. Now for the fun part: You need to weight the sandwich so the juices from the vegetables meld with the bread, and it has to be refrigerated with the weights for at least 2 hours. If you can balance some cans or other heavy items on top, that's the easiest thing; or, you could put another baking sheet on top of the sandwich and put various refrigerator items on that sheet. Whatever you come up with, the sandwich should be refrigerated, weighted, for at least 2 hours and as long as a day. When you're ready to eat, unwrap the bread and slice into individual portions.

Variations and substitutions:

- Substitute ¼ cup canned chopped black olives for the whole olives
- Substitute ¼ cup purchased or homemade vinaigrette for the olives, garlic, olive oil, lemon juice and mustard; chop the anchovy fillets coarsely (if using) and mix in with the vinaigrette. Scatter ¼ cup sliced olives over the bottom piece of the bread after brushing it with the vinaigrette.
- Substitute several good-sized slices of roasted bell pepper (purchased, or homemade as described on page 299) for the fresh bell pepper
- Substitute slices of leftover grilled or pan-fried zucchini for the cucumber
- Add 3 to 4 ounces of finely shredded or thinly sliced chicken to the layers
- Add 1 can tuna, drained and flaked, to the layers

THREE-COLOR PASTA SALAD

4 to 6 servings

Tri-color pasta—red, green and white—adds a festive touch to this salad. But the flavor really is no different from plain pasta, so feel free to substitute regular rotini, shells or other small pasta shape for the tri-color rotini.

1 pound three-color rotini or other small pasta shape (uncooked)
1 teaspoon vegetable oil or olive oil
Half of a medium cucumber
2 green onions, cut into ¼-inch lengths
1 large tomato, diced
½ cup crumbled feta cheese (about 2 ounces)
¾ to 1 cup Hearty Italian Vinaigrette (page 99) or other vinaigrette dressing

Cook the pasta in a very large pot of boiling, salted water, stirring frequently to prevent sticking, until tender. Drain and refresh immediately with lots of cold water; shake colander after rinsing to get rid of excess water. Transfer pasta to a large mixing bowl and toss with the oil (this prevents the pasta from sticking together as it cools). Set aside to cool completely.

Meanwhile, cut the cucumber into 4 quarters lengthwise; use a spoon to scrape away and discard seeds. Cut cucumber into ¼-inch dice. When pasta is cool, add diced cucumber, onion, tomato and feta cheese; stir gently to mix. Add ¾ cup of the vinaigrette and stir to coat; add additional dressing if desired until the salad is the consistency you like. Cover and refrigerate at least 1 hour before serving.

GAZPACHO WITH VARIATIONS

This cold soup originates in Spain, where the long, hot summers produce a bounty of vegetables. The typical Spanish version is a purée of tomatoes and other vegetables, thickened by bread and oil. But like many classic dishes, there are a number of American variations on the theme, ranging from blender purées to almost stew-like mixtures rich with cubed vegetables. Below are two versions: the classic, bread-thickened version you'd likely get in Spain, and a chunky version enlivened with white wine, with a puréed variation. Try all three, especially when the farmer's market is loaded with fresh local vegetables.

CLASSIC SPANISH GAZPACHO

About 1 quart; 4 or 5 servings

2 thick slices stale French or Italian bread (each about 1x2x3 inches), crusts removed
1 pound ripe tomatoes, peeled and seeded (about 3 medium tomatoes)
2 garlic cloves
Half of a small onion, cut into 1-inch chunks
Half of a cucumber, peeled and seeded, cut into 1-inch chunks
Half of a green or red bell pepper, cored, cut into 1-inch chunks
½ teaspoon salt
¼ teaspoon sugar, optional (use if the tomatoes are not sweet)
3 tablespoons olive oil
3 tablespoons sherry vinegar or white wine vinegar
⅔ cup tomato juice, optional
Optional garnishes: chopped hard-cooked egg, chopped green or red bell peppers, chopped onion, chopped cucumber, croutons

Soak bread in water to cover for about 5 minutes, then gently squeeze dry. Place tomatoes, garlic, onion, cucumber, bell pepper, salt and sugar in blender or food processor and process until smooth, scraping down occasionally. Add the bread and pulse on and off until the bread is incorporated and the mixture is thick. Add the oil and vinegar and process until blended. Add the tomato juice if the soup is thicker than you like; it depends on the juiciness of your tomatoes. Chill for at least 1 hour before serving; serve with garnishes, letting each diner add garnishes to his or her own bowl.

CHUNKY AMERICAN-STYLE GAZPACHO

About 5½ cups; 6 servings

I like to keep a quart jar of this in the refrigerator for a quick lunch or snack on a hot summer afternoon; it will keep for several days.

2 cans (11½ ounces each) V-8 juice or tomato juice, or about 2¾ cups
2 tablespoons olive oil (reduce or omit for a low-fat gazpacho)
2 cloves garlic
1 tablespoon chopped fresh basil or cilantro leaves
1 tablespoon chopped fresh parsley
½ teaspoon salt
1 medium cucumber, washed but not peeled
1 stalk celery, diced
Half of a small red or green bell pepper, diced
3 tablespoons finely diced red onion
1 cup dry white wine

In blender container, combine V-8 juice, olive oil, garlic, basil, parsley and salt. Process until garlic and herbs are finely minced. Cut the cucumber into 4 quarters lengthwise; use a spoon to scrape away and discard the seeds. Cut cucumber into ¼-inch dice; add half the cucumber to the blender. Add the celery to the blender. Pulse on and off for a few seconds at a time until the mixture is coarse but not completely puréed. In large bowl or glass jar, combine V-8 mixture with remaining cucumber and other ingredients; mix well and refrigerate at least 1 hour before serving.

Variation:

Blender Gazpacho: Follow recipe above for Chunky American-Style Gazpacho, but place all the vegetables in the blender container. Purée to desired consistency.

Creamy Vegetable-Cheese Soup

4 to 6 servings

For a delicious vegetarian soup, use vegetable broth in place of the chicken broth, and omit the ham. Leftovers, of the regular or the vegetarian version, make a surprisingly good pasta sauce.

4 cups chicken broth or vegetable broth
½ cup coarsely chopped carrot (about 1 large carrot)
3 tablespoons butter or stick margarine
4 green onions, sliced into ¼-inch pieces
1½ cups diced mixed-color bell peppers (try to use a mix of red, green and/or yellow)
¼ cup flour
½ cup frozen green peas, or fresh shelled peas
1 can (12 ounces) evaporated skim milk, or ¾ cup half-and-half or cream
A pinch of nutmeg, optional
¾ cup diced ham (about 3 ounces)
1 cup shredded pepper-Jack or Monterey Jack cheese

In Dutch oven, combine broth and carrot. Heat to boiling, then reduce heat to medium and cook until carrot is very tender and broth has reduced somewhat; this will take 10 to 15 minutes. Meanwhile, melt butter in a medium skillet over medium heat. Add onions and bell pepper; cook, stirring occasionally, until vegetables are tender. Sprinkle flour gradually into the skillet, stirring constantly. Cook, stirring constantly, until flour clings to vegetables and turns golden in color. Remove from heat; stir in peas and set aside until needed.

When carrot-broth mixture is ready, add evaporated milk and nutmeg to Dutch oven. Cook over medium heat until liquid barely comes to a boil. Add ham and bell pepper mixture, stirring constantly. Cook, stirring frequently, until the mixture comes to a gentle boil. Taste for salt and adjust if necessary; canned chicken broth probably is salty enough that no additional salt will be needed. With heat still on medium, add shredded cheese slowly, stirring constantly, and cook until cheese melts. Serve immediately.

Appetizers and Snacks

CHUNKY GUACAMOLE

3 to 5 servings, depending on use

Most of the guacamole you see has been mashed to a paste. This chunky version is quite different from that, and has a ton of flavor. It's also easier to make, and once you try it, you may find that the mashed version seems boring by comparison. This is excellent with warmed tortilla chips—freshly fried chips are especially good.

1 small tomato, peeled, seeded and diced
1 tablespoon minced onion
1 clove garlic, pressed or very finely minced
2 tablespoons freshly squeezed lime or lemon juice (from about 1 lime, or half a lemon)
3 tablespoons minced cilantro leaves
¼ teaspoon salt
A few dashes of Tabasco or other liquid hot pepper sauce, optional
A generous pinch of sugar, optional (use if the tomato is not very sweet)
1 ripe pebbly-skinned avocado (they have more flavor than the smooth-skinned ones)

In medium mixing bowl, combine all ingredients except the avocado; stir well to mix. This can be mixed in advance and set aside for up to an hour at room temperature (in fact, the taste is improved if the tomato mixture is allowed to stand for a while), or you can proceed with the final step immediately.

When ready to serve, peel the avocado and remove the pit. Cut the avocado into chunks ½ inch square or slightly smaller. Add immediately to the tomato mixture, stirring gently to combine.

Layered Dips

Look through any Junior-League or church cookbook, or in ads sponsored by food companies in family magazines, and you'll see dozens of recipes for layered dips. These are great for parties or casual weekend snacking, and as an added bonus, kids love them. Here are just a few recipes to get you started; feel absolutely free to vary them to suit the ingredients you have on hand and your personal taste.

LAYERED SEAFOOD DIP

1 package (8 ounces) cream cheese, softened
2 tablespoons minced green onion, optional
8 ounces cooked or canned crabmeat, imitation crabmeat, or tiny or finely chopped cooked shrimp
¾ cup bottled seafood cocktail sauce
Crackers, small party rye bread, and/or fresh vegetables for dipping

Spread cream cheese over a serving plate. Sprinkle with green onions. If using canned crab or shrimp, drain meat and pick out any cartilage or shell; if using imitation crabmeat, shred finely with your fingers. Distribute seafood evenly over cream cheese. Pour cocktail sauce over the center of the seafood, allowing an edge of seafood to show. This may be prepared several hours in advance; cover with plastic wrap and refrigerate until serving time. Serve with crackers, party rye bread and/or vegetables.

LAYERED MEXICAN DIP

1 can (16 ounces) refried beans
1 cup sour cream (reduced-fat works fine)
Half of a package (1.25-ounce package) taco seasoning mix
1 cup prepared guacamole (an 8-ounce container from the supermarket is fine)
1 cup (4 ounces) shredded Monterey Jack, marble Jack, or other cheese
1 cup thick salsa, chopped fresh tomatoes, or drained Mexican-style diced canned tomatoes
1 can (4 ounces) diced green chiles, drained, optional
1 can (2¼ ounces) sliced ripe olives, drained, optional
1 cup shredded lettuce, optional
½ cup sliced green onions, optional
Corn chips or plain tortilla chips for dipping

Spread beans over a large serving plate. In small bowl or the sour-cream container, blend sour cream and taco seasoning mix. Spread over beans, leaving a slight edge of beans showing. Spread guacamole over sour cream, leaving a slight edge of sour cream showing. Sprinkle cheese evenly over all. Top with salsa and any or all of the optional vegetable toppings. This may be prepared several hours in advance; cover with plastic wrap and refrigerate until serving time. Serve with chips.

HOT LAYERED MEXICAN DIP

8 ounces ground beef
½ cup chopped onion
1 package (1.25 ounces) taco seasoning mix
1 can (16 ounces) refried beans
1 can (4 ounces) diced green chiles, drained
1 cup bottled taco sauce
2 cups (8 ounces) shredded Monterey Jack, marble Jack, or other cheese
1 cup sour cream (reduced-fat works fine)
½ cup sliced green onions, optional
Corn chips or plain tortilla chips for dipping

In medium skillet, brown ground beef over medium heat, stirring to break up. Add onion and cook, stirring occasionally, about 5 minutes. Drain excess grease. Blend taco seasoning mix with ½ cup hot water; stir into ground beef mixture. Cook, stirring occasionally, until thickened, about 10 minutes.

Spread refried beans in pie pan or 8-inch-square dish (use a pyrex pan or dish if you'll be microwaving the dip). Distribute ground beef evenly over beans. Sprinkle evenly with chiles. Drizzle taco sauce evenly over all. Sprinkle evenly with cheese. This can be prepared in advance; cover and refrigerate until you're ready to heat.

When you're ready to heat the dip, remove the plastic wrap. If using the oven, heat oven to 325°F. Bake, uncovered, until cheese is bubbly, about 25 minutes. If using the microwave, heat at MEDIUM-HIGH/70% power until cheese is bubbly, about 8 minutes. Dot with sour cream; sprinkle with green onions. Serve with chips.

Layered Cucumber-Ham Dip

1 package (8 ounces) cream cheese, softened
1 packet (.65 ounce) dry Italian salad dressing mix
1 cup diced ham (about 4 ounces), or 4 ounces sliced honey ham from the deli
1 cup diced cucumber
Small party rye or pumpernickel bread and/or buttery crackers such as Ritz

In small mixing bowl, blend cream cheese and Italian dressing mix. Spread over a serving plate. If using diced ham, distribute evenly over the cream cheese; if using ham slices, roll slices up and cut into ¼-inch-wide strips, then cut the strips into 1-inch-long pieces and distribute evenly over the cream cheese. Sprinkle cucumbers evenly over the ham. Serve with bread or crackers.

Layered Two-Cheese Dip

1 package (8 ounces) cream cheese, softened
1 jar (8 ounces) pasteurized process cheese sauce such as Cheez Whiz, or 1 can (10¾ ounces) condensed cheddar cheese soup
1 cup salsa
Crackers, small party rye bread, and/or fresh vegetables for dipping

Spread the cream cheese in a microwave-safe 8-inch dish or pie pan. Spread cheese sauce or soup evenly over the cream cheese. Top with salsa. Microwave on HIGH 3 minutes. Serve with crackers, party rye bread, and/or vegetables.

SATAY: THAI GRILLED MEAT SKEWERS

About 12 pieces

For total authenticity, use Thai fish sauce in place of the soy sauce in the recipe below, substituting an equal amount. However, the satay will still taste wonderful using the soy sauce as written. These are traditionally served with Peanut Dipping Sauce and Thai Cucumber Relish (recipes on page 144); for a change of pace, serve the satays instead with the Noodles with Thai Peanut Sauce (page 87) and fresh cucumber wedges.

Marinade:
2 or 3 cloves garlic, pressed or finely minced
2 tablespoons freshly squeezed lime juice (from about 1 lime)
2 tablespoons soy sauce or Thai fish sauce
1 tablespoon packed brown sugar
1 tablespoon vegetable oil
1 teaspoon turmeric,* optional (adds the traditional color)
1 teaspoon ground cumin*

1 pound pork tenderloin or boneless, skinless chicken breast
About a dozen skewers

In nonaluminum mixing bowl, combine all marinade ingredients. Slice the meat with the grain into ⅛-inch-thick strips. Add the meat to the marinade and stir to coat. Cover and refrigerate from 1 to 4 hours, stirring occasionally. If using wooden skewers, soak them in cold water for about 30 minutes, then drain and pat dry.

Prepare medium-hot grill. Thread the meat strips onto the skewers. Grill until just cooked through, about 2 minutes per side. Serve with Peanut Dipping Sauce and Thai Cucumber Relish (recipes on page 144) on the side.

*You may substitute 1½ teaspoons curry powder blend for the turmeric and cumin.

PEANUT DIPPING SAUCE

½ cup crunchy peanut butter
½ cup unsweetened canned coconut milk, or ½ cup heavy cream
2 tablespoons soy sauce (or 1 tablespoon soy sauce and 1 tablespoon Thai fish sauce)
1 tablespoon lemon juice
1 tablespoon packed brown sugar
A good pinch of cayenne pepper, optional

In small saucepan, combine all ingredients. Heat to a gentle boil over medium heat, stirring frequently. Remove from heat and set aside until cool.

THAI CUCUMBER RELISH

Half of a medium cucumber
About 1 teaspoon salt
3 tablespoons white vinegar
3 tablespoons finely chopped red onion
2 tablespoons finely shredded carrot
2 tablespoons water
1 tablespoon teriyaki sauce or Thai fish sauce
2 teaspoons sugar

Cut the cucumber into 4 quarters lengthwise; use a spoon to scrape away and discard seeds. Cut cucumber into ⅛-inch dice. In a small bowl, toss the cucumber with the salt; set aside for about 30 minutes. Drain and rinse very briefly, then drain well. Combine drained cucumber with remaining ingredients, stirring to mix well.

Nachos

Nachos suit cabin life very well. It's easy to whip together a batch—large or small, depending on the crowd—and heat them quickly in the oven or microwave. They make a great appetizer, lunch, or light supper. And the ingredients are easy to come by, even in small-town grocery stores.

The base for nachos, as I make them, is tortilla snack chips. I recommend using plain, salted chips rather than those with "nacho" or cheese flavoring added. The larger triangular chips work best, but you may use round chips, small triangles or whatever you have.

For a big batch of nachos, lay down half of the total amount of tortilla chips on an appropriate-sized baking dish, top with half of the other ingredients, and repeat the layers. If you're making a smaller batch, you won't need to use this double-decker scheme; simply lay out the tortillas, top them and bake. A cookie-sized baking sheet is great for a big batch that you'll be heating in the oven. For microwave preparation, you'll need to keep the batches smaller and use nonmetallic plates or baking dishes. For a light supper for two, a stoneware dinner plate stacked with double-decker ingredients is about right, and works in either the microwave or oven.

Besides the chips, the only element that is really essential for nachos is shredded cheese. I like to use colby-Jack cheese or the four-cheese "Mexican blend" that has recently appeared in dairy cases (note: this is not the "seasoned" blend, which has chili powder and other flavorings; this is just a blend of four shredded cheeses). Colby, cheddar or Monterey Jack all work well, as does shredded pepper-Jack cheese. Plan on a generous amount of cheese; I recommend 1¼ cups of cheese per 4 cups of tortilla chips. Finely shredded cheese melts more quickly than thicker shreds, which can be a bonus when you're using a microwave to heat the nachos.

Meat is always optional on nachos, but is a nice topping if you're serving the nachos for something more substantial than a snack. Leftover taco meat works great, as does leftover fajita fillings (cut the strips of meat and vegetables into smaller pieces before using for nachos). You can also fry a batch of ground beef for use in nachos. On the following page is a recipe I use frequently, which can be varied depending on your mood and your pantry supplies. This also makes a quick taco filling.

The only other "messy" topping I use is beans. When I use the more paste-like refried beans, I dab them over the chips in small spoonfuls. Most of the time, I prefer whole black beans. Look for those with cumin or chili spices for best flavor. Drain the beans, then scatter them over the chips.

continued

Vegetables are the most fun and attractive toppings for nachos. Typical vegetable toppers include diced onion and bell peppers (use both red and green peppers for best color), diced and drained tomatoes, slices of pickled jalapeño peppers (or minced fresh jalapeños if you really like it hot), sliced green onions and sliced ripe olives. Use two or more of these vegetables. One word of caution: if you use too many toppings, the nachos will be soggy. Ideally, no more than 75 percent of the tortilla chips should be covered with toppings, except cheese, which can be put on more heavily. A word about salsa: I serve salsa, and other wet condiments such as guacamole and sour cream, on the side as dippers. If you put these wet toppings on the nachos before baking, the result will be a sodden mass. Also, the contrast of cool sour cream and guacamole to warm, crisp nachos is part of the nacho experience. I prefer the salsa to be room temperature, but it can be served straight from the refrigerator, if you like.

Cheese goes on last, after the meat, beans and vegetables. If you're building double-decker nachos, top the first layer of ingredients with a layer of cheese, then add the second layer of chips and other toppings, followed by a final layer of cheese. For oven nachos, bake them at 375°F until the cheese melts. This usually takes 15 minutes or so, depending on the size of the batch, and double-decker nachos take a bit longer. A microwave plate of nachos will take between 3 and 5 minutes on HIGH. Again, a double-decker batch takes longer than a single layer.

To help you put this all together, on the facing page is a basic, double-decker version of nachos that will work in either the microwave or the oven.

QUICK NACHO MEAT MIXTURE

4 to 6 servings

½ pound ground beef
½ cup diced onion
½ to ¾ cup salsa

In medium skillet, brown ground beef, stirring to break up. Drain excess grease. Add onion and cook until the onion is tender. Stir in salsa and heat through.

Double-Decker Nacho Plate

4 appetizer servings; 2 light main-dish servings

4 cups plain, salted tortilla snack chips
¾ to 1 cup Quick Nacho Meat Mixture (page 146) or leftover taco filling
½ cup diced green and/or red bell peppers
½ cup diced onion
¾ cup canned black beans with cumin, drained
3 tablespoons sliced ripe olives
1¼ cups shredded colby-Jack cheese
Salsa and sour cream for dipping

Place half the tortilla chips on a stoneware dinner plate (or any type of plate that is microwave- or oven-safe); spread the chips out evenly so there are no gaps between chips. Scatter half the meat mixture over the chips. Scatter half the peppers and onions over everything. Top with half the beans, and scatter half the olives on top. Sprinkle half the cheese over everything. Repeat the layers. Microwave on HIGH 4 to 5 minutes or until cheese bubbles, rotating plate frequently; or, bake at 375°F about 15 minutes, or until cheese bubbles. Serve with salsa and sour cream for dipping.

CONEY ISLAND SAUCE

2 cups sauce; enough for 10 to 12 hot dogs or burgers

Traditionally served on hot dogs, this sauce is also great on burgers, baked potatoes, or scrambled eggs. It freezes well, if there's any left over.

2 tablespoons chili powder blend
1 tablespoon paprika
1 tablespoon flour
2 teaspoons salt
1 pound lean ground beef
¼ to ½ teaspoon Tabasco sauce
¾ cup diced onion
¾ cup tomato juice (one 5½-ounce can), plus additional if needed

In mixing bowl, combine chili powder, paprika, flour and salt; stir with a fork until blended. Add ground beef and Tabasco sauce, and mix very well with your hands. Fry in a large skillet over medium heat until browned, stirring frequently and pressing with a fork so the meat mixture is as fine as possible. Add onion and cook about 5 minutes, stirring occasionally. Add tomato juice and ¼ cup water; reduce heat to very low and cook 10 minutes longer, stirring occasionally. Thin with additional tomato juice if you want a thinner consistency.

DECADENT CHEESY CONEY FRIES

Variable servings

Not exactly health food! But when you're craving a really ooey, gooey, messy snack, this is just the thing. (Don't tell your doctor where you got this recipe!)

Coney Island Sauce (facing page)
Pasteurized process cheese sauce such as Cheez Whiz
Frozen French fries, thawed according to package directions
(or, make your own French fries from fresh potatoes if you prefer)
Oil for deep frying

In separate dishes or pans, heat Coney Island Sauce and cheese sauce in microwave or on stovetop over low heat; add a little water, milk or beer to the cheese sauce to thin if necessary. Keep both sauces warm while you prepare the fries.

Fry French fries in deep fryer or large pot; drain well and place on serving dish. Sprinkle with salt. Pour warm cheese sauce over the fries, then top with Coney Island Sauce.

Visions of Blueberries Dance in Their Heads

Although they are cultivated in over half the states in America, blueberries are best suited to the cooler northern tier. Native to North America, the wild blueberry was prized by indigenous peoples wherever the scrubby plants grew. An old Eskimo recipe for ice cream calls for whipping seal oil until fluffy, then stirring in sugar and a large amount of blueberries until the berries are sugar-coated. This confection was usually chilled before eating. Plains Indians dried blueberries, then pounded them together with dried meat and combined the mixture with animal fat. The resulting "pemmican" was then packed into cleaned animal intestines for storage. In addition to these exotic recipes, indigenous peoples used blueberries in ways we think of today as standard: stewed with sugar as a dessert sauce, combined with fat and flour to make pudding or sweet fritters, infused in hot water to make tea.

Blueberries have been cultivated and harvested commercially since the Civil War era, with modern cultivars being developed at the turn of the century. Michigan and Maine compete for blueberry bragging rights. Recent data has Michigan producing nearly 45 percent of the blueberries eaten in the U.S., while Maine lays claim to being America's largest blueberry-growing state, with over 90 percent of the low-bush blueberries in the U. S. How can both these statements be true? The key is the variety. Low-bush blueberries are the "wild" strain, while the berries grown commercially in Michigan (and 30 or so other states) are an "improved" cultivar called highbush blueberries. With apologies to the Wolverine State, I'm going to focus exclusively on wild blueberries in this writing.

Wild blueberries are one of the great opportunists of the plant community. They thrive in areas where forest fires have burned within the previous year or two. Some people say that the first type of cultivation practiced by indigenous peoples was the occasional burning of selected areas to promote blueberry growth the following year. Many plants tolerate the cooler temperatures, short growing season and long winter dormancy common throughout wild blueberry growing areas. But blueberries actually prefer thin, acidic soil rather than the richer loam found deep in the forest, where many plant species compete for nutrients and water. In contrast, the areas where blueberries thrive are so harsh that many taller plants can't survive there. These areas, although in a cool region, are subject to intense sunlight and heat during much of the summer growing season due to the lack of any type of leafy canopy.

The blueberries love it! Spring and early summer rains swell the flowers, promoting the develop-

ment of tiny, hard, green berries. Soon, increasing sunlight and heat cause the berries to swell and grow rapidly, developing anthocyanin, a water-soluble pigment that puts the "blue" in "blueberry." Actually, blueberries go from green, to pink, to currant-red, to deep purple during their ripening stages. The slightly under-ripe red berries have a much tarter flavor, and lend interest to jam when combined with fully ripe berries.

But it is the fully ripe, deep purple berries that are most prized. Ripe berries last for just a few days before withering and falling off the bush, but they are quickly replaced by the slightly younger ripening berries. The wild blueberry harvest is generally a month long, or slightly more. In most years, the Fourth of July signals the start of the wild blueberry season in northern tier states such as Minnesota.

Picking a pailful of wild berries is serious work. Blueberry patches along trails or canoe portages are quickly stripped of berries by casual pickers, so the serious forager needs to go off the beaten path. Blueberries also tend to grow best on high ridgelines. Generally, you'll have to hike a parcel of woods and brushy country to get up the ridge. Once you emerge from the woods into the open area favored by blueberries, the heat can be intense on a sunny day. Fortunately, these higher ridges often enjoy cooling breezes, which are a lifesaver on a sticky July day. A bottle of water is a necessity when picking blueberries on a hot day. If you're bringing your dog, bring water and a dish for the dog also.

The actual picking is a knee-stretching, jeans-spoiling job. Blueberries are rhizomes that spread by means of branching stems, much like creeping Charlie. The easiest way to pick is to sit down next to a cluster of loaded bushes and start plucking. No matter how careful you are, you'll end up sitting or kneeling in a few berries; stained pants are a mark of honor among blueberry fanatics. Serious pickers use the two-handed method, in which one hand holds the stem of the plant and acts as a receptacle for berries rolled off the plant by the other hand. The plucked berries are then transferred to a pail or plastic sack. Some people pluck "cleanly," with few leaves or stems mixed in with the berries, while "dirty" pickers end up with many twigs, stems and leaves in the pail that will need to be removed when the berries are washed.

continued

What is the reward for all this work when you could go to almost any grocery store and buy a pint of berries that are cleaned, plump, and ready to use? Like most wild foods, wild blueberries are far more flavorful than their domestic counterparts. Next time you have a fresh blueberry in hand—whether wild or domestic—take a small bite of it, concentrating on the skin. Now, take a bite of the flesh of the berry. You'll immediately notice that the flavor is concentrated in the skin; the flesh is just moist pulp. Because wild blueberries are so much smaller than domestic berries, they have a much higher proportion of skin to flesh and thus, more intense flavor. I counted out some blueberries as I added them to a measuring cup recently. It took 400 wild berries to make up the measure, while it takes approximately 50 domestic blueberries to fill a cup. More skin, more flavor.

Also, like most wild foods, blueberries have good years and bad years. If the spring and early summer are dry, there will be few berries to pick in July. In years like this, bears can get out of hand and become a nuisance to humans who venture into wilderness areas such as the massive Boundary Waters Canoe Area Wilderness in northern Minnesota. It's hard to imagine a huge bear depending on tiny wild blueberries for food, but in fact, the sweet fruit is a big part of the black bear diet. Areas where bears have feasted on blueberries are easy to spot. Bears are not "clean" pickers, preferring to swipe the entire plant from the ground before stripping the berries, and often turning rocks over in the process. They also uncover tasty ants by overturning rocks, so perhaps the ants are like a garnish for the berries … or is it the other way around?

If you manage to bring in a haul of wild blueberries, you may want to freeze some so you can enjoy a taste of summer on a cold winter's day. I wash the berries just before freezing, picking out all leaves and stems during washing (I am a "clean" picker by nature, but my pail usually contains a few stray bits of non-blueberry material). I dry the berries well by laying them out on a towel, then I place them in a single layer on a cookie sheet, which I put in the freezer for an hour or two. If the berries are placed on the sheet while still wet, they may become mushy and watery upon thawing. For the same reason, it's best not to pack fresh berries into a container and freeze it. Once the berries are frozen individually, I remove them from the sheet and pack them into heavyweight plastic containers or freezer-weight plastic bags. This way, I can shake out a few berries to enliven a batch of pancakes or to heap on a dish of ice cream. Or, I can thaw a larger amount for pie, sauce or jam. If you've picked berries at the cabin, keep them refrigerated for up to several days and bring them home in a cooler. Freeze them when you get home, rather than trying to transport blueberries that you've frozen at the cabin. Whether you're using the berries fresh or freezing them, don't wash them until you're ready to use them, or they may become soft and prone to spoilage.

Here are some recipes you may enjoy trying with wild blueberries.

WILD BLUEBERRY JAM

About 2/3 cup jam per cup of fresh berries

It's not as far-fetched as it may sound to cook jam at the cabin; from start to finish, this jam takes about 45 minutes, and you'll really appreciate the flavor so shortly after you've picked the berries. You may cook a larger batch of jam than this recipe indicates, increasing quantities proportionally, but don't try to cook more than 4 cups of fresh blueberries in one batch.

1 cup fresh wild blueberries (about 4½ ounces)
2 tablespoons water
¾ cup sugar

Wash and pick over blueberries, discarding stems, leaves or other detritus. Drain briefly, and transfer to a small, heavy-bottomed stainless-steel saucepan (it is very important to use a heavy-bottomed pan for making jam; otherwise, it will surely scorch during the final stages of cooking). Add the water, and crush a few of the berries with a wooden spoon to start the juices flowing. Heat over medium-low heat, stirring occasionally, until the berries have released juices to almost reach the top of the berries; this will take 5 to 8 minutes. Stirring constantly, sprinkle the sugar slowly into the pan ¼ cup at a time, stirring well between additions to dissolve the sugar. Decrease heat to low and cook, stirring frequently, until the jam has thickened and will hold a soft shape, without weeping juices, when scooped with a clean spoon. This will take 20 to 30 minutes; stir very frequently near the end of cooking time, as the jam is prone to scorching at this time. Transfer jam to a glass jar* or dish and cool completely before refrigerating.

*If you're making a larger batch and plan to keep some of the jam a while, sterilize the jars with boiling water before using, and cap with sterilized lids.

BLUEBERRY PANCAKES

Variable servings

Use any good pancake mix (Sturdiwheat mix, packed in Red Wing, Minnesota, is a favorite of mine); buttermilk mix is traditional, but wild rice pancake mix adds a delightful North woods accent. Mix the pancakes as directed, then gently stir in about ¼ cup cleaned wild blueberries (or a bit more if you prefer) per cup of pancake batter. Cook in the normal fashion, and serve with butter and maple syrup.

Main Dishes

PERFECT GRILLED CHICKEN WITH FLAVOR VARIATIONS

4 or 5 servings as written; easily adjusted for more or less servings

The secret to grilled chicken that is juicy and cooked throughout without burning is the indirect heat at the start of cooking.

1 skin-on chicken, cut up, or about 4 pounds skin-on parts
Garlic salt, seasoned salt or plain salt
Seasoned pepper or plain pepper (lemon pepper is very good on chicken)

To prepare a grill for indirect heat: If using a charcoal grill, bank coals along two sides of the grill, leaving the center clear; light and allow to burn until covered with grey ash. If using a gas grill, pre-heat one of the burners of a two-burner grill (if you have three or more burners, pre-heat the burners on the edges, leaving the center burner off).

When you're almost ready to grill, sprinkle chicken parts generously with seasoned salt and pepper; rub into the chicken with your fingertips. Place the chicken on the grill over the non-heated area (in the center of the charcoal grill, or over the unlit area of a gas grill). Cover and cook 35 minutes, turning chicken about every 10 minutes. Now transfer the chicken to the grill over the heated area. Cover and cook 10 to 15 minutes longer, turning every 5 minutes, until chicken is crispy and cooked through: If you poke a piece, the juices should run clear. You can also check the temperature with an instant-read thermometer; temperature should read 165°F at the thickest part. If the chicken is getting too browned before it is done, simply transfer it back to the grill over the non-heated area.

Flavor variations: *Use plain salt and pepper rather than seasoned salt and pepper, or omit the salt and pepper as directed in the variation:*

- Rub chicken pieces with ¾ cup barbecue sauce before grilling. Just before the chicken is done, brush with ¼ cup additional barbecue sauce and cook, turning once, for 5 minutes.
- Rub chicken pieces with teriyaki sauce before grilling; omit salt and pepper.
- Rub chicken pieces with ¾ cup prepared pesto. During cooking, baste the chicken each time you turn it with additional pesto (you will need about ½ cup for the basting).
- Before grilling, marinate chicken in the refrigerator for 1 to 4 hours in bottled or homemade Italian dressing.

- Dust the chicken lightly with cayenne pepper and sprinkle liberally with plain salt; omit the black pepper. Just before you remove the chicken from the grill, squirt a fresh lemon over the chicken pieces.
- Combine ¼ cup Dijon mustard with 1 tablespoon olive oil and 1 tablespoon orange juice; rub over the chicken before grilling.
- Rub chicken pieces with ½ cup Thai peanut sauce (purchased, or made from recipe on page 144); omit salt and pepper. Let stand at room temperature 10 minutes before grilling. Sprinkle cooked chicken with chopped cilantro leaves.

CHICKEN-BREAST STACKERS

4 servings; easily adjusted for more or less servings

It's surprising how good a simple recipe like this is! The flavors complement each other well, and the marinating and cooking methods help keep the chicken juicy.

4 boneless, skinless chicken breast halves
⅓ cup barbecue sauce (the Spiked Barbecue Sauce on page 299 is great with this)
About ⅓ pound sliced ham (sliced relatively thinly, as for sandwiches)
4 slices Swiss or other cheese (about the same size as the chicken breasts)

Place chicken breasts in a small baking dish and add barbecue sauce, turning chicken pieces to coat. Cover and refrigerate 1 to 3 hours, turning once or twice.

When ready to cook, prepare grill for indirect heat (page 154). Remove breasts from barbecue sauce and place on grate away from fire. Cover grill and cook chicken about 7 minutes. Turn chicken, then quickly top each piece with one-quarter of the ham; top the ham with a slice of cheese. Re-cover grill and cook until chicken is cooked through and cheese melts, 5 to 7 minutes.

GRILLED CHICKEN AND VEGETABLE SALAD

3 or 4 servings; easily increased

For a complete grilled meal, serve this main-dish salad with Grilled Flatbread (page 289).

Dressing:
¼ cup olive oil
2 tablespoons white wine vinegar
1 tablespoon minced fresh oregano, or 1 teaspoon crumbled dried oregano
2 teaspoons Dijon mustard
1 clove garlic, pressed or finely minced, optional
½ teaspoon salt
A few grindings of black pepper

1 yam or sweet potato (about 8 ounces)
1 medium onion
1 red, yellow or green bell pepper, cored and cut into 4 wedges
8 ounces fresh asparagus spears, tough ends snapped off
About 2 tablespoons olive oil or vegetable oil
6 cups mixed salad greens, torn into large bite-sized pieces
2 boneless, skinless chicken breast halves (about 12 ounces total)
Seasoned pepper and salt, or your favorite grill seasoning dry rub or blend
1 medium tomato, peeled, seeded and cut into ½-inch pieces
4 ounces crumbled blue cheese (about 1 cup)
8 to 10 leaves fresh basil, optional but very good

In a pint-sized jar, combine dressing ingredients. Cover jar tightly and shake well to blend. Set aside for up to 1 hour at room temperature, or refrigerate for up to 8 hours.

Scrub yam skin very well, and prick with a fork in several places. Cook until just tender by microwaving 3 to 4 minutes, or by baking at 350°F for 40 minutes (this may be done a day or two in advance; refrigerate cooked yam until needed). Cut yam into 4 wedge-shaped quarters; place on a large plate. Peel onion and slice ½ inch thick. Slide wooden toothpicks into the rings in several locations; this helps hold the onion together during grilling. Add onion slices to the plate with the yam. Add the bell pepper wedges and the asparagus to the plate. Brush all with olive oil on all sides. Arrange salad greens on a large serving platter; refrigerate until serving time if it is warm or if you are preparing platter in advance.

Prepare medium-hot grill; before placing the grate over the heat, clean it well and rub lightly with vegetable oil. Sprinkle chicken breasts generously with seasoned pepper and salt, or work dry-rub seasoning into the meat. Place seasoned chicken breasts on grate. Arrange all vegetables (except the tomato) on the grate, placing the asparagus spears perpendicular to the grate. Sprinkle vegetables lightly with salt. Cover grill and cook, turning frequently, until chicken is cooked through and vegetables are tender-crisp (yam should be golden-brown and nicely marked), about 15 minutes; as each vegetable is done, transfer to a plate and keep warm until everything is done. Working quickly, cut vegetables into 1-inch chunks and scatter over the prepared salad greens. Top vegetables with the tomato pieces. Slice chicken breasts into strips or cut into chunks, and arrange on vegetables. Sprinkle blue cheese over all. Roll up basil leaves and cut into thin strips; scatter over entire salad. Shake dressing well and pour evenly over salad.

Variations:

- Substitute 6 ounces trimmed fresh green beans for asparagus. Sprinkle with water and wrap tightly in foil. Place foil packet of green beans on grate with other vegetables, and cook about 10 minutes or until tender-crisp.
- Add one or two of the following to the salad:
  - ½ cup halved, pitted kalamata olives
  - 1 small jar marinated artichoke hearts, drained
  - 1 hard-boiled egg, cut into wedges
  - Half of a small cucumber, cut into ½-inch cubes
- Cook a baking potato, or several smaller red potatoes, with the yam; cut into wedges, brush with oil and grill along with the yam
- Slice a small zucchini or summer squash in half lengthwise, then brush with oil and grill for about 6 minutes (zucchini cook very quickly, so they don't need to be on the grate as long as the other vegetables)
- Substitute 1 turkey tenderloin for the chicken breast halves
- For a vegetarian salad, omit the chicken breast halves
- Substitute 4 ounces cubed mozzarella cheese for the blue cheese
- Substitute 4 ounces crumbled feta cheese for the blue cheese
- Sprinkle salad with croutons before serving
- Substitute raspberry vinegar for the white wine vinegar in the dressing; sprinkle ⅔ cup fresh raspberries over the salad

Even easier: Substitute ½ cup prepared Italian vinaigrette dressing for the homemade dressing.

CHICKEN-SHRIMP KABOBS

4 servings

Marinating the shrimp and chicken in separate mixtures lends interest to this attractive kabob dish.

Juice from 2 fresh limes (about ¼ cup)
3 tablespoons Angostura bitters (from liquor store, or in bar-mix area of a supermarket)
8 ounces boneless, skinless chicken breast or thigh meat, cut into 1-inch chunks
3 tablespoons butter or margarine, melted
3 tablespoons soy sauce
3 tablespoons packed brown sugar
1 pound raw shrimp, shelled and deveined

In a medium nonaluminum mixing bowl, combine lime juice and bitters. Add chicken pieces; mix well. In another bowl, mix melted butter, soy sauce and brown sugar. Add shrimp; mix well. Cover both bowls; refrigerate 1 to 3 hours, stirring occasionally.

Prepare a hot grill, or the broiler. Thread shrimp and chicken chunks alternately on skewers. Grill or broil just until done, about 10 minutes, turning occasionally.

CHICKEN PACKETS WITH VARIATIONS

2 servings per packet

This basic packet recipe is designed for cooking on the grill; however, if the weather turns on you at the last minute (or if you don't have a grill), you can bake these in the oven instead. Several flavor variations are given, but don't be afraid to try your own creations. To serve more than two people, make additional packets; if you overload a packet with too much food, it won't cook properly, so it's better to make packets with two servings apiece. These are great served with rice.

¾ pound boneless, skinless chicken meat (breast or thigh meat, as you prefer)
Other ingredients as specified in desired variation (see pages 160–161)
12 x 18-inch sheet heavy-duty foil, or 12 x 36-inch sheet regular foil

Cut chicken into chunks roughly 1½ x 2 inches. Combine in a bowl with the other ingredients and toss gently to combine. You may cover and refrigerate any of these variations for an hour or so to marinate; or, proceed directly to cooking. When you are ready to cook, you'll need a medium-hot fire ready in the grill; if you're baking the packets, the oven should be heated to 425°F.

Place the combined ingredients on the center of the shiny side of the foil (if using regular-weight foil, fold it in half, shiny-side in, and place the ingredients in the center). Flatten the pile of ingredients slightly; the ingredients will cook more evenly if the packet is somewhat flattened rather than shaped like a log. Bring up the long sides and make a triple or quadruple fold over the ingredients to seal. Roll-fold the ends in, making sure each end has at least 2 folds. When you make the packet, don't smash the ingredients together tightly; leave a good bit of room in the packet, keeping it somewhat flattened.

For grilling: Place packets, seam-side down, on grate over direct heat. Cover grill and cook about 12 minutes, turning packet(s) after about 5 minutes; be careful not to puncture the foil when you turn the packet(s). To serve, unroll one end of the packet carefully to avoid escaping steam, then either pour the contents out the end or open the top and spoon them out.

For baking: Place packet(s), seam-side up, on baking sheet and bake 20 minutes; turning is not necessary. To serve, unroll one end of the packet carefully to avoid escaping steam, then either pour the contents out the end or open the top and spoon them out.

continued

Honey-Mustard Chicken Packet

Half of a small onion, cut into ½-inch-wide strips
1 tablespoon honey
2 teaspoons Dijon-style mustard
2 teaspoons olive oil or vegetable oil
A generous pinch of crumbled dried thyme leaves, optional
A light sprinkle of salt and pepper

Island Chicken Packet

½ small red or green bell pepper, cored and cut into 1-inch chunks
½ cup sweet onion chunks (1-inch chunks)
½ cup diced fresh or canned pineapple
2 tablespoons teriyaki sauce (purchased or homemade, page 301)
1 teaspoon Asian sesame seasoning oil

Orange BBQ Chicken Packet

½ cup frozen pearl onions, thawed, or sweet onion chunks (1-inch chunks)
2 tablespoons barbecue sauce
1 tablespoon frozen orange juice concentrate, thawed
1 tablespoon butter or margarine, cut into small chunks
A light sprinkle of salt and pepper

Italian Chicken Packet

½ small red or green bell pepper, seeded and cut into 1-inch chunks
½ cup sweet onion chunks (1-inch chunks)
8 fresh white button mushrooms, quartered
3 tablespoons bottled Italian dressing or Hearty Italian Vinaigrette (page 99)

Ginger-Lemon Chicken Packet

Half of an apple, cored and cut into 1-inch chunks
1 tablespoon butter or margarine, cut into small chunks
1 clove garlic, minced
½ teaspoon fresh gingerroot, minced
1 teaspoon sherry
1 teaspoon freshly squeezed lemon juice
A generous sprinkle of salt and pepper

Orange-Tarragon Chicken Packet

2 green onions, cut into 1-inch chunks (white and green parts)
Half of a medium orange, seeded, peeled and sectioned, cut into 1-inch chunks
1 tablespoon butter or margarine, cut into small chunks
1 teaspoon Dijon mustard
1 tablespoon fresh tarragon leaves
A generous sprinkle of salt and pepper

Chili-Lime Chicken Packet

½ cup sweet onion chunks (1-inch chunks)
2 teaspoons olive oil or vegetable oil
1 teaspoon chili powder blend
1 teaspoon freshly squeezed lime juice
A light sprinkle of salt and pepper

ITALIAN-STYLE GRILLED STEAK

Variable servings, depending on size of steak(s)

Nothing could be easier than this classic Italian method of grilling steak. If you happen to have fresh rosemary or thyme, toss a few sprigs on the coals just before adding the steaks to the grill.

Top-quality inch-thick steaks like porterhouse, T-bone or New York strip
Whole peeled garlic cloves
Freshly ground black pepper
Salt, preferably kosher or sea salt flakes
Fresh lemon, cut into quarters

Pat steaks dry with paper towels. Squeeze a little garlic over each steak with a garlic press (or, chop garlic very finely and put a little on each steak); rub in with your fingers. Sprinkle each steak generously with pepper. Repeat on remaining side, then let steaks stand at room temperature while you prepare a hot grill.

When grill is ready, sprinkle one side of each steak generously with salt. Place steaks on grate, salt-side down, and sprinkle second side with a little additional salt. After about 2 minutes, rotate the steaks 45 or 90 degrees to create a diamond pattern from the grate; cook 2 or 3 minutes longer. Turn steaks and cook on second side to desired doneness, preferably rare to medium-rare. Just before removing from grill, squeeze a generous amount of fresh lemon juice on each steak.

GRILLED STEAK "MARGARITA"

4 servings

A basket of warm flour tortillas and a bowl of Citrus Salsa (page 217) make nice accompaniments to this grilled steak. Garlic Mashed Potatoes (page 290) and grilled corn on the cob (page 178) are another serving option.

¾ cup bottled margarita mixer (the kind with no alcohol)
¼ cup vegetable oil
2 cloves garlic, thinly sliced
¼ cup coarsely chopped fresh cilantro leaves, optional
1- to 1½-pound top round or other beef steak, about an inch thick

Combine margarita mixer and oil in measuring cup or bowl, and whip together with a fork or whisk. Stir in garlic. Place steak in a nonaluminum dish and pour margarita mix over, turning to coat steak. Cover and refrigerate 8 to 16 hours, turning occasionally.

Prepare hot grill. Remove steak from marinade; discard marinade. Salt and pepper steak generously and place on grate. Cook about 3 minutes, then rotate the steak 45 or 90 degrees to create a diamond pattern from the grate; cook 3 minutes longer. Turn steak over and repeat on second side, then cook until desired doneness. Place on serving platter; let rest 5 minutes, loosely covered, before slicing into thin slices across the grain.

TWICE-GRILLED STEAK BURRITOS

4 servings

These are rather like chimichangas, but without all the fat and mess! Salsa Rice (page 85) or refried beans make a nice side dish.

1 pound boneless round or sirloin steak, about ¾ inch thick
1 or 2 bell peppers, depending on size and your personal preference (a mix of red and green bell peppers is very nice)
1 small onion, or half of a large onion
Juice from 1 fresh lime (about 2 tablespoons)
3 tablespoons vegetable oil
2 cloves garlic, pressed or minced
1 small fresh hot pepper, minced; or, ½ teaspoon crushed dried hot red pepper flakes
¼ teaspoon ground cumin, optional
4 burrito-sized flour tortillas (about 10 inches)*
1 cup shredded Monterey Jack or colby-Jack cheese (about 4 ounces)
A little additional vegetable oil
Cilantro Sour Cream (facing page) and prepared salsa for garnish, optional

Place steak in a glass baking dish that is large enough to hold the steak comfortably. Remove and discard stems and seeds from peppers, then cut peppers into strips and scatter over the steak. Cut the onion into strips also and scatter over the steak. In a small jar, combine lime juice, oil, garlic, hot pepper and cumin; cover tightly and shake well to mix. Pour lime-juice mixture over steak and vegetables, then stir with your hands so the steak and vegetables are coated with the marinade. Cover and let stand at room temperature 1 hour, or refrigerate up to 4 hours, turning steak occasionally.

Prepare medium-hot grill. When you're almost ready to cook, tear off a 12x18-inch piece of heavy-duty foil (or a 12x36-inch piece of regular foil, folded shiny-side in). Use a slotted spoon or your hands to transfer the vegetables to the shiny side of the foil; let any excess marinade drip back into the pan with the steak. Fold foil into a tight packet, using the "Drugstore Wrap" technique (page 284). Place foil packet over hot coals and cook about 10 minutes, turning once. Move the foil packet slightly off to the side, turning it again, and transfer the steak to the grate; sprinkle generously with salt. Cook until steak is medium doneness, turning steak and vegetables once. Remove steak and vegetables from grill, but keep the grill going for the final step.

Working quickly, slice the steak across the grain into thin strips. Place one-quarter of the strips and one-quarter or less of the vegetables (depending on total amount you cooked; extras are good served on the side) at the bottom of a flour tortilla; top with ¼ cup shredded cheese. Fold up the bottom of the tortilla, fold in the sides and then roll up the tortilla tightly. Repeat with remaining ingredients. Brush all sides of each burrito with oil, then place on the grill, seam-side down. Cook about 2 minutes, or until the burrito has become firm and lightly browned; the tortilla should be firm enough to be turned without coming unwrapped. Carefully turn the burrito and cook the other side until lightly browned. Serve each burrito garnished with a dollop of Cilantro Sour Cream and a dab of salsa, or with other desired toppings and garnishes.

*If you can't get these large tortillas, use smaller tortillas; you'll probably need 5 or 6 of the smaller ones. Divide filling ingredients accordingly, and proceed as directed.

Variation:

Twice-Grilled Chicken Burritos: Substitute 1 pound boneless, skinless chicken breast for the steak. Marinate no longer than 1½ hours (refrigerated). Proceed as directed.

CILANTRO SOUR CREAM

½ cup sour cream (reduced-fat works fine)
3 tablespoons chopped cilantro leaves
1 teaspoon lemon or lime juice

Combine all ingredients in a small bowl. Refrigerate at least 1 hour before serving.

Juicy Lucy Burgers

3 servings; easily doubled

Several bars in Minneapolis serve versions of this tasty burger. Probably the most famous is Matt's on 35th and Cedar; they call theirs the Jucy Lucy (note spelling). This version is similar to the ones made at Matt's, but you will have to provide your own ambience!

1 pound extra-lean ground beef
1 teaspoon Worcestershire sauce, optional
¾ teaspoon garlic salt or seasoned salt, or ½ teaspoon plain salt
¼ to ½ teaspoon freshly ground pepper
3 thin, square slices Monterey Jack or cheddar cheese ("sandwich slices" work great)
2 teaspoons vegetable oil, needed for pan-fried burgers and/or fried onions
1 yellow onion for frying, sliced ¼ inch thick, optional but traditional
3 hamburger buns
Condiments of your choice: thinly sliced raw onions, pickles, ketchup, etc.

You have a decision to face: grilling on an outdoor grill, or pan-frying as they do at most bars. I think grilling tastes best, and it is less fatty; however, if you want the traditional fried onions on your grilled Lucy, you'll have to use a skillet.

Combine ground beef, Worcestershire sauce, salt and pepper; mix very well with your hands. Divide into 6 even portions. Make a thin round patty about 4½ inches across from each portion. Trim the corners from the cheese slices and place one slice on each of 3 patties. Top with remaining 3 patties; press the edges together very well to seal, patting the edges in slightly with your hands so the edges are the same thickness as the rest of the burger.

For grilled burgers: Prepare medium-hot grill. Heat oil in large skillet (on the stove) and add onions; reduce heat to medium and cook, stirring occasionally, until onions are very tender. Meanwhile, place stuffed patties on the grill and cook to desired doneness, turning once; medium doneness will take 4 or 5 minutes per side. Because of the cheese stuffing, the burgers will feel less firm to the touch when done than regular burgers. Serve with fried onions, if you have made them, and buns with condiments.

For pan-fried burgers: If you're pan-frying, you really should fry some onions with the burgers. Heat a large skillet over medium-high heat. Add the oil and heat briefly. Add burgers, reducing heat to medium. Cook about 4 minutes, then turn the burgers and add the sliced onion to the skillet. Cook, stirring the onions around frequently but not moving the burgers, about 5 minutes. Lift the burgers out, turning them and placing on top of the onions; stir the onions as you make the switch. Cook about 4 minutes longer, or until burgers are desired doneness and onions are tender. Because of the cheese stuffing, the burgers will feel less firm to the touch when done than regular burgers. Serve with the fried onions, buns and condiments.

BARBECUED FLANK STEAK

3 or 4 servings

A simple marinade adds flavor and tenderness to this steak. If you have any leftovers, fry up some peppers and onions, and gently re-warm the sliced steak; tuck everything into warmed flour tortillas for easy fajitas.

Marinade ingredients:
¼ cup orange juice
2 tablespoons soy sauce
2 tablespoons honey
1 tablespoon vegetable oil

1 flank steak, 1 to 1¼ pounds

Combine all marinade ingredients in measuring cup or small bowl and blend with fork. Prick steak on both sides with a fork. Place steak in glass baking dish, or in large zip-top bag. Add marinade, turning steak to coat. Cover dish, or seal bag and place in a baking dish. Refrigerate 6 to 12 hours, turning meat occasionally. Prepare hot grill. Place steak on grate over hot coals. After about 2 minutes, rotate the steak 45 or 90 degrees to create a diamond pattern from the grate; cook 2 or 3 minutes longer. Turn steak and cook 4 or 5 minutes on second side for medium-rare, or a bit longer to desired doneness; flank steak is best when it is medium-rare to medium doneness. Slice thinly across the grain while still hot, holding your knife at a 45° angle to the cutting board (rather than straight up-and-down) to get wider slices.

BARBECUED CABBAGE ROLLS

4 servings of 2 cabbage rolls each

Grilling adds a nice flavor and texture to these traditional cabbage rolls, and the added bonus is that you won't heat up the cabin on a warm summer day. If the weather turns poor for grilling, don't despair; variations are also given for cooking in an oven or on the stovetop.

8 large cabbage leaves
1 pound lean ground beef or turkey
1 carrot, shredded
1 egg, lightly beaten
¾ cup cooked rice, cooled
¼ cup finely crumbled cornbread or wheat bread
2 tablespoons minced onion
1 tablespoon chopped fresh parsley, optional
2 teaspoons Worcestershire sauce
16 pieces kitchen twine (about 10 inches long), soaked in cold water for 10 minutes
1 can (16 ounces) tomato sauce
2 tablespoons packed brown sugar
1 tablespoon cider vinegar
¼ teaspoon salt

Carefully pare away the thick rib of the cabbage leaves so each leaf is of fairly uniform thinness. Heat a large pot of salted water to boiling and add the cabbage leaves; cook until bright green and pliable, about 5 minutes. Drain, and rinse with cold water until cool; set aside to drain while you prepare the stuffing.

To prepare the stuffing, combine ground beef, carrot, egg, rice, cornbread, onion, parsley and Worcestershire sauce; mix gently but thoroughly. Pat a cabbage leaf dry and place one-eighth of the stuffing at the rib end, shaping the stuffing into a log wide enough to leave about an inch and a half of cabbage on each side. Fold up the bottom of the leaf, then the sides, and roll up tightly, making sure that the meat is completely encased in cabbage. Tie the roll in 2 places with soaked kitchen twine. Repeat with remaining ingredients. Cover and refrigerate until ready to cook; this can be done up to a day in advance.

To prepare the sauce, in a small nonaluminum saucepan, combine tomato sauce, brown sugar, vinegar and salt. Cook over medium heat, stirring occasionally, until mixture comes to a boil.

Prepare grill for indirect heat (page 154). Brush cabbage rolls with the tomato sauce and place on grate away from heat. Cover grill and cook until stuffing is cooked through, about 35 minutes, basting with sauce and turning every 5 or 10 minutes. Re-heat remaining sauce to boiling, and serve with the cabbage rolls.

Variations:

Baked Cabbage Rolls: Assemble as directed, but don't use the string; as each roll is made, place it, seam-side down, in a 9-inch-square baking dish. Prepare tomato sauce as directed and pour over the cabbage rolls. Cover the dish and bake in a 350°F oven 45 minutes, or until sauce is hot and bubbly and stuffing is cooked.

Stovetop Cabbage Rolls: Prepare the tomato sauce first, using a large nonaluminum skillet and adding an additional ¼ cup water. Assemble as directed, but don't use the string; as each roll is made, place it, seam-side down, in the skillet with the sauce. Cover the skillet and simmer the cabbage rolls about 45 minutes, moving the rolls to prevent sticking and spooning the sauce over the rolls several times during the cooking. If the sauce becomes too thick during cooking, add a few more tablespoons of water.

GRILLED MEATLOAF

6 servings

Even if your cabin has an oven, you should try this easy way of baking a meatloaf. Grilling won't heat up the cabin on a hot day, and the grilled flavor is really wonderful. Cold leftover meatloaf makes an outstanding sandwich.

½ cup seasoned or plain bread crumbs
¼ cup plus 2 tablespoons barbecue sauce or ketchup, divided
¼ cup finely chopped onion
1 egg
1 teaspoon seasoned or plain salt
1½ pounds ground beef (or the mix of beef, pork and veal sold as "meatloaf mix")
2 strips bacon, optional

Prepare grill for indirect heat (page 154). Cover a standard-sized (8½ x 4½ x 2½ inches) metal loaf pan, inside and out, with foil; set aside. In a large mixing bowl, combine the bread crumbs, ¼ cup of the barbecue sauce, the onion, egg and salt; mix very well and let stand 5 minutes. Add the meat to the bowl and mix very well with your hands. Pack the meat mixture firmly into the loaf pan, smoothing the top and mounding it slightly. Place the pan on the grate away from the coals; cover the grill and cook 30 minutes, rotating the pan occasionally. Spread the remaining 2 tablespoons barbecue sauce over the top of the meatloaf. If using the bacon, cut the strips in half and arrange on top of loaf. Continue cooking the meatloaf on the grill another 30 to 40 minutes, or until the meatloaf is cooked through.

Pork with Maple-Mustard Sauce

4 servings

Boneless butterflied loin chops, about an inch thick, are the best for this dish; however, you may use whatever type of pork chops you like.

1 tablespoon butter or margarine
3 tablespoons whole-grain mustard
2 tablespoons maple syrup
1 tablespoon white wine vinegar
¼ teaspoon minced fresh gingerroot, optional
4 serving-sized pork chops, bone-in or boneless
1 cup chicken broth
2 teaspoons flour

In stainless-steel saucepan, melt the butter over medium heat. Stir in mustard, maple syrup, vinegar and gingerroot. Set aside until completely cooled. Add pork chops, turning to coat all sides with mustard mixture. Cover and refrigerate 1 to 3 hours, turning chops once or twice.

Prepare medium-hot grill, or the broiler. Lift chops from mustard mixture, shaking excess mixture back into saucepan. Cook chops until just barely done; if you overcook them, they will be tough and dry. While chops are cooking, add the chicken broth to the saucepan with the remaining mustard mixture. Heat to a gentle boil. Reduce heat slightly and cook, stirring occasionally, 10 to 15 minutes. When the chops are cooked, transfer to a plate; cover to keep warm. Blend flour with 2 tablespoons water, then stir into the simmering broth/mustard mixture. Boil gently, stirring constantly, until sauce is somewhat thickened. Taste for seasoning and add salt if necessary. Serve sauce with chops; if you prefer a smooth sauce, strain the finished sauce into a gravy boat through a wire-mesh strainer.

Cioppino: Italian-Style Shellfish Stew

4 or 5 servings

If you live or vacation near the coast, you can buy shellfish at reasonable prices to make this great party dish. Feel free to substitute or add other types of shellfish; mussels are also good.

3 tablespoons olive oil
1 medium onion, chopped
3 cloves garlic, pressed or minced
8 ounces bottled clam juice
1 can (28 ounces) Italian-style plum tomatoes packed in juice, cut up, juice reserved
1 pound fettuccini (uncooked)
⅓ pound lobster meat (frozen lobster is OK; thaw in refrigerator before cooking)
1 pound snow crab claws (frozen claws are OK; thaw in refrigerator before cooking)
½ pound raw green shrimp, shelled and deveined
½ pound bay scallops
2 tablespoons coarsely chopped fresh Italian flat-leaf or regular parsley (do not substitute dried)
1 tablespoon coarsely chopped fresh basil leaves (do not substitute dried)
1 tablespoon coarsely chopped fresh marjoram leaves, or 1 teaspoon dried
2 tablespoons butter

Bring a large pot of salted water to the boil and keep hot; this will be needed to cook the fettuccini. In nonaluminum Dutch oven or stockpot, heat the oil over medium heat. Add the onion and garlic and sauté until just tender. Add clam juice and tomatoes with their juice. Heat just to boiling, then reduce the heat so the sauce bubbles gently. When the tomato sauce has been simmering about 5 minutes, add the fettuccini to the large kettle of boiling water, stirring frequently to prevent sticking, and cook until it is not quite done; stir the tomato sauce occasionally while the fettuccini is cooking. Meanwhile, cut the lobster into smaller pieces if it is a large chunk.

When the fettuccini is almost ready to drain and the tomato sauce has cooked for about 20 minutes, add the seafood and herbs to the tomato sauce. Return the tomato sauce to a simmer and cook about 5 minutes, stirring occasionally; seafood should be opaque in center when done. Meanwhile, check the pasta and when it is al dente (tender but still slightly firm in the middle), drain it and place in a serving bowl; quickly stir in the butter.

Give each person a wide, shallow bowl or very deep plate. Each person places a heaping portion of pasta in his or her dish, then ladles seafood and tomato sauce over. Have a big bowl in the center of the table for shells, and make sure there are plenty of napkins on hand; this is messy to eat but worth it!

CIOPPINO FOR A CROWD

8 to 10 servings

Double the quantities of the oil, onion, garlic, clam juice, tomatoes, fettuccini, herbs and butter from the recipe on the facing page

For the seafood, use:
1 lobster tail, in the shell (about 1 pound)
1 pound snow crab claws
1¼ pounds stone crab claws
1 pound green shrimp, shelled and deveined
1 pound bay scallops
1 pound mussels, shells scrubbed and beards removed

Proceed as directed on facing page, except place the whole lobster tail in the tomato sauce as soon you reduce the heat (after adding the clam juice and tomatoes and bringing to a boil). The lobster tail should be done by the time you are ready to add the other seafood; pull it out and set it aside to cool slightly while the other seafood cooks. Just before serving, remove the lobster meat from the shell; cut up the meat and return it to the tomato sauce, discarding the shell. The lobster shell will have added a bit of extra flavor to the tomato sauce.

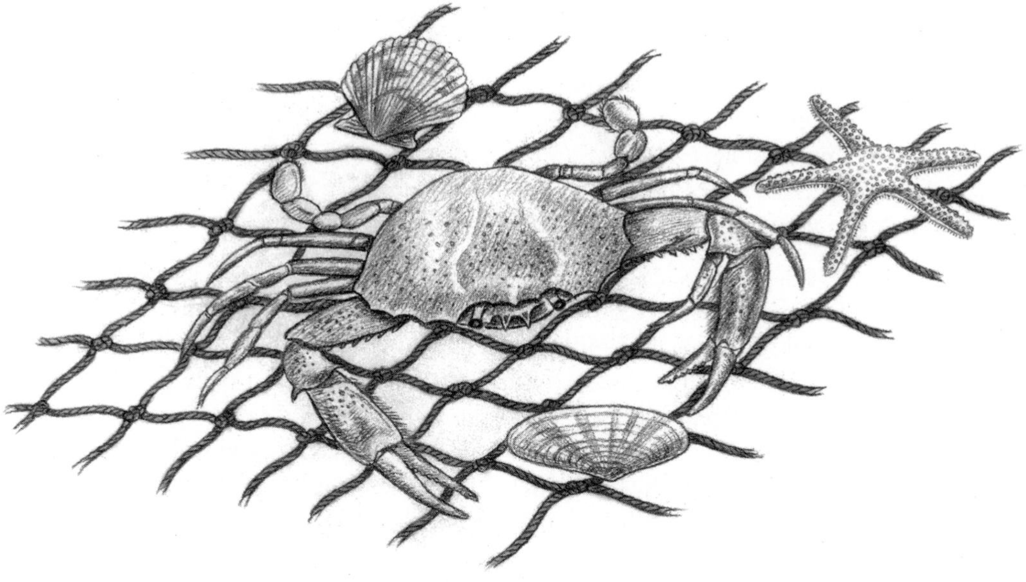

Stuffed Catfish Fillets on the Grill

4 servings; easily increased

Grilling adds a wonderful flavor to these fish fillets; however, you can also bake them in a 375°F oven for about 25 minutes, then pop them under the broiler for a final crisping.

4 boneless, skinless catfish fillets (5 to 6 ounces each)
½ cup finely diced red and/or green bell peppers
½ cup minced onion
¼ teaspoon minced jalapeño pepper, optional
1 clove garlic, pressed or minced
¼ cup butter or margarine (half of a stick), divided
1 cup finely crumbled cornbread
2 tablespoons chopped fresh parsley
About ¼ cup chicken stock
2 tablespoons freshly squeezed lemon juice (from about half of a lemon)
1 teaspoon chopped fresh sage leaves, or ¼ teaspoon rubbed dried sage

Pat fillets dry with paper towels. Sprinkle with salt and pepper; set aside. In medium skillet over medium heat, sauté bell peppers, onion, jalapeño pepper and garlic in 1 tablespoon of the butter until vegetables are tender. Remove from heat and stir in the crumbled cornbread and parsley; set aside until cooled completely. When the vegetable mixture is cool, add enough chicken stock to make a moist mixture. Spread one-quarter of the mixture over each fillet. Roll up fairly tightly, starting with the top of the fillet closest to where the head of the fish used to be. Some of the filling will fall out the sides; pat this firmly back onto the sides of the roll-up where the rest of the filling is exposed. Secure the roll-up by running 2 toothpicks through the tail of the fish. Refrigerate for about 30 minutes while you prepare a medium-hot grill. In the meantime, melt the remaining 3 tablespoons butter; stir in the lemon juice and sage, and cook about a minute.

Place fish, toothpick-side up, on oiled grate off to the side of the coals (the fish should be just barely over the edge of the hot coals; or, you can use indirect heat); brush with the butter-lemon mixture. Cover the grill and cook, brushing with butter-lemon mixture and rotating every 10 minutes while keeping the toothpick side up, until center of fish is just done; this will take 20 to 25 minutes. To check for doneness, probe the center of the stuffing with an instant-read thermometer; it should read about 150°F (or, stick a metal skewer into the center for about 30 seconds and pull it out; the skewer should be hot). Flip the fish over so the toothpick side is down during the last few minutes of grilling; this marks the fish nicely and also ensures that the fish at the top is cooked completely.

Spaghetti with Grill-Roasted Tomato Sauce

4 servings

Fresh tomatoes, basil and garlic marry perfectly with spaghetti, but usually the weather is so warm when home-grown tomatoes are ripe that I don't feel like heating up the kitchen by making a long-simmered sauce. This wonderful sauce cooks on the grill and really tastes great. Now, if I could only figure out how to boil pasta on the grill ...

2 pounds plum tomatoes or regular tomatoes
Disposable aluminum roasting pan, approximately 13x9x2 inches
⅓ cup chopped fresh parsley
3 tablespoons olive oil
1 to 2 tablespoons minced garlic
½ teaspoon sugar (if the tomatoes are garden-fresh and sweet, don't use the sugar)
20 to 25 fresh basil leaves (use more if the leaves are small)
8 ounces spaghetti (uncooked)
Grated Parmesan cheese for serving

Prepare grill for indirect heat (page 154). To prepare tomatoes, remove core and cut tomatoes from top to bottom into quarters (or eighths if using larger tomatoes); remove and discard the seeds, then cut the tomato wedges into 1-inch chunks. Place tomatoes in aluminum pan. Add parsley, olive oil, garlic and sugar; sprinkle generously with salt and freshly ground pepper. Stir well with a spoon, and place on the grate away from the fire. Cover the grill and cook 45 minutes, stirring tomatoes every 15 minutes.

While the tomatoes are grilling, prepare the basil by stacking the leaves 5 or 6 at a time, rolling them up tightly, then cutting into thin ribbons; set aside. Near the end of the tomato cooking time, heat a very large pot of salted water to boiling, then add the spaghetti, stirring vigorously to prevent the spaghetti from sticking together; right after you put the spaghetti in the boiling water, stir the basil into the tomato mixture and continue grilling. When spaghetti is tender yet still has a slightly firm center, carefully scoop out about ½ cup of the spaghetti cooking water and set aside; drain the spaghetti and turn into a large serving bowl (or, return it to the cooking pot). Pour the tomato mixture and all juices over the spaghetti. Toss well to combine; if the mixture is dry, add a bit of the reserved cooking water until it is the consistency you prefer. Serve the spaghetti with Parmesan cheese on the side.

Grilled Pizza

Two 9- to 10-inch pizzas; 2 generous servings each

Try this when you don't want to heat up the oven (or if your cabin doesn't have one!). You can use any toppings you like, but don't use toppings with a lot of liquid or your pizzas will be soggy. Since the pizza doesn't stay on the grill very long, the toppings won't get much cooking time; most vegetables are best if lightly cooked before using to top the pizza. Follow the list below for guidelines, or try your own combinations.

1 loaf (1 pound) frozen yeast bread dough, or homemade dough for 1 loaf
A small amount of olive oil (oil seasoned with garlic is very good)
A little minced garlic, optional (very good if you are using plain olive oil)

A total of 1½ to 2 cups toppings: *Choose* ***up to*** *4 from the following:*

- **Roasted bell peppers, cut into ½-inch dice (see page 299 for roasting instructions, or buy already-roasted peppers in a jar)**
- **Asparagus that has been cooked until tender-crisp, cut into 1-inch pieces**
- **Up to ½ cup of diced red or yellow onions**
- **3 or 4 green onions, sliced ¼ inch thick**
- **Marinated or cooked mushroom pieces or slices**
- **Up to ¼ cup sliced ripe olives**
- **Lightly sautéed sliced celery**
- **Canned marinated artichoke hearts, drained and cut up**
- **Very ripe fresh tomatoes, seeded and drained, cut into ½-inch pieces (or substitute up to ½ cup canned diced tomatoes, very well drained)**
- **Cut-up cooked chicken or turkey**
- **Smoked trout or salmon, broken into large flakes**

3 tablespoons shredded Romano or Parmesan cheese
1½ to 2 cups shredded mozzarella cheese

Thaw the dough according to package directions, or prepare homemade dough and let rise once. When you're ready to start cooking, you'll need to have a grill ready, but the heat should be only medium (place the coals only in the center of the grill, leaving the sides clear, and let coals burn down a bit; if using propane, adjust heat to medium-low, and use just the center burner). Punch dough down if necessary, and divide into 2 pieces. Roll each into a circle about 9 inches across; don't worry if the circles aren't perfect, as this pizza looks great with an "organic" shape. Place the rounds on a lightly greased cookie sheet and bring them outside to the grill.

Oil the grill rack lightly. Remove one round, which probably began shrinking to a smaller diameter as soon as you stopped rolling it. Drape it over your fists and gently move your fists outward, stretching and turning the dough, until it is the proper diameter again (if you've seen pizza cooks do this in movies or commercials, here's your chance to try it!). When the dough is 9 or 10 inches across and roughly even in thickness, place it on the grill rack over the heat. Cook for about 45 seconds, then rotate the dough one-half turn and cook about 30 seconds longer; it should be an uneven medium-brown with a few darker spots, but should not be burned. Turn and cook the second side about 30 seconds. Transfer the grilled crust to the cookie sheet, and repeat with the remaining dough round.

Brush the darker sides of each grilled crust with olive oil; if you're using unseasoned olive oil, you may want to sprinkle with a little minced garlic. Arrange the toppings evenly on each crust. Sprinkle each pizza evenly with the Romano cheese, then with the mozzarella.

Use a spatula and your hands to place the pizzas on the grill rack, away from the coals (off to the sides). Cover the grill and cook, rotating the pizzas very frequently, until the cheese melts. This usually takes 5 to 10 minutes; watch the crust carefully to make sure it isn't burning.

Vegetables, Starches and Side Dishes

Roasted Fresh Corn on the Cob

1 serving per ear of corn

Fresh corn on the cob that's been roasted on a grill or over a campfire is one of the best summertime treats there is. Ignore any advice you may have read about peeling back the husks to remove the silk before roasting; this destroys the integrity of the husk, causing dried-out corn. The silk peels off easily after the corn is roasted, and the folded-back peel makes an ideal handle to hold the steaming ear.

Fresh, unhusked corn on the cob
Melted butter (seasoned with chopped garlic or herbs, if you like)
Salt and pepper for serving

Soak the corn in clean, cool water for 30 minutes before roasting; you'll have to tie the ears together or weigh them down with a large rock or log to keep them submerged.

Prepare grill or campfire; if cooking over a campfire, the wood should be burned down to glowing coals rather than a hot, roaring flame. Place wet ears on grate over the grill or campfire and cook 20 to 25 minutes, turning occasionally, until corn is tender and spotted with occasional golden brown kernels (check an ear for doneness before removing them all from the fire); the husks will be charred and this is OK. Holding the corn with oven mitts or towels, peel back the husks and silk, leaving the husks attached to use as a handle. Let the diners brush their corn with melted butter, and season to taste.

For campfire cooking without a grate: Simply toss the soaked ears directly onto glowing embers. Turn frequently, and move occasionally to cooler embers to prevent premature burning. Cooking time will be about 15 minutes, or slightly less.

ROASTED FROZEN CORN ON THE COB

1 small serving per mini cob

Let me state this right up front: There is no comparison between fresh sweet corn and frozen mini cobs. But the season for fresh corn is so short (especially in my home state of Minnesota) that sometimes the frozen stuff seems an acceptable alternative. This method makes the best out of it and is lots better than boiling or microwaving.

Frozen mini cobs, thawed
1 teaspoon butter or seasoned butter per cob
Salt and pepper, or seasoned salt/seasoned pepper if you're using plain butter

Spread butter on all sides of each cob. Place 2 mini cobs end-to-end on a square of foil. Bring the sides of the foil (parallel to the cobs) together and roll-fold snugly over the corn; you'll need at least 3 complete roll-folds. Roll the ends in tightly. Place the wrapped corn on a grate over a prepared grill or campfire and cook 15 minutes, turning frequently.

SUMMER SQUASH CASSEROLE

6 servings

Use yellow squash, zucchini squash or crookneck for this dish. It's great hot or at warm room temperature, so it makes a good carry-along dish for a potluck.

1 package (6 ounces) complete stuffing mix such as Stove Top
6 tablespoons butter or margarine (three-quarters of a stick), melted
3 cups diced yellow squash or other summer squash
½ cup diced onion
1 tablespoon vegetable oil
1 can (10¾ ounces) condensed cream of mushroom, cream of chicken or cream of celery soup
1 cup sour cream (reduced-fat works fine)
1 cup shredded cheddar or other cheese (about 4 ounces)

Heat oven to 350°F. Spray an 8x10x2-inch baking dish with nonstick spray or grease lightly. In a mixing bowl, combine stuffing mix and melted butter, stirring to coat evenly. Pat half the stuffing into the prepared baking dish; set aside.

In a large skillet, sauté the squash and onion in oil until the squash is just tender. Remove from heat; stir in the condensed soup and sour cream. Spread evenly over the stuffing in the baking dish. Top with remaining stuffing; sprinkle evenly with shredded cheese. Bake until mixture is hot and bubbly and cheese melts, 30 to 40 minutes.

CRISPY GREEN BEANS

4 servings; easily adjusted for more or less servings

Green beans can be rather a ho-hum vegetable … they overcook easily, and lose their bright green color. This easy recipe produces beautiful, bright-green beans with a wonderful texture. It's based on a technique used in Chinese cooking.

1 pound fresh green beans, ends removed (do not use frozen beans)
Vegetable oil for skillet deep-frying (or enough to fill a deep fryer)
2 teaspoons butter or margarine
¼ cup sliced or slivered almonds

Rinse green beans and drain well; place on paper towels to dry completely. Heat about ¾ inch of oil in a skillet over medium-high heat (or, fill deep fryer with oil as recommended by manufacturer). Heat oil to 375°F; if you stick a toothpick or wooden chopstick into the oil, small bubbles should immediately rise from the wood. Add a small layer of green beans; do not overcrowd the skillet or deep fryer. Cook until beans have bubbles on the surface and are bright green, about 30 seconds. Transfer to paper-towl-lined plate and keep warm while you repeat with remaining beans. When all beans are cooked, pat them all over with paper towels to remove excess oil.

In large skillet, melt butter over medium heat. Add almonds and cook, stirring constantly, until almonds are golden brown. Add beans and cook, stirring constantly, until beans are just re-warmed; do not overcook. Sprinkle with salt to taste before serving.

STUFFED ZUCCHINI

3 or 4 servings; easily doubled

When your zucchini patch produces one of those monster zucchini (or the neighbors insist you take one from their patch), turn it into a delicious light meal with this recipe. Actually, you'll still be stuck with the other half of the zucchini, since this recipe uses just half; consider doubling the recipe and inviting the neighbors over!

1 very large zucchini, about a foot long
12 ounces bulk pork sausage such as Jimmy Dean's
⅔ cup chopped onion
⅓ cup thinly sliced celery
About 2 teaspoons vegetable oil
1 large tomato, diced
1 cup cooked rice, or slightly more as needed
1 egg, beaten
½ teaspoon garlic salt, seasoned salt or plain salt
¼ teaspoon pepper
1 cup shredded cheddar or other cheese (about 4 ounces)

Slice the zucchini horizontally so you have 2 long halves; wrap and refrigerate 1 half for other uses (unless you are making a double recipe). Use a grapefruit spoon or soup spoon to scrape out the seeds and soft core along the whole length of the zucchini, leaving a rounded trench up the middle of the zucchini. Discard the seeds and core. Sprinkle the cut side of the zucchini generously with salt; set aside for about 30 minutes, then rinse off the salt and drain the zucchini (the salt helps remove any bitterness sometimes found in mature zucchini).

While the zucchini is salting, fry the pork sausage in a large skillet over medium heat, stirring frequently to break up. When the meat has lost its pink color, add the onion and celery and cook, stirring occasionally, until the sausage is cooked through and the vegetables are tender. Transfer the sausage mixture to a large mixing bowl and allow to cool slightly. Pat the rinsed and drained zucchini dry with paper towels. Rub the outside of the zucchini with the oil and place on a large baking sheet. Heat the oven to 350°F.

Add the tomato, rice, egg, salt and pepper to the cooled sausage mixture and mix well; if there doesn't seem to be quite enough stuffing, add a bit more rice. Mound the sausage mixture into the trench in the zucchini, packing fairly firmly and rounding the top. Sprinkle the grated cheese over the top. Bake until the zucchini is tender-crisp, the stuffing is hot and the cheese melts, about 35 minutes. To serve, slice into 3- or 4-inch-wide pieces.

GRILLED ITALIAN POTATO SPEARS

4 servings; easily adjusted for more or less servings

These are great with any grilled meat and are quick-and-easy to prepare using pre-baked potatoes. Bake the potatoes with another dish while the oven is on and refrigerate the cooked potatoes until needed.

3 already-baked skin-on russet potatoes (about 8 ounces each)
½ cup bottled or homemade Italian dressing (such as Hearty Italian Vinaigrette, page 99)
1 tablespoon shredded or grated Parmesan or Romano cheese

If the potatoes are hot, allow them to cool enough to handle. Cut each potato lengthwise into 4 wedges (if the potatoes are very large, you can cut them into 6 wedges each). Place the wedges in a baking dish. In a small bowl, stir together the dressing and Parmesan cheese, then pour the dressing mixture over the potato wedges. Turn the potato wedges carefully to coat all sides. Let the potatoes stand at room temperature for 30 minutes to an hour; if warm potatoes were used, the shorter time will be sufficient, but if the potatoes were cold from the refrigerator, the longer time is recommended.

Prepare medium-hot grill; if cooking these along with another grilled dish, start cooking the potatoes about 10 minutes before the other dish is ready to serve. Remove potato wedges from dressing, retaining the dressing. Place potato wedges on grate above hot coals; cover grill if possible, although this is not essential (and depending on what else you're cooking, it may not be desirable). Cook the potatoes until golden brown and crispy on all sides, turning carefully every few minutes and dipping into the remaining dressing as you turn them. Sprinkle with salt before serving.

GRILLED CORN, PEPPER AND CUCUMBER SALAD

4 or 5 servings

Grill the corn, onions and peppers for this salad while you are fixing another meal on the grill, then assemble the salad and let it marinate overnight. You'll have a delicious salad with a wonderful grilled flavor for the following day.

2 ears fresh corn, unhusked
Half of a small red onion
About 2 teaspoons olive oil or vegetable oil
1 red or green bell pepper
1 fresh Anaheim chile pepper, optional
Half of a cucumber, cut into ¼-inch cubes

Dressing:

Juice of 1 lemon (about ¼ cup)
2 tablespoons vegetable oil
2 tablespoons sugar
1 clove garlic, pressed or minced
½ teaspoon fresh thyme leaves, minced, or ¼ teaspoon crumbled dried

Soak corn in a bucket of water for about an hour (see page 178). Slice onion into ½-inch-thick rings; brush with oil. Prepare medium-hot grill. Place onion slices, peppers and corn on grate over coals. Cook as directed below; the onion and peppers will be done before the corn.

Onion: Grill over hot coals until nicely marked and tender-crisp, about 5 minutes per side. Let cool, then cut into ½-inch pieces. Place in a large mixing bowl.

Peppers: Grill over hot coals until peppers are completely blackened, turning as each side becomes blackened. Transfer the peppers to a paper bag and roll up the top; let stand 10 minutes, then peel off and discard the charred skin. Remove and discard seeds and stem. Cut peppers into ½-inch pieces and add to the mixing bowl.

Corn: Grill over medium coals (or off slightly to the side of the grill), turning frequently, until corn is tender when pressed; the husks will be quite charred. Peel back a bit of the husk and check the corn for doneness; if necessary, replace husk and continue grilling until corn is cooked (I like this best when the corn kernels have toasted slightly, so some are browned). Remove corn from grill. You may husk the corn immediately, or let it stand for a while before husking, depending on your schedule.

When you pull back the husks, the silk will come along; pull off any stray silk that doesn't come off with the husks. Cut the corn off the cob and add to the mixing bowl with the onion and peppers.

Combine all dressing ingredients in a jar. Seal tightly and shake to blend. Add cucumber and dressing to mixing bowl with other vegetables. Stir well. Cover and refrigerate 12 to 24 hours.

FRIED GREEN TOMATOES

4 servings

These are a traditional end-of-the-season dish in Minnesota when the frost is coming and the tomatoes aren't ripe yet. But it's good enough to fix anytime during tomato season. Don't try this with ripe tomatoes, as they will fall apart during cooking.

1 cup flour
½ cup cornmeal
1 teaspoon paprika, optional
1 teaspoon seasoned or plain salt
2 or 3 large green or greenish-red tomatoes, cut crosswise into ½-inch-thick slices
1 cup whole milk or half-and-half
Olive oil or vegetable oil for frying (about ½ cup)

In wide bowl or dish, combine the flour, cornmeal, paprika and salt, stirring well to mix. Add tomatoes to another wide bowl or dish, and pour milk over. Heat ¼ inch oil in heavy skillet over medium heat just until a drop of water sizzles when flicked into the oil. Quickly remove a tomato slice from the milk and coat both sides with the flour mixture; add to the skillet and repeat until you have a single layer of tomatoes. Cook until golden brown and crisp on both sides, turning only once. Transfer cooked tomatoes to a warm plate lined with paper towels; set aside and keep warm. Add additional oil to skillet if necessary, and repeat until all tomato slices are cooked.

Picnic Potato Casserole on the Grill

6 to 8 servings

This easy-to-make dish is simple to transport for a picnic and also works great for camping when you have a cooler to carry the ingredients (it's not suitable for lightweight or pack-in camping). Of course, it's just as good cooked in the back yard of your home or cabin.

8 x 8 x 1¾-inch disposable aluminum pan, and a sheet of foil to cover the pan
1 teaspoon oil, butter or stick margarine
1 bag (28 ounces) frozen O'Brien potatoes
2 cups shredded Colby or cheddar cheese, divided
1 can (10¾ ounces) condensed cream of mushroom or cream of chicken soup (reduced-fat works fine)
1 teaspoon seasoned salt, garlic salt or celery salt

This should be assembled just before cooking. If you'll be cooking this at a picnic or campsite, carry the potatoes and cheese in a cooler; the potatoes can be packed in the cooler while still frozen. Check the potatoes about 45 minutes before you plan to start cooking and if they are still frozen, remove the bag from the cooler and allow them to thaw before assembling the casserole.

Prepare medium grill, or prepare for indirect heat (page 154). Smear the inside of the aluminum pan liberally with the oil, butter or margarine. Add the potatoes, half the cheese, the undiluted soup and the salt to the pan, and mix as best you can. Pour ½ soup can (about ¾ cup) water evenly over the potatoes and cover the pan tightly with foil. Place the pan on the grate where it will get indirect or medium heat. Cook about 40 minutes, rotating pan every 10 minutes. Check the potatoes by lifting a corner of the foil; they should be bubbling after 40 minutes (if they are not, move potatoes to a hotter area of the fire and continue cooking, covered, until bubbly). When potatoes are bubbly, remove the foil and sprinkle remaining cheese over the potatoes. Cook, uncovered, about 10 minutes longer, until the cheese melts.

The Many Faces of Potato Salad

Potatoes are a New World vegetable, and no side dish is more American than potato salad. From the mustard-tinted potato salad found at delis and picnic tables across the country, to hot German-style potato salad rich with bacon, to warm potato slices dressed with olive oil and vinegar, few dishes are as varied as potato salad. There's really no "right" or "wrong" way to make it. Even cooks who have a favorite recipe will vary it to suit the ingredients on hand.

Even the type of potato used is subject to debate. Probably the most commonly used potato is the russet potato, also called Idaho or baking potatoes. This starchy potato crumbles somewhat into the dressing, and is usually featured in the ubiquitous yellow potato salad. Red potatoes are waxier than the starchy russet potatoes, and keep their shape better when cooked. They are often used in potato salads featuring a vinaigrette-type dressing, although this is not a hard-and-fast rule either. Yukon gold potatoes, which are appearing more frequently in large city supermarkets, are intermediate in characteristics between the two types.

All potatoes should be well scrubbed before further preparation. Even if you're peeling the potatoes, you should wash them first to remove soil and any pesticides or sprays (this is a good rule to follow with all vegetables). Red potatoes have tender skins, and are often used with the peels intact, while most cooks peel russet potatoes for use in potato salad. Russets can be boiled whole in their jackets, and the peels will easily slip off the hot cooked potato under cold running water; I think potatoes cooked and peeled this way are less watery than those that have been peeled and cut up before cooking. However, if you're in a hurry, there's no doubt that cut-up potatoes—peeled or not—cook more quickly than whole potatoes.

The cooked potatoes are generally cooled before combining them with mayonnaise-based dressings. Oil-based dressings work best when tossed with still-warm potatoes, as this allows the flavors to permeate the potatoes. Mayonnaise-based potato salads are more perishable than vinaigrette-based salads, and once chilled, they must be kept absolutely cold until serving. Vinaigrette-based potato salads are more forgiving, and are good at almost any temperature.

On pages 188–192 are some potato salad variations for you to try (for another variation that is a bit more involved, see Warm Potato Salad with Caesar Dressing, page 82). All recipes are based on two pounds of potatoes (3 or 4 baking-sized russets, 6 Yukon gold, or 10 medium-sized red potatoes), which usually makes enough salad for 6 to 8 servings. You can cut the recipes in half with ease to make 3 or 4 servings. Feel free to vary the ingredients—within reason—based on your personal preferences and the ingredients you have on hand. Keep in mind that potatoes tend to suck up salt like a sponge, and cold foods taste less salty than warm foods. Therefore, you may want to add a lesser amount of salt to a salad that will be chilled, then add a bit of additional salt just before serving.

CLASSIC GOLDEN POTATO SALAD

2 pounds russet potatoes
¼ cup minced onion
1 cup salad dressing such as Miracle Whip, or mayonnaise (salad dressing is sweeter)
2 teaspoons yellow mustard
1 tablespoon vinegar
½ teaspoon salt or celery salt
⅛ teaspoon white pepper (preferably, but you can use black pepper if that's all you have)

Cook the potatoes until tender, then peel and cube them into bite-sized pieces, or whatever size you prefer (typical size is ½ to ¾ inch). Place cubed potatoes and onion in large mixing bowl, and let stand until potatoes are warm room temperature. In smaller bowl, combine remaining ingredients; stir well to blend. Add dressing to potatoes and toss gently to coat. Cover and refrigerate until well chilled; serve cold.

Variations and additions:

- Add one or more of the following:
  - -½ to 1 cup diced or thinly sliced celery
  - -½ to 1 cup finely diced red or green bell pepper
  - -A tablespoon or so of chopped fresh parsley leaves
  - -2 hard-cooked eggs, cut up; decorate the top of the salad with a third egg cut into wedges
  - -2 or 3 tablespoons sweet pickle relish or finely chopped pickles
  - -5 or 6 radishes, cut into thin slivers; decorate the top of the salad with radish roses
- Replace ¼ to ½ cup of the salad dressing with sour cream
- Add 1 tablespoon sugar to the dressing if you prefer a sweeter taste
- Add ¼ teaspoon celery seeds to the dressing
- Sprinkle with paprika before serving; add a few parsley sprigs as garnish

WARM HERBED POTATO SALAD

2 pounds potatoes (any type you prefer)
½ cup olive oil or vegetable oil
¼ cup white wine vinegar
2 tablespoons dry white wine or chicken broth*
¾ teaspoon Dijon mustard
¾ teaspoon salt, or to taste
¼ teaspoon pepper
¼ cup minced red onion
3 tablespoons minced fresh parsley
2 tablespoons minced fresh herbs of your choice (I like a mix of tarragon and oregano), or 1½ teaspoons dried

Cook the potatoes until tender. While potatoes are cooking, combine oil, vinegar, wine (if using), mustard, salt and pepper in large mixing bowl; whisk well. When potatoes are tender; peel or not, as you prefer (I prefer to peel russets or Yukon gold potatoes, but leave the peels on red potatoes). Cut potatoes into lengthwise quarters, then slice ¼ inch thick; add to the bowl with the dressing (give the dressing another quick whisk if it has separated). Add the onion, parsley and herbs, and toss all gently to combine. Serve warm; leftovers can be served cold, or reheated gently in a microwave.

*Necessary only if you are using russet potatoes; russets need a little more liquid because they soak up more moisture. Wine or chicken broth will not be needed if you use waxy red potatoes.

GERMAN POTATO SALAD

2 pounds red potatoes
¼ pound bacon (about 6 regular slices), cut into ¼-inch pieces
Half of a medium onion, thinly sliced into quarter-rings
¾ cup thinly sliced celery
¾ cup cider vinegar
2 to 3 tablespoons sugar, depending on personal preference
½ teaspoon dry mustard powder, optional
½ cup cold water
1 tablespoon flour
3 tablespoons chopped fresh parsley, optional

Cook potatoes with skins on until tender. While potatoes are cooking, fry the bacon in a large skillet over medium heat until just crisp, stirring frequently. Add the onion and celery; cook until vegetables are tender-crisp. Add the vinegar, sugar and mustard to bacon mixture in skillet; cook, stirring frequently, until mixture bubbles. In measuring cup or small bowl, blend the water and flour; add to the skillet in a thin stream, stirring constantly and maintaining medium heat. Cook until the mixture thickens and bubbles, stirring frequently; if this is done before the potatoes are ready, remove from heat and set aside.

When potatoes are tender, drain and slice thinly when cool enough to handle. Add to the skillet with the bacon dressing mixture; cook over medium heat, gently stirring occasionally, until potatoes are warmed and permeated with dressing. Stir in parsley, or sprinkle on top before serving. Serve warm.

DILLED POTATO SALAD

2 pounds potatoes (any type you prefer)
Half of a medium cucumber
½ cup mayonnaise (reduced-fat works fine)
½ cup sour cream (reduced-fat works fine)
2 tablespoons minced fresh dill leaves
1 tablespoon white wine vinegar or white vinegar
2 teaspoons honey
¾ teaspoon salt

Cook the potatoes until tender. While potatoes are cooking, slice cucumber into 4 lengthwise quarters; scrape away and discard seeds and pulpy seed core. Cut cucumbers into ¼-inch dice; set aside. In a large mixing bowl, combine mayonnaise, sour cream, dill, vinegar, honey and salt; stir to blend well. When potatoes are tender, peel or not, as you prefer (I prefer to peel russets or Yukon gold potatoes, but leave the peels on red potatoes); set aside until potatoes are cool room temperature. Cut potatoes into lengthwise quarters, then slice ¼ inch thick; add to the bowl with the dressing. Add cucumbers and toss all gently to combine. Cover and refrigerate until well chilled; serve cold.

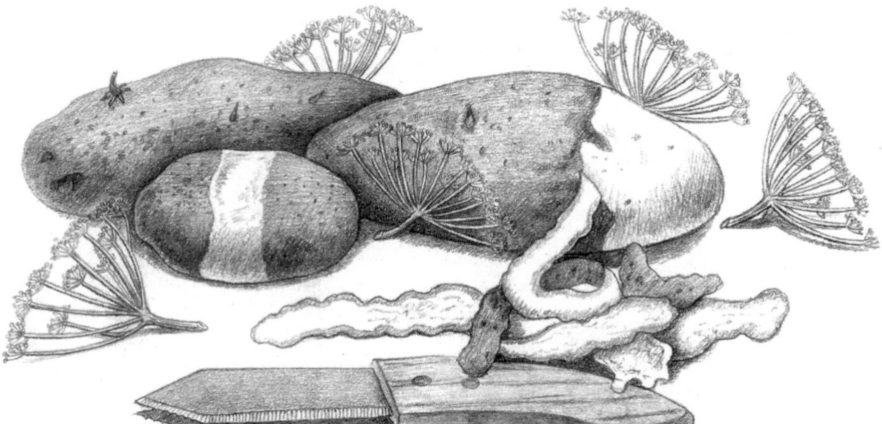

GREEK POTATO SALAD

2 pounds red potatoes
⅓ cup olive oil
2 tablespoons red wine vinegar
2 tablespoons chopped fresh oregano leaves
¾ teaspoon salt
¼ teaspoon pepper
Half of a medium cucumber
½ cup pitted, sliced kalamata olives or other black olives
½ cup diced red or green bell pepper
Half of a small red onion, thinly sliced into quarter-rings
4 or 5 pepperoncini peppers,* cores and stems discarded, chopped coarsely, optional
1 cup crumbled feta cheese (about 4 ounces)

Cook the potatoes until tender. While the potatoes are cooking, combine oil, vinegar, oregano, salt and pepper in a large mixing bowl; whisk well. Slice cucumber into 4 lengthwise quarters; scrape away and discard seeds and pulpy seed core. Cut cucumbers into ¼-inch dice; set aside. When potatoes are tender, drain and refresh with cold water until cool. Cut into ¾-inch cubes. Add to the mixing bowl with the dressing (give the dressing another quick whisk if it has separated); stir gently to coat potatoes with dressing. Add diced cucumber and remaining ingredients; toss gently to combine. Cover and refrigerate until well chilled; serve cold.

*Pepperoncini peppers are brined, light-green peppers, usually 2 inches long. They can be hard to find in smaller grocery stores, but the taste is wonderful so they are worth looking for. Try an ethnic grocery that specializes in Italian or Greek foods, or look near the olives in large city supermarkets.

Skillet Potato Casserole

4 servings

Sinfully delicious! This recipe is so simple that you could even make it on a primitive stove or campfire while camping. Serve for brunch, or as a hearty side dish; it also works well for an open-air breakfast.

¼ pound bacon (about 6 regular slices)
2½ cups shredded potato, freshly grated or thawed frozen shreds (slightly thicker shreds work better than thin, watery shreds)
½ cup diced onion
½ cup diced green bell pepper, optional
4 eggs
⅓ cup milk
½ teaspoon garlic salt, celery salt, seasoned salt or plain salt
¼ teaspoon Tabasco sauce, optional
¾ cup shredded cheddar or other cheese (about 3 ounces)

In 9-inch cast-iron or other heavy-bottomed skillet, cook bacon over medium heat until crisp. Transfer bacon to paper towels to drain, retaining drippings. Add shredded potato, onion and green pepper to skillet with drippings; cook, stirring occasionally, until potatoes are nicely browned. Meanwhile, beat together eggs, milk, salt and Tabasco sauce. When potatoes are crispy, add egg mixture and stir gently to combine. Cook without stirring until the mixture begins to set. Crumble the bacon over the top, and sprinkle shredded cheese over all; cook until cheese melts and eggs are set. Cut into wedges to serve.

Parmesan-Grilled Yams

2 servings per yam; make as many as you wish

The yams used for this dish are the ones with rich, moist orange flesh; you may even be able to find garnet yams, which have a lovely color and flavor. The "true yam" is dry and mealy, with pale flesh; it will not work well for this recipe.

1 orange- or garnet-fleshed yam (choose evenly shaped yams)
1 tablespoon grated Parmesan or Romano cheese
1 teaspoon snipped fresh chives
1 tablespoon butter, softened
Black pepper to taste

Scrub the yam(s) well, but do not peel. Prick the skin in several places with a fork. Cook the yam(s) until just tender by one of the following methods:

- Microwave on HIGH, rotating and turning over occasionally. One yam will take 4 to 5 minutes; 2 will take 5 to 10 minutes; 4 will take 10 to 15 minutes.
- Bake: Place yam(s) on a baking sheet; this will catch any juices that the yam will drip during baking. Bake at 400°F for 45 to 55 minutes.
- Boil yams in a large pot of water until tender, 20 to 30 minutes; drain.

Let the yams cool to room temperature. In a small bowl, mix Parmesan cheese and chives. Prepare medium-hot grill. Cut cooled yams lengthwise into quarters. Rub butter over the whole yam (cut sides and peel); grind some black pepper over the cut sides of the yam. Sprinkle the Parmesan mixture evenly over the cut sides of the yam, pressing to help it adhere. Place yams, skin-side down, on grate over medium- to medium-cool coals, or grill using indirect heat (page 154). Cook until yams are warmed through and cheese has melted slightly, 8 to 12 minutes.

Hush Puppies

About 16 hush puppies; 4 to 6 servings

Traditional with fried fish, these also go well with any stew or barbecued meat.

1 cup cornmeal
½ cup flour
2 teaspoons baking powder
1 teaspoon sugar
¾ teaspoon salt
¾ cup milk
1 egg
½ teaspoon Tabasco sauce or cayenne pepper, optional
¼ cup minced onion (green onion is very good in this recipe)
Oil for deep frying

In mixing bowl, combine cornmeal, flour, baking powder, sugar and salt; stir with a fork to blend. In measuring cup or small bowl, combine milk with egg and Tabasco sauce; beat with a fork. Stir onion into milk mixture. Add milk mixture to dry ingredients, and stir until just combined (do not overmix). The batter can be refrigerated up to an hour before cooking.

Heat oven to 225°F to keep cooked hush puppies warm (if you don't have an oven, set a paper-towel-lined ceramic serving bowl over a pan of boiling water; place the cooked hush puppies into the bowl and cover with a towel between batches). Line a heatproof serving dish with paper towels. Heat recommended amount of oil to 375°F in deep fryer (if you stick a toothpick or wooden chopstick into the oil, small bubbles should immediately rise from the wood); or heat 2 inches oil to 375°F in a deep skillet or Dutch oven. Drop batter by the heaping tablespoonful into the hot oil; you can fry 4 or 5 hush puppies at a time. Cook until deep golden brown and crisp, turning frequently; total cooking time will be about 2 minutes. Transfer cooked hush puppies to paper-towl-lined dish and keep warm in the oven while you fry the remaining batter.

Wild Rice Salad

4 to 6 servings

A friend of mine told me about this easy salad, with its simple dressing. It's just as good as she said it would be, and twice as easy! She actually uses currants instead of apples, but these can be hard to find; however, feel free to substitute 1/2 cup currants for the apple in the recipe, and see what you prefer. I have a feeling that a little curry powder in the orange juice mixture would be good also, but I haven't tried this.

3 cups cooked, cooled wild rice (sometimes available frozen; thaw before using)
1 can (8 ounces) sliced water chestnuts, drained and cut into halves
2 tablespoons grated orange zest (orange part of the peel, with no white)
¼ cup olive oil or vegetable oil
¼ cup orange juice
1 teaspoon celery salt
Half of a small apple
¾ cup frozen green peas, thawed, or cooked fresh peas
Lettuce leaves for serving, optional

Drain wild rice if necessary; there shouldn't be any water in the rice, or the salad will be weak in flavor. In a large bowl, combine wild rice, water chestnuts and orange zest. In glass jar, combine oil, orange juice and celery salt; cover tightly and shake well to blend. Pour over wild rice mixture, and stir gently to combine. Cover and refrigerate 1 to 3 hours. Just before serving, core the apple and cut into chunks that are not quite ½ inch in size. Add apples and peas to rice mixture, stirring gently to combine. Serve on lettuce leaves, if desired.

Desserts and Sweets

OPEN-FACED FRESH FRUIT TART

6 to 8 servings

This is best prepared in a two-piece tart pan, but a regular pie plate will also work.

Half (one ball) of the Easy Low-Fat Pie Crust recipe (page 198)
½ cup ground almonds or other nuts
⅓ cup sugar
5 Granny Smith or other tart apples (do not use Delicious apples)
¼ cup apricot or peach preserves
2 tablespoons rum, brandy, sherry or apple juice

Heat oven to 350°F. Prepare pie crust as directed; fit into tart pan or pie plate. Bake crust 10 minutes. Remove from oven; increase oven temperature to 375°F.

In small bowl, mix together ground almonds and sugar. Sprinkle evenly into pie crust. Peel apples and cut each in half from top to bottom; scoop out seed core with a grapefruit spoon or cut carefully away with a paring knife. Place apples cut-side down on cutting board, and slice 7 halves into ⅛-inch-thick slices, keeping the slices together so the shape of the apple half remains intact. Place the apples, core-side down and in their half-round shape, on top of the ground almonds; typically, you'll be able to fit one in the center and surround it with 6 apple halves. Shred remaining apples coarsely, and pack the shreds in the spaces between the apple halves. In a small saucepan, heat preserves and rum until runny, then brush over the apple halves and shreds. Bake at 375°F until apples are tender and edge of crust is nicely browned, 35 to 45 minutes. (For a prettier appearance, make a second batch of the apricot-rum glaze, and brush over the fruit just after removing from the oven.) Cool slightly or completely before serving.

Variation:

Substitute 5 or 6 pears for the apples; or mix them half-and-half, alternating an apple half with a pear half as you fill the crust.

EASY LOW-FAT PIE CRUST

Makes a double crust

Regular pie crust takes a bit of practice to make; in fact, I never attempt it without my Cuisinart food processor, so it's not in my cabin repertoire. But this low-fat crust (based on a recipe from the Culinary Institute of America) is delicious, and much easier to put together than a standard crust. For best texture, the ricotta, milk and egg white should be very cold.

½ cup part-skim ricotta cheese
¼ to ½ cup sugar (depending on how sweet you want the crust to be)
3 tablespoons milk
1 egg white
2 tablespoons vegetable oil
1½ teaspoons vanilla extract, dry sherry or apple juice
⅛ teaspoon salt
1¾ to 2 cups flour, plus additional for rolling crust
2 teaspoons baking powder

In a chilled mixing bowl, combine all ingredients except flour and baking powder; stir to blend. Add 1¾ cups of the flour and the baking powder, and stir until just combined; if mixture is too wet, add remaining ¼ cup flour. Pat into a firm ball with your hands, then divide into two portions; pat each into a ball with your hands. Sprinkle work surface with a tablespoon or so of additional flour, then roll out 1 ball to form a 10-inch circle; fit into ungreased pie or tart pan. Repeat with remaining ball, or wrap tightly and refrigerate up to 3 days.

For an open-faced pie or tart, pre-bake the crust at 350°F 10 minutes before filling. For a double-crust pie, fill the unbaked bottom crust, then top with the second rolled-out crust; seal as usual.

Frozen Desserts on a Stick

There are many variations to these homemade frozen pops. All you need are small paper bathroom cups and a few basic ingredients that are available from any convenience store, some wooden sticks from the craft store or variety store, and a corner of the freezer. Kids love to help make these treats, and they're a great way to help kids—or adults—get their daily servings of fruit.

Smaller pops freeze more quickly, but you can make these in any size you like. I think the 3- or 5-ounce cups work best, but you can go all the way up to a 7-ounce cup if you like. These keep for a week or more in the freezer—if they last that long!

ICE CREAM PARFAIT POPS

No specific quantity; make as many as you wish

Required: Ice cream or frozen yogurt (2 or 3 flavors make more interesting parfaits)
Optional layers: *Choose **several** that sound good together:*

- **Chocolate, butterscotch or other flavor ice cream topping**
- **Fruit preserves**
- **Reese's Peanut Butter Cups, Almond Joy bars, or other soft-filled candy bars**
- **Chocolate chips**
- **Chopped nuts**
- **Grated sweetened coconut**
- **Frozen strawberries or peaches, thawed and cut into small pieces**
- **Finely crushed cookies, such as vanilla wafers, Oreo cookies or peanut butter cookies**

Here's the basic technique: Pour a little ice cream topping, preserves or runny frozen fruit into the bottom of a small paper cup. Top with a layer of ice cream. Add a contrasting layer of filling, or some cut-up candy or nuts; top with more ice cream. Repeat the layers once more, work the stick into the center, and freeze until solid. If you're using super-premium ice cream, it probably needs to be softened a bit before you can pack it into the cup; softer ice creams are easier to pack, but don't freeze up as well, so you need to experiment to see which suits you. I find it helpful to freeze the cups between packing ice cream layers; otherwise, when I pack a new layer of ice cream into the cup, it ends up squishing into the ingredients below it and the parfait effect is lost. By the way, of all the "stick treats" in this section, this one has the least need for sticks since it's pretty enough to serve in a dish all by itself. So if you can't get the sticks into the frozen layers, or just don't want to fiddle with it, don't worry; just serve them in a dish.

continued

Here are two layering suggestions; feel free to experiment! The ingredients are listed in the order they go into the cup, starting at the bottom.

Peanut Butter Ice Cream Cup

- 2 teaspoons chocolate ice cream topping
- A few sprinkles of chopped peanuts
- A layer of vanilla ice cream
- Half of a Reese's Peanut Butter Cup, cut into small pieces
- A layer of chocolate ice cream
- 2 teaspoons caramel ice cream topping
- A few sprinkles of chopped peanuts
- A layer of vanilla ice cream

Mint Parfait

- 2 teaspoons chocolate cookie wafer crumbs
- A layer of mint ice cream
- A layer of crème de menthe ice cream topping, or mint jelly
- A few mini chocolate chips
- A layer of vanilla ice cream
- 1 tablespoon chopped cookies-and-cream white chocolate bar
- 2 teaspoons chocolate ice cream topping
- A layer of chocolate ice cream

FROZEN PUDDING POPS

6 to 10 pops, depending on size

1 box (4-serving size) instant pudding mix, any flavor
2 cups skim milk
*Choose **one** of the following:*

- **½ cup chopped-up cookies such as oatmeal or peanut butter**
- **½ cup chocolate chips**
- **1 cup fresh raspberries or cut-up strawberries**
- **1 banana, cut into ½-inch pieces**
- **6 to 10 large marshmallows**
- **Use your imagination; almost anything will work!**

Choose a pudding flavor that will go well with the optional ingredient you've selected. Prepare the pudding as directed on the package, using 2 cups of skim milk.

- If you're using chopped-up cookies or chocolate chips, stir them into the pudding mix
- If you're using fresh fruit, sprinkle a bit in the bottom of each cup, then stir the rest into the pudding
- If you're using large marshmallows, push one onto the end of each stick

Divide the pudding, with add-ins as noted above, evenly between the cups. If using the marshmallows, push the stick, marshmallow-end first, into the cup until the marshmallow is covered with pudding; otherwise, just push a plain stick into each cup. Freeze until firm.

CHUNKY FRUIT POPS

5 to 8 pops, depending on size

2 cups plain or vanilla yogurt (nonfat works fine)
1 cup chopped canned or thawed frozen fruit (canned crushed pineapple; frozen strawberries or peaches, thawed and chopped; canned apple slices, chopped; canned blueberries; etc.)
1 can (12 ounces) frozen juice concentrate, any flavor, thawed
1 small can (6 ounces) frozen orange juice, thawed

In mixing bowl, stir together all ingredients. Spoon into paper cups, filling about ⅔ full. Freeze for about an hour, then insert sticks and freeze until solid.

Turnovers on the Grill

4 turnovers

Imagine being in a setting where you don't have an oven—of any sort—and serving up hot, fresh turnovers! These are really great, and are a big hit with kids and adults alike.

Pie crust dough for single-crust pie (purchased or homemade; see Easy Low-Fat Pie Crust on page 198 for an option)
A little flour for rolling crust
1 can (generally 20 ounces) apple, blueberry or other pie filling
4 squares of foil, approximately 12x12 inches each
Nonstick spray, or butter, margarine or shortening

Divide the crust into 4 equal portions. Roll each into a ball, then roll each on a floured surface into a circle or square about 7½ inches across. Spoon about a quarter of the filling (or a little less; don't overfill the turnovers or they will be difficult to seal) into the center of each individual crust, keeping the filling an inch away from all edges. Dab the edges with water, then fold the crust over to form a semicircle or triangle, depending on what shape you've rolled the crust. Pinch the edges very well with your fingers to seal. Dab the edges again with water, and roll the edges in again to form a double seal.

Spray the center of each foil sheet on the shiny side with nonstick spray, or butter lightly. Place 1 folded and crimped turnover in the center of each square. Bring the sides together and roll-fold until fairly snug against the turnover. Roll the ends in, making sure each end has at least 3 rolls.

Prepare medium-hot grill; an indirect fire (page 154) is best, but depending on what else you're cooking, this may not be practical. Place the turnovers over the hot portion of the grill and cook 5 minutes on each side, then move the packets off to the cooler area of the grill (not directly over coals or a lit bank of propane). Cook 15 to 20 minutes longer, turning every 5 minutes; check 1 packet after 15 minutes by partially unrolling and checking for doneness. The pastry should be nicely golden brown with a few deeper brown spots, and the turnover should be quite hot. When the turnovers are done, remove from the grill and open a corner of each packet to allow steam to escape; this prevents the turnovers from getting soggy. Cool slightly or completely before eating.

No-Bake Peanut Butter Graham Bars

24 pieces

Even if your cabin doesn't have an oven (or if you don't want to heat it up), you can make a batch of these rich, delicious bar cookies.

½ pound butter or stick margarine (2 sticks)
1 cup peanut butter, smooth or chunky
2 cups powdered sugar
1¾ cups graham cracker crumbs
1½ cups semisweet chocolate chips (three-quarters of a 12-ounce bag)

In a large saucepan, melt the butter over medium-low heat. Add the peanut butter and stir until blended; remove from heat. Stir in the powdered sugar and graham cracker crumbs, mixing well. Press mixture into 9x13x2-inch pan. Melt chocolate chips by one of the following techniques:

Microwave: Place chips in microwave-safe mixing bowl. Microwave on HIGH for 1 minute; stir. Continue microwaving in 15-second intervals, stirring between each interval, until smooth.

Stovetop: Place chips in heavy-bottomed small pan. Cook over lowest possible heat until the chips just begin to melt. Remove from heat and stir. Return to heat for a few seconds at a time, stirring until smooth.

Spread melted chocolate chips over the peanut-butter mixture in the pan. Cool 10 minutes in the refrigerator, then cut into 2-inch squares without removing from the pan. Return the pan to the refrigerator for 20 minutes longer, then remove the bars from the pan. Keep refrigerated, especially if the weather is warm.

Cobblers, Crisps, Crunches and Bettys: Baked-Fruit Desserts

I noticed something interesting when I started writing out recipes for this book. The first baked-fruit dessert I wrote down was a cherry cobbler, which is basically stewed fruit topped with a biscuit-like mix (for convenience, I use canned refrigerated biscuit dough in this book). Next, I tested a mixed-berry crisp. When I started writing it down, I realized that the basic procedure was almost identical to the cherry cobbler. The main difference was that the fruit for the crisp was topped with an oatmeal mixture instead of biscuits. So, I delved into the old-fashioned cookbooks, and discovered that there is a host of fruit desserts that are basically the same fruit preparation, with variations in the topping.

Here are the differences between these desserts.

- A cobbler has a base of stewed fruit, topped with a biscuit-like mixture
- A crisp has a base of stewed fruit, topped with a flour-butter mixture that usually—but not always—includes oatmeal (the British apparently call this oatmeal-enhanced version a crumble)
- A crunch is like a crisp, but with a layer of the flour-butter mixture under the fruit as well as on top of it
- A Betty sandwiches the fruit between three layers of seasoned breadcrumbs
- A pandowdy features a pie crust topping over the fruit, so it's like a pie without a bottom crust

One of the features of these desserts is that they are flexible and open to adaptation. If you have some blueberries, but not quite enough for one of these desserts, simply add cherries, raspberries or other fruit to make up the difference. You could also use a smaller baking dish and a bit less topping. If pears look good at the market, try them in one of these recipes. You may never have heard of pear cobbler, but I bet you'll love it! If the apples are a bit tart, toss in a bit more sugar, or even some honey. Frozen fruits also work well for these desserts. So even if the nearest orchard is hundreds of miles away—or if it's the middle of winter—you can still bake up a warm, comforting dessert. The point is, these easy recipes allow you to use whatever you have on hand or can readily buy.

continued

The basics

Although you can vary the size of the desserts, or even make individual ones, you need to have a starting point. Here are specifics for these recipes; each will make about 6 servings.

- **Fruit:** If using fresh fruit, use 5 to 6 cups prepared fruit (slightly less for a Betty). If using frozen fruit, use less because the fruit will not cook down and lose as much volume as fresh fruit; 4 or 5 cups is about right, but you can vary the amount depending on how the fruit is packaged. Also, feel free to add dried fruit if it seems appropriate. Raisins are great in apple desserts, for example. If you're using peaches or other dried fruits that are large, cut them into smaller pieces and steep in boiling water for 10 minutes before mixing with the other fruit.
- **Sugar:** Frozen fruit is sometimes packed in a light syrup glaze, and doesn't need any sweetening; other frozen fruit could benefit from a bit of added sugar. Fresh fruit usually is best with a little added sugar. Rhubarb, tart apples and cherries need more sugar than sweeter fruits such as peaches or pears. The best advice is to taste the fruit, and add sugar as needed. As a rule of thumb, add up to 1 cup sugar for rhubarb or tart apples, ¾ cup for cherries, ½ cup for berries or pears and ⅓ cup for peaches or nectarines. You may use brown sugar, white sugar, or a combination.
- **Thickeners:** If the fruit is juicy (blueberries, raspberries, peaches, etc.), add up to 2 tablespoons cornstarch or flour; medium-juicy fruit, such as pears or rhubarb, needs less thickener—try 2 teaspoons. Apples may not need any thickener at all unless they're very juicy. In all cases, if you're using frozen fruit and it has let off a lot of juice as it thawed, increase the thickener slightly.
- **Juice:** Apples can be tossed with a tablespoon or two of lemon or orange juice if they are particularly dry, although this is not essential. Berries, peaches and other stone fruits don't need any juice unless they're of poor quality, in which case you shouldn't be making a baked dessert out of them!
- **Spices:** Feel free to add a sprinkle of cinnamon, nutmeg, cardamom or whatever else you think would complement the fruit, but don't overdo it; you want to taste the fruit, not the spice. A splash of vanilla or other extract is often good, too, although not traditional.
- **Baking dish:** The standard dish used in these recipes is an 8-inch-square baking dish that is about 2 inches deep; a 9-inch-round dish holds the same amount and needs the same amount of baking time. If you're using a glass dish rather than a metal one, lower the oven temperature by 25 degrees. For all recipes, spray the dish with nonstick spray, or butter lightly.

The recipes all start with the same procedure for the fruit. Wash fresh fruit, and peel if appropriate; apples, pears and peaches are generally peeled, but if you want to leave the peels on for fiber, who's to say that's wrong? Remove any pits, stones, leaves, cores or seeds in the way that's normal for that fruit. The fruit should be in bite-sized pieces, ¾ inch or less; blueberries and raspberries are fine with no further preparation, while cherries are generally cut into halves after pitting. Larger fruit such as apples, peaches or pears should be cut into wedges, then into chunks. Frozen fruit needs to be thawed (save the juices and add them to the dish with the fruit), and cut into smaller pieces if necessary.

For cobbler, crisps and pandowdies, I prefer to combine the fruit mixture right in the baking dish to avoid dirtying a mixing bowl. Spray the dish first with nonstick spray (or grease lightly with butter or margarine), then add the fruit, sugar, thickener, spices and any juice to the dish. Stir gently to combine, then add the topping. Fruit for crunches and Bettys must be mixed in a separate mixing bowl, since part of the crust mixture goes on the bottom of the baking dish.

All of these desserts are best when baked an hour or so before serving, so they are still warm. Ice cream or whipped cream are heavenly on these desserts. Leftovers should be refrigerated, and can be eaten cold, or re-warmed slightly in the oven or microwave. Most are great for a quick breakfast the next morning.

COBBLER WITH BISCUIT TOPPING

Prepared fruit as instructed on page 206
1 small tube (10.8 ounces/5 biscuits) large refrigerated flaky biscuits, such as Pillsbury Grands!
¼ cup butter or stick margarine (half of a stick), melted
Sugar for dusting biscuits (about ½ cup)

Heat oven to 400°F. Mix fruit as directed, and place in prepared baking dish. Cut each biscuit into quarters. Use a fork to dip each piece into the melted butter, then roll lightly in sugar and place on top of the fruit. Bake 25 minutes, or until biscuits are golden and fruit is bubbling around edges.

FRUIT CRISP

Prepared fruit as instructed on page 206
½ cup butter or stick margarine (1 stick), cut into ½-inch pieces
⅔ cup packed brown sugar
½ cup flour
¼ teaspoon salt
¼ teaspoon nutmeg, optional
½ cup rolled oats

Heat oven to 400°F. Mix fruit as directed, and place in prepared baking dish. In large mixing bowl, combine the butter, brown sugar, flour, salt and nutmeg. Toss together with your hands,* rubbing the butter to break it into smaller pieces and coat them with the flour and sugar. When the mixture is the size of peas, add the rolled oats and mix gently. Sprinkle the rolled-oats mixture evenly over the fruit. Bake 35 to 45 minutes, or until the topping is golden brown and the fruit is bubbling.

*If you have a food processor, combine all ingredients in work bowl and pulse on-and-off until mixture is combined but still coarse in texture.

ZUCCHINI OR GREEN TOMATO CRISP

Follow Fruit Crisp recipe above, substituting peeled, sliced zucchini or diced green tomatoes for the fruit (remove the seeds if the zucchini is large). Use 2 teaspoons cornstarch, ¾ cup sugar, and ½ teaspoon cinnamon; also add 2 tablespoons lemon juice to the zucchini or tomatoes before adding the topping. Proceed as directed.

Fruit crunch

The fruit used for a crunch should not be very juicy, so be sure to add thickener, or drain off excess juice from frozen fruit.

Prepared fruit as instructed on page 206
½ cup butter or stick margarine (1 stick), cut into ½-inch pieces
1 cup packed brown sugar
¾ cup flour
¼ teaspoon salt
¾ cup rolled oats

Heat oven to 350°F. In mixing bowl, mix fruit as directed; set aside. In another mixing bowl, combine the butter, brown sugar, flour and salt. Toss together with your hands,* rubbing the butter to break it into smaller pieces and coat them with the flour and sugar. When the mixture is the size of peas, add the rolled oats and mix gently. Press half the rolled-oats mixture gently into prepared baking dish; top with fruit, smoothing evenly with a spoon. Sprinkle remaining oatmeal mixture evenly over the fruit. Bake 50 to 60 minutes, or until the topping is firm and golden brown.

*If you have a food processor, combine all ingredients in work bowl and pulse on-and-off until mixture is combined but still coarse in texture.

FRUIT BETTY
(TRADITIONALLY PREPARED WITH APPLES)

Use a slightly smaller amount of fruit for this recipe; include some raisins if you like.

Prepared fruit as instructed on page 206
4 cups cubed bread or biscuits (cut into ½-inch cubes before measuring)
¾ cup sugar
¾ teaspoon cinnamon
¼ teaspoon nutmeg
½ cup butter or stick margarine (1 stick), melted

Heat oven to 300°F. In mixing bowl, mix fruit as directed; set aside. Spread bread cubes on a baking sheet and cook, stirring occasionally, until crisp and lightly browned on the outside, about 15 minutes. Remove from oven and set aside to cool. Increase oven temperature to 375°F. When bread cubes have cooled, add them to a large mixing bowl with the sugar, cinnamon, nutmeg and about half the melted butter; toss gently but thoroughly. Place one-third of the bread in the prepared baking dish; top with half of the fruit mixture. Top fruit with half the remaining bread, pressing gently into the fruit; top with remaining fruit. Sprinkle remaining bread over the top, pressing gently into the fruit. Drizzle remaining melted butter over the top. Bake 30 to 40 minutes, or until the topping is nicely browned and the fruit is bubbling.

FRUIT PANDOWDY (TRADITIONALLY PREPARED WITH APPLES)

For a colonial touch, substitute ½ cup maple syrup for the brown sugar when using apples or pears.

Prepared fruit as instructed on page 206
2 tablespoons butter or stick margarine, cut into very small pieces
Prepared, rolled-out crust for single-crust pie
1 tablespoon cream or milk
2 teaspoons sugar

Heat oven to 400°F. Mix fruit as directed, and place in prepared baking dish. Distribute butter pieces evenly over the fruit. Gently place crust on top of the fruit, tucking the edges of the crust inside the dish. Brush the top of the crust with cream, and sprinkle with sugar. Bake 30 minutes, or until the crust is lightly browned. Remove from the oven; reduce oven to 375°F. Use a spatula to cut the crust into 2-inch squares, pressing the crust edges gently into the fruit as you cut it. Return the dish to the oven and bake 15 to 25 minutes longer, until the crust is nicely browned and the fruit is bubbling.

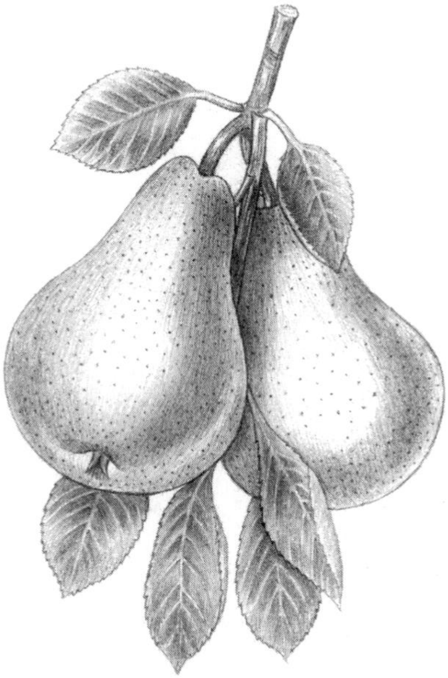

HOMEMADE ICE CREAM SANDWICHES

About 7 sandwiches

Great fun for kids to make, and you can use any flavor of ice cream you like for the filling. If you buy ice cream in a different shape than the one listed, simply figure out what size to cut the cookies, allowing for a bit of expansion during baking; you could even make big round cookies if you buy a round pint of ice cream.

1 egg
½ cup shortening
¼ cup butter (half of a stick), softened
1 teaspoon vanilla extract
1 box (18.25 ounces) devil's food cake mix, divided
About ¼ cup flour
A half-gallon rectangular carton (about 5x3½x6¾ inches) ice cream, any flavor
Tiny chocolate chips, nuts, shaved chocolate, or other edible decorations, optional

Heat oven to 375°F. In mixing bowl, beat together egg, shortening, butter and vanilla until smooth and creamy. Add half of the box of cake mix and beat until smooth. Add remaining cake mix, and stir with a large spoon until completely mixed (the mixture will be too stiff to use a mixer at this point). Dust work surface liberally with flour, and roll out the dough to ¼ inch thickness. Cut into 4½x3-inch rectangles, re-rolling scraps once to cut more cookies; transfer to an ungreased baking sheet, leaving an inch between cookies. (The dough is not very firm, so the cookies will be hard to put on the baking sheet without ruining them. Here's what I do: I lift each rectangle carefully with a spatula and flip it onto my hand, then flip my hand over to drop the cookie on the baking sheet.) Bake until the centers spring back when touched lightly, 10 to 12 minutes. Remove from oven and prick holes all over the cookies with a fork. Cool on baking sheets 10 minutes, then transfer to racks to cool completely.

When ready to assemble the sandwiches, peel away the front half of the ice cream carton, and cut the ice cream into front and back halves; each piece should be about 5x3½x6¾ inches. Re-wrap the back half of the carton and re-freeze for another use. Quickly slice the ice cream block into slices that are ½ to ¾ inch thick. Place an ice cream slice on one of the cookies; top with a second cookie and press lightly together. Tip: The sides that were up on the baking sheet are prettier than the sides that were down, and look better on the outside of the sandwich.) If you want a decorated cookie, quickly roll the edge of the assembled sandwich in the tiny chocolate chips or whatever you're using, pressing firmly to embed the chips in the edge of the ice cream. Wrap tightly in plastic wrap and freeze until ready to eat.

Beverages and Miscellaneous

CREAMY TROPICAL FREEZE

3 or 4 servings

This is an easy recipe to modify. Simply substitute other sherbet flavors and different frozen juice concentrates. You can make a pretty good imitation of the orange freeze served at a national chain by using orange sherbet and orange juice concentrate, for example.

1 pint tropical-flavor sherbet (mango, pineapple, coconut, lemon, etc.)
1 small can (6 ounces) frozen pineapple juice concentrate, or other flavor as you like
1 cup milk (reduced-fat works fine), or a little more if you prefer a thinner freeze
Optional fruit garnish: maraschino cherries, pineapple chunks

In blender, combine sherbet, juice concentrate and milk. Blend until just smooth, stirring down a few times if necessary. Pour into chilled serving glasses. Garnish each with fruit; for a festive touch, spear the fruit on a long, frilly toothpick.

SUN TEA

Servings depend on jar size

Take advantage of free solar energy on a hot day to make a jar of sun tea. I like to use a mix of tea flavors; one of my favorites is 4 bags of Irish breakfast tea and 2 bags of orange spice tea. Experiment!

Tea bags: 3 or 4 for a 1-quart jar, 6 to 8 for a ½-gallon jar
Optional garnishes: lemon slices, fresh mint leaves
Sugar or honey to sweeten the tea, optional

Fill 1-quart or ½-gallon jar with cold water. Place the tea bags in the jar, dunking each a few times to get it thoroughly wet; let the tags hang out over the rim. Seal the jar, catching the strings on the tags to prevent them from falling into the jar. Place the jar in full sun for 2 to 3 hours, or until the tea is the strength you like. Remove and discard bags, then chill tea before serving in glasses full of ice. Garnish with lemon or mint, and add sugar to taste.

MINT-LIMEADE GIN FIZZ

Enough syrup for about 12 cocktails

I can't remember where I first heard about this refreshing summertime drink, but it is a real winner. Make a big pitcher of the mix for a summer patio party.

1 can (12 ounces) frozen limeade concentrate, thawed
¾ to 1 cup fresh whole mint leaves, washed and dried
Gin or vodka
Club soda or sparkling water

In blender, combine limeade concentrate and mint leaves (the more mint leaves, the more pronounced the mint taste; try your first batch with ¾ cup leaves, and increase for the next batch if you like). Process on LIQUEFY until smooth. Keep refrigerated until needed.

For each individual cocktail, add 2 tablespoons of the limeade syrup and a jigger of gin to a tall glass; stir well to mix. Fill the glass with ice cubes, then add club soda to the top of the glass. Stir and serve.

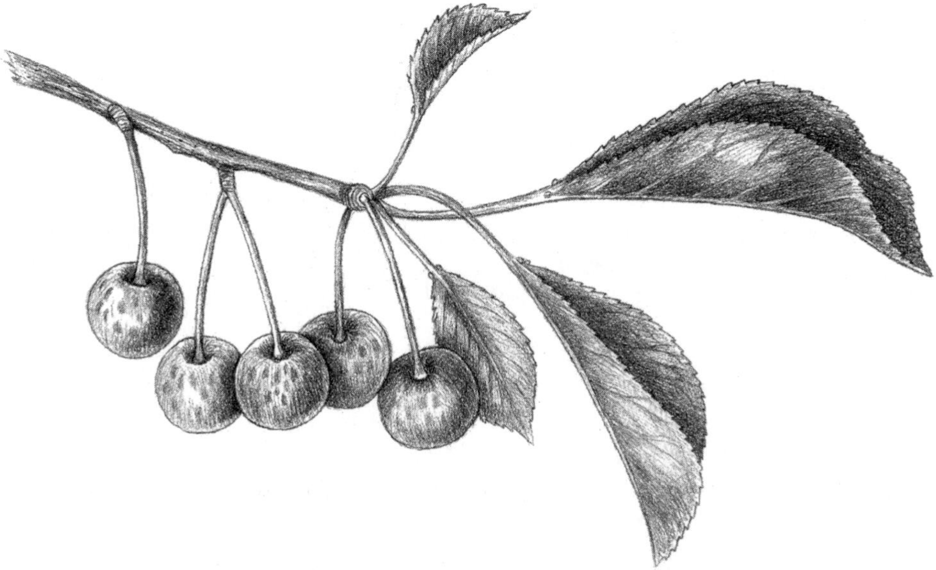

Planning for Leftovers

When you pack the cooler for the trip home, the last thing you want to deal with is an odd assortment of leftovers. On the other hand, it doesn't seem right to throw them away. To avoid this dilemma, why not plan ahead and turn ho-hum leftovers into delicious meals? This is an especially useful trick for couples or small families. For example, leftover sliced meatloaf makes wonderful cold sandwiches for another day, especially when slathered with mayonnaise and mustard and topped with lettuce and some thinly sliced red onion. Here are some other quick ideas to help you get the most out of your meals.

- **Fajitas:** For easy fajitas, fry up some sliced onions and peppers until tender-crisp, then toss in thinly sliced leftover grilled steak or chicken breast. Serve with warmed flour tortillas, shredded cheese and salsa, and optional guacamole or sour cream.
- **Potato Pancakes:** Make from leftover mashed potatoes: beat an egg with a little grated raw onion and some seasonings, then mix in about 1 cup of mashed potatoes. Spoon onto a hot, greased griddle or skillet and flatten slightly; cook until browned on one side, then carefully turn with a spatula and cook the second side until browned. These are great with applesauce and/or sour cream.
- **Fried Rice:** Make easy fried rice from leftover cooked rice. Scramble an egg, stirring constantly so the curds are small; transfer to a small bowl and set aside. Add diced fresh, cooked or frozen vegetables to the same skillet (frozen peas and sliced green onion are particularly good) and fry for a few minutes. If you have some leftover meat, slice that thinly and fry it with the vegetables. Add a little more oil, then stir in cold, cooked rice; stir constantly until heated through. Toss in some soy sauce and the scrambled egg at the last minute.
- **Squash Soup:** Mash cooked winter squash (such as acorn, butternut, Hubbard, or pumpkin) with a little chicken broth. Add additional broth or milk to desired soup consistency; season with a dash of curry powder blend or other hearty spice, then heat just to boiling for a delicious cream soup.
- **Chef's Salad:** Assemble a big chef's salad from leftover sliced meats and any handy vegetables (broccoli, carrots and cauliflower work well either raw or cooked). Slice up some cheese and cut into strips to arrange on top, or sprinkle with crumbled blue or feta cheese. Complete the arrangement with anything else in the refrigerator that looks good: olives, salad peppers such as pepperoncini, sliced hard-cooked egg, etc. Serve with your favorite dressing on the side. Hot breadsticks are great with this meal.
- Cut up cooked ham, and sprinkle between the layers as you're assembling au gratin or scalloped potatoes. A green salad or vegetable is enough to complete this meal.
- See pages 102-103, "Fun with Flatbreads," for pizza ideas using leftovers.

Here is a delicious sandwich based on leftover pork roast (you'll need to have some rolls, cheese and an onion on hand also). You could substitute a beef roast, or even cooked chicken. Thinly sliced pork or beef roast from the deli would also work well if you don't have leftovers.

OPEN-FACED PORK SANDWICHES

4 servings as written; feel free to adjust quantities as needed

1 small onion, cut into quarters and sliced moderately thinly
1 tablespoon butter or margarine
A sprinkle of sugar
3 cups cubed cooked pork (remove fat, bones and gristle, then cut into cubes ½ inch or smaller)
¼ cup chicken broth, beer, leftover white wine or water
¼ teaspoon of any or all of the following: paprika, garlic powder, caraway seed
4 crusty French or Italian rolls, 5 or 6 inches long; or equivalent in pieces from a French loaf
Sliced Havarti-dill or other creamy, mellow cheese, to taste (the more, the better!)

In medium skillet, slowly cook onion in butter over low heat, stirring frequently, until onion is very soft and a rich golden color. Allow about 20 minutes for this step; the onion should not brown before it is soft. Near the end of the cooking time, sprinkle onion with sugar. When the onion mixture is ready, add the pork cubes, broth and seasonings. Continue cooking over low heat about 15 minutes, or until most of the liquid cooks away; don't raise the heat above low or the meat will become tough.

To assemble, split the rolls and pull out some of the soft center to make room for the pork. Arrange the opened rolls on a baking sheet and divide the pork evenly among the rolls. Top with cheese. Broil or bake until the cheese is bubbly. These are easiest to eat with a knife and fork, rather than with the hands.

CITRUS SALSA

About 1½ cups

Vary the amount of jalapeño to suit your tolerance for heat.

1 medium orange, peeled, seeded and cut into ½-inch pieces
3 green onions, sliced ¼ inch thick
¼ cup diced red bell pepper
2 tablespoons coarsely chopped fresh cilantro leaves
1 tablespoon minced fresh jalapeño pepper (remove and discard seeds before mincing)
1 tablespoon olive oil or vegetable oil
½ teaspoon salt
¼ teaspoon minced garlic

Combine all ingredients in nonaluminum bowl; stir well. Cover and refrigerate at least 1 hour to allow flavors to blend. This keeps well for several days in the refrigerator.

Variation:

Substitute half of a red grapefruit, cut up as directed, for the orange. Add ¼ teaspoon honey. Proceed as directed.

AVOCADO-PINEAPPLE SALSA

About 2 cups

Fabulous with warmed tortilla chips, or as a topper for grilled burritos.

1 medium pebbly-skinned ripe avocado, peeled and cut into ¼-inch pieces
¾ cup diced fresh pineapple
¼ cup diced red onion
3 tablespoons coarsely chopped fresh cilantro leaves
1 fresh hot red pepper, chopped (remove and discard seeds before chopping)
2 tablespoons lime juice or orange juice
1 tablespoon olive oil or vegetable oil
½ teaspoon salt

Combine all ingredients in nonaluminum bowl; stir well. Cover and refrigerate 1 to 3 hours to allow flavors to blend. Best served the day it is made, as the avocado will turn brown if kept longer.

Fall

Table of Contents

Beverages and Miscellaneous

Autumn Pursuit

For a surprising number of people, the reason to own a cabin in the first place is to have a base for annual deer hunting trips; all other cabin use is incidental.

Larger hunting parties, or those in remote areas, may choose to take a small deer at the beginning of the trip in order to have meat during the rest of the hunt. For most hunters, however, the venison they hope to acquire is not included in menu planning for the hunting trip itself, because the deer is taken to a butcher for processing after the hunt is over. But even if this is the case with your hunting party, you should still plan on a meal of fresh venison tenderloins at hunting camp.

Many hunters also enjoy walking the woods for squirrel, rabbit and grouse (or partridge, as this bird is called in the East) during their deer-hunting trips. After bagging a deer on opening morning, I've often enjoyed walking the woods in subsequent afternoons with my shotgun, trying to flush out a few ruffies for dinner. And of course, sometimes birds or small game are the primary quarry being sought from the hunting shack.

In contrast to some modern lakeshore cabins equipped with blenders, microwaves and a full range of kitchen gadgets, deer-hunting cabins often have minimal cooking facilities. One of my favorite places I've stayed during a deer hunt was a primitive log cabin in the middle of the woods. There was no running water, no electricity and no heat other than a fireplace; all cooking was done on a wood-burning stove or outside, on a grill. Other times, a motel—with a hot plate, refrigerator and sink but no stove—has been home base, and cooking is limited to fast-and-easy skillet dishes or crock pot food. This works very well indeed for hunting camp. Plug the crock pot in when you head to the woods in the morning, and when you come back in at the end of the day, dinner is ready, and it always smells great!

On the following pages are a few recipes that are specifically geared for hunting camp. You'll find many other suitable recipes throughout this book, as well. Simply look for those that work with the kitchen facilities you have.

Venison Tenderloins

The tenderloins are two small boneless pieces of meat you'll find inside the cavity of a dressed deer (or elk, moose, antelope, etc.). They're the most tender pieces of meat on the animal, and are a traditional opening-day feast. If the deer was taken in the morning, you can enjoy the tenderloins for dinner that evening; if it was taken later in the day, let it hang overnight before removing the tenderloins. Tenderloins from a freshly dressed animal are apt to be tough because the meat fibers haven't had the necessary time to relax.

Always wipe the tenderloins off immediately after field dressing. I carry a small sponge and a few paper towels in my dressing kit, and when I've finished the rest of the dressing chores, I moisten the sponge with water from my canteen and wipe out the entire body cavity, paying special attention to those precious tenderloins. This step ensures better-tasting meat, and is especially important if the intestines or other internal organs have been accidentally punctured. After wiping the cavity down well, I use the paper towels to remove excess moisture. I want the cavity to be clean but fairly dry, so it will have a smooth, firm finish after hanging. If the cavity is sopping wet, mold and unwanted bacteria can grow while the deer is hanging.

To remove the tenderloins from a hanging deer, have someone hold the rear legs apart so you have room to work. Look inside the deer's body, down toward the lower back, and you'll see two elongated bulges of meat on either side of the backbone. These are the tenderloins, and are the same cut that compose the "tender" part of a porterhouse steak (in the beef world, they are also called "fillet mignon"). They're easy to remove; simply slip the tip of a sharp hunting knife, or a stiff boning knife, underneath the tip of the meat and cut it away from the cavity, keeping your knife angled toward the outside of the deer, scraping as close to the bone as possible. You should end up with two long, thin pieces of meat that come to a point on each end. On a good-sized white-tailed deer, these weigh about 8 ounces apiece. On moose or elk, tenderloins can add up to several pounds of toothsome meat.

A good way to handle the tenderloins is to butterfly them into medallions. This makes it possible for everyone to have a taste. Butterflying also works well for the loin (often called the backstrap), making it easy to cut a nicely sized steak from even a smaller-diameter loin. Trim the meat of any tendons, fat or shot-damaged areas before butterflying. If the deer has been hanging for several days when you remove the tenderloins, you may also have to trim away some of the outer surface of the meat, which has probably become dried and hardened.

To butterfly a tenderloin, loin or other boneless cut, lay it on a cutting board and slice off a piece that is twice as thick as you want the final piece to be. (In other words, if you want an inch-thick steak, cut off a piece that is 2 inches wide.) Now slice the meat into two "wings" of equal thickness, taking care not to slice all the way through. Open the meat up like a book, and whack it lightly with the flat side of your knife to give it a better shape.

You can also cook the tenderloin whole; grilling, broiling or pan-frying are the methods of choice. However you choose to prepare it, take care not to overcook it. Like all prime venison, tenderloin is best when served somewhere between medium-rare to medium doneness. If cooked to well done, prime venison will likely become tough.

BACON-SMOKED GRILLED TENDERLOIN

Servings depend on size of tenderloin

1 pair of venison tenderloins, trimmed as described previously
Seasoned salt
1 or 2 strips bacon per tenderloin, depending on size

Prepare medium-hot grill. Tuck the thin ends of the tenderloin under so the meat is of fairly even thickness. Sprinkle generously with seasoned salt. Wrap a piece (or two, if necessary) of bacon around the meat in a spiral, securing it on both ends with a wooden toothpick. Grill the meat, turning frequently, until the bacon is crisp and the tenderloin is desired doneness. Slice into chunks and serve with toothpicks as an appetizer; or, cut into serving-sized portions and serve as a main dish.

MARINATED VENISON TENDERLOIN

Servings depend on size of tenderloin

1 pair of venison tenderloins, trimmed as described previously
¼ to ⅓ cup Italian dressing, bottled or homemade (see recipe on page 99)

Place the tenderloins in a dish, bowl or plastic zip-top bag. Add dressing and turn the meat to coat. Let marinate 30 minutes at room temperature, or up to 2 hours refrigerated. When ready to cook, drain the meat, sprinkle lightly with salt and pepper, then cook on hot grill, or under the broiler, until the meat is desired doneness. Slice into chunks and serve with toothpicks as an appetizer; or, cut into serving-sized portions and serve as a main dish.

CAJUN BUTTERFLIES

Servings depend on size of tenderloin

These make a tasty appetizer. The cooking method produces a lot of smoke, so it's best to cook this outdoors over a very hot grill or campfire. You must have a cast-iron skillet to prepare this; a regular skillet can't handle the high heat required for this dish.

1 pair of venison tenderloins, trimmed as described previously
1 cup milk (canned milk works fine)
2 to 4 tablespoons butter
1 to 3 tablespoons Cajun spice blend, such as Paul Prudhomme's Steak Magic, or the homemade blend on page 300

Butterfly the tenderloins as described on page 224, ending up with pieces that are ½ inch thick (so your initial cut needs to be 1 inch thick). Place in a bowl with the milk; cover and let marinate 45 minutes at room temperature, or up to 2 hours refrigerated. Drain and discard milk; pat venison dry with paper towels.

Place a clean, dry cast-iron skillet over a very hot fire or grill, and let it heat until it is extremely hot; this could take 15 minutes or longer. While the skillet is heating, melt the butter and place 2 tablespoons of it in a small bowl. Put a tablespoon of the seasoning blend in another small bowl. When the skillet is as hot as it will get, dip each piece of butterflied meat into the melted butter to coat, then dip both sides into the seasoning blend, making sure to keep the meat "open" in the butterfly shape. Add the meat to the hot skillet and cook until deeply browned on both sides. The key to this dish is to have the skillet so hot that it sears and colors the meat almost immediately; if it takes more than a minute or two to cook each side, the meat will be overdone.

Other Hunting-Camp or Game Recipes

OVEN-BARBECUED SQUIRREL

2 or 3 servings

Bourbon Barbecue Sauce:
1 cup chopped onion
1 tablespoon butter
½ cup cider vinegar
½ cup ketchup
3 tablespoons packed brown sugar, or molasses or honey
3 tablespoons bourbon, apple juice or orange juice
1 teaspoon dry mustard powder, or 2 teaspoons prepared mustard
¼ teaspoon Tabasco sauce

2 squirrels, whole or cut up

Heat oven to 300°F. In nonaluminum Dutch oven, cook onion in butter over medium heat until just tender, stirring occasionally. Add remaining sauce ingredients. Heat just to boiling, then reduce heat and simmer about 5 minutes, stirring occasionally. Add squirrels to the Dutch oven, turning to coat with sauce. Cover Dutch oven tightly and place in oven. Bake, turning squirrels occasionally, until the meat is extremely tender, about 2 hours. (Older squirrels may take even longer. If the meat is still not tender after 2 hours, add about ¼ cup additional water and continue cooking another 30 minutes, or until tender. If one squirrel is tender before the other, remove the tender one and continue cooking the other one until tender.) Remove squirrels from sauce and set aside until they are cool enough to handle. Pull the meat from the bones and shred coarsely with your fingers; discard bones. Return meat to sauce and re-heat on the stovetop for a few minutes. Serve over hot cooked rice or noodles. Leftovers make a great barbecue sandwich.

Make-ahead note: You may prepare the barbecue sauce up to a few days in advance; keep refrigerated until needed. If you want to prepare the entire dish in advance, follow instructions above for cooking; then, after you've shredded the meat and returned it to the sauce, cover the dish and refrigerate it for as long as 2 days. Re-heat gently over medium-low heat before serving (don't re-heat over high heat or the meat will become tough).

TEXAS VENISON STEW

4 to 6 servings

Hot cornbread and coleslaw are great with this easy stew. Non-hunters note: Boneless beef round or rump works just as well as venison.

1½ pounds boneless venison round steak or roast
2 tablespoons bacon drippings or vegetable oil
2 cans (14½ ounces each) diced tomatoes with garlic and onion, or 2 cans plain diced tomatoes plus ½ cup salsa
1 envelope (1½ ounces) dry onion soup mix (Lipton's is good)
1 cup flat beer (dark beer adds a nice flavor)
1½ cups peeled mini carrots, or 4 regular carrots peeled and cut into 2-inch chunks
1 can (4 ounces) diced green chiles, drained
1 can (14½ ounces) hominy, drained*
1 lime, cut into wedges

Trim and discard any fat, silverskin or gristle from venison; cut meat into 1-inch cubes and sprinkle liberally with salt. Heat bacon drippings in Dutch oven over medium-high heat until very hot. Add venison cubes and brown well on all sides. Add tomatoes with their juices, onion soup mix and beer to the Dutch oven. Heat just to boiling, then reduce heat and simmer, stirring occasionally, about 45 minutes. Add carrots, chiles and hominy; cook 1 to 1¼ hours longer, or until venison and carrots are tender (if the gravy gets too thick before the venison is tender, stir in a little water or more beer). Serve with lime wedges; diners can squeeze as much lime as they like onto their stew.

*If you can't get hominy (or if you don't like it), feel free to substitute 2 Idaho potatoes, peeled and cut into ¾-inch cubes.

VENISON STEAKS WITH MUSHROOM PAN SAUCE

4 servings

The loin (also called the backstrap) is a very tender piece of meat that corresponds to the loin or rib-eye area of beef. Feel free to substitute beef loin or tenderloin steak for the venison in this recipe.

4 inch-thick boneless venison loin steaks, butterflied if necessary
3 tablespoons butter, divided
1 tablespoon olive oil
8 ounces coarsely chopped fresh mushrooms
1 clove garlic, pressed or minced
2 tablespoons brandy or cognac, optional
½ cup dry red wine or good-quality unsalted venison or beef stock

Season steaks on both sides with salt and freshly ground black pepper. Melt 2 tablespoons butter in the oil in a large heavy-bottomed skillet (do not use aluminum or nonstick) over medium-high heat. As soon as the butter stops foaming, add steaks and cook until well browned on one side. Turn and cook until not quite desired doneness, preferably rare to medium-rare. Transfer steaks to a plate and keep warm.

Pour off all but a small amount of fat. Add the mushrooms and cook until nicely browned, stirring frequently. Add garlic and cook about 30 seconds, stirring constantly. Add brandy if using and cook, stirring frequently, until brandy has cooked almost completely away. Add wine, stirring well to loosen any browned bits. Cook over high heat, stirring frequently, until reduced to a saucelike consistency. Remove the pan from the heat and add the remaining tablespoon of butter, swirling the pan and stirring until the butter melts. To serve, spoon sauce and mushrooms over steaks.

GRILLED VENISON LOIN WITH BROWN SUGAR BASTE

2 or 3 servings per pound of meat

Any boneless, tender venison cut works well for this easy recipe.

Boneless venison loin portion, or other prime boneless cut
3 tablespoons butter
3 tablespoons soy sauce
3 tablespoons packed brown sugar

Remove all fat and silverskin from meat. In microwave-safe measuring cup, combine butter, soy sauce, and brown sugar. Microwave at MEDIUM/50% power, stirring occasionally, until butter is melted and brown sugar is dissolved (you may also do this in a small pan on the stovetop, but be careful that the brown sugar doesn't burn). Brush sauce over the meat. Grill to medium doneness, turning and brushing with sauce frequently. One pound will serve 2 or 3 people. If you are preparing more than a pound, increase basting ingredients proportionally.

DUCK BREAST WITH CHERRY SAUCE

4 servings

This recipe works equally well with duck or goose breasts, or venison loin steaks.

2 boneless, skinless duck breasts (4 halves), 1 goose breast or 4 venison loin steaks
1 can (15½ ounces) pitted dark cherries, drained and juice reserved
½ cup port
½ teaspoon crumbled dried thyme leaves
1 tablespoon butter or margarine
1 tablespoon olive oil
1 cup chicken or beef broth
2 teaspoons cornstarch

Pat duck breasts dry and season with salt and pepper; set aside. Combine drained cherries, port and thyme in a small bowl; set aside to marinate for 15 minutes or so.

When ready to cook, melt butter in oil in large skillet over medium heat. When butter stops foaming, add duck breasts and cook until nicely browned on both sides and desired doneness; medium to medium-rare is best. Transfer meat to a plate and keep warm. Add the broth to the skillet, stirring to loosen any browned bits. Cook over medium-high heat, stirring frequently, until liquid is reduced to about half. Drain port into skillet; add reserved cherry juice and heat to boiling. Stir in cherries. While cherries are heating, blend cornstarch with 2 tablespoons water, then add to the skillet in a small stream, stirring continuously. Cook, stirring constantly, until sauce is thickened and glossy. Slice duck breast thinly on the diagonal and serve with cherry sauce.

PHEASANT WITH APPLES, MUSTARD AND CREAM

2 or 3 servings

Serve with rice or noodles, and a brightly colored vegetable.

1 boned pheasant or equivalent
½ cup flour seasoned with salt and white pepper
2 tablespoons butter
½ cup chopped onion
1 cup chardonnay, Piesporter or other medium-dry fruity white wine
2 teaspoons Dijon mustard
¾ cup cream or 1 can (12 ounces) evaporated milk
1 Granny Smith or other firm, tart apple, cored and sliced

Dredge pheasant in seasoned flour; reserve flour. In medium skillet, melt butter over medium-high heat. Add pheasant; brown on both sides. Transfer pheasant to a plate; cover to keep warm and set aside. Add chopped onion to skillet. Cook over medium heat, stirring frequently, until tender, about 5 minutes. In the meantime, blend a generous tablespoon of the reserved flour into the wine. When the onions are tender, add the wine mixture, mustard and the cream to the skillet; stir to blend. Arrange pheasant on top of onion/cream mixture; top with apple slices. Simmer (do not boil), uncovered, until pheasant is just cooked; this will probably take 10 to 15 minutes. Stir occasionally during cooking if it seems to be sticking.

Breakfast and Brunch Dishes

APPLE-CHEDDAR BRUNCH PIZZA

6 to 8 servings

Cheddar and apples are a traditional New England combination, and they work very well together in this easy dish. Remember to take the frozen bread dough out of the freezer and place it in the refrigerator the night before, so it's ready to go when you are.

About ¼ cup flour, divided
1 loaf (1 pound) frozen yeast bread dough, thawed; or equivalent in homemade dough
5 cups sliced apples (use Granny Smith or other tart apples)
½ cup packed brown sugar
½ cup white sugar
2 teaspoons cinnamon or apple pie spice
¼ teaspoon nutmeg (omit if using apple pie spice)
5 tablespoons butter or stick margarine, cut into small pieces
8 ounces shredded cheddar cheese (about 2 cups)

Heat oven to 350°F. Spray a rimmed cookie sheet (15¼ x 10½ inches) with nonstick spray, or butter lightly. Sprinkle your work surface with a little flour and roll out the bread dough slightly larger than the sheet. Place the dough on the prepared sheet, stretching to fit; roll edges slightly to form a shallow rim. Spread apples evenly over the dough. In a mixing bowl, combine brown and white sugars, 2 tablespoons flour, cinnamon and nutmeg; mix well and sprinkle over the apples. Dot with the butter. Sprinkle cheese evenly over all. Bake until the apples are tender and the cheese is bubbly, 25 to 35 minutes. Serve warm.

Waffle Bar

Years ago, I worked with a fellow who used to accompany six or eight friends to deer-hunting camp each year. Bill wasn't a hunter, but he liked to go along on the trips anyway and so got elected to the position of camp cook (on a wood-burning stove, yet!). I used to try to help him in his efforts to come up with meals that would be easy to fix for a crowd, yet impressive and tasty. One year, I suggested a Waffle Bar, and the guys liked it so well that it became an instant tradition.

Organization is the key to a successful Waffle Bar. Everything needs to be set out and ready so that when the waffles start coming off the iron, there are no delays. If you're serving ham, sausage or bacon, cook it before you start the waffles, place it in a serving dish and keep warm in the oven (or place the covered serving dish over a pan of very hot water, then cover the whole thing with a towel to keep in the heat). Plan on scrambled eggs rather than eggs cooked-to-order, and have them ready in advance also. If you have a large enough serving dish, heap the eggs in the center and surround them with any meat, then keep the whole thing warm until the waffles are ready. Syrup, jam, butter, stewed fruit and any other accompaniments should be set out and ready to go, as should all the plates, forks, napkins and other utensils you'll need. A selection of juices is nice, and coffee or milk should be available for those who like it.

For the waffles, there are many excellent mixes available from which to choose. I usually use one of these, rather than making my own waffle batter from scratch. However, if you want to really lay out an impressive spread and don't mind a little work, try the Sourdough Waffles recipe (page 236). An electric waffle iron works well. This is almost the only kitchen piece I own that features a nonstick coating, which I think is a great help when making waffles (I don't like nonstick skillets, because they emit toxic fumes when overheated, which is much easier to do with a skillet than with a plug-in, temperature-controlled waffle iron). Waffles really are best when served hot and crisp, right off the iron, but you can put them on a large plate in a 250°F oven while you prepare as many as you'll need. Don't cover the plate or stack the waffles more than two deep, or they will become soggy.

Here are some suggestions for your Waffle Bar; offer as many as you like. Some may seem unusual, but they work really well. Just ask Bill and his hunting buddies!

Waffle toppers

- Butter, margarine (best served at room temperature)
- Hot syrup: maple, and fruit-flavored syrup if you like
- Warm honey and/or Honey Butter
- Maple-Stewed Apples (page 241) or other stewed fruit, served warm

- Jam or preserves
- Whipped cream (add a little vanilla, brandy or other flavorings for more flavor)
- Yogurt (plain or vanilla) or sour cream
- Vanilla ice cream (set carton in a bed of ice to keep it cold)
- Ricotta cheese, beaten with a little honey and crushed nuts
- Fresh blueberries or raspberries
- Cut-up fresh strawberries, tossed 30 minutes in advance with a little sugar
- Sliced peaches (canned peaches work fine and are heavenly with whipped cream)
- Sliced bananas (toss with a little orange juice to keep them from browning)
- Spiced honey pineapple topping (see Spiced Honey Pineapple Sundaes, page 294)
- Maraschino cherry halves
- Lemon curd (a sort of clear, custardy mixture; look in the supermarket with the jams)
- Chocolate chips or shaved chocolate
- Chopped pecans or other nuts
- Granola
- Cinnamon-sugar (¼ cup sugar mixed with ½ teaspoon cinnamon)
- Crisp bacon crumbles, if you're not serving bacon alongside

Beverages

- Orange juice, grapefruit juice, apple juice, tomato juice
- Bloody Mary cocktails, or Virgin Mary drinks (no vodka)
- Champagne, champagne punch, or Mimosas (champagne and orange juice)
- Coffee, tea
- Milk
- Chilled hard apple cider (also called cider beer; very refreshing for brunch)
- Nonalcoholic sparkling cider (apple or pear)

Meats, eggs

- Crisp bacon strips
- Fried ham slices
- Breakfast sausage patties or links
- Scrambled eggs (stir in some chives and a little shredded cheese for variety)

Sourdough Waffles

Begin fermenting the starter 4 or 5 days before you need it. If you're serving more than 4 people, plan on using the entire batch from the first fermentation, adding additional flour and water for the second fermentation as needed (you won't have any starter left over for future batches if you do this). If you are boiling peeled potatoes, save the water to use in sourdough starter; it gives a better flavor.

The sourdough starter:

1 tablespoon sugar
2 cups warm water (ideally 110°F; do not use hot water, as this kills the yeast)
1 package dry yeast
2 cups flour for the first ferment, plus 1½ cups for the second

In large bowl, dissolve sugar in water. Stir in yeast and let stand 10 minutes, or until foamy. Stir in 2 cups flour and mix well. Cover with a clean towel and let stand at room temperature 3 or 4 days, stirring several times each day; when ready, the sourdough should have a vinegar-like smell, but should not be discolored. When the starter is ready, refrigerate it until needed (it will be OK for weeks, but if you keep it that long, "feed" it every 5 days with a mixture of ¼ cup flour and ¼ cup warm water), or proceed to the second fermentation, below.

The night before you'll be making the waffles, begin the second fermentation: Measure out 1 cup starter into a large ceramic bowl, and refrigerate the remaining starter for future batches (if you'll be making a larger batch of waffles, measure out all the starter and increase flour and water proportionally). Add 1½ cups flour and 1 cup warm water to the bowl with the starter; stir well, and add a little more water if the batter seems too thick. Cover loosely with a towel and let stand in a warm place overnight. The resulting batter is now called sourdough, and is ready to use.

Thr waffles:

1½ cups sourdough from the second fermentation above (see note on page 237)
2 eggs
3 tablespoons melted butter or margarine
¼ cup nonfat dry milk powder
2 tablespoons sugar
1 teaspoon baking soda
½ teaspoon salt
1 tablespoon cold water

Begin heating the waffle iron. In very large bowl combine starter, eggs, melted butter, dry milk and sugar; beat well with a whisk or fork. When the waffle iron is hot, mix the soda, salt and cold water in a small bowl, then stir into the batter. The batter will increase rapidly in volume; when it has stopped increasing, ladle out the appropriate amount for your waffle iron, keeping in mind that it will expand further as it cooks. Cook until golden brown. Repeat until all batter is used, keeping waffles warm until ready to serve.

Note: The waffle recipe as written will make enough waffles for 4 to 6 people. If you need to make a larger quantity, mix up only one batch at a time, cook that entire batch, then make up a second batch. Also, if the batter is thicker than you like, add a little more water to the batter to thin it out. Don't mix the soda water into the batter until you're ready to cook!

SOURDOUGH PANCAKES

Follow procedures for Sourdough Waffles, using only 1 tablespoon melted butter in the final batter.

PFANNKUCHEN: BAKED PANCAKE PUFF

4 servings

Make sure everyone is seated at the breakfast table a few minutes before this is done; it's most impressive when it's fresh, hot and puffy right from the oven.

4 eggs
¾ cup milk (2% milk works fine)
2 tablespoons butter or margarine, melted, plus a small amount for greasing the skillet
1 teaspoon vanilla extract, optional
¼ teaspoon salt
¾ cup flour
Powdered sugar for dusting, optional
Optional toppings: Maple-Stewed Apples (page 241), other stewed fruit, cut-up fresh fruit, yogurt, whipped cream

Heat oven to 400°F. In mixing bowl, beat the eggs with a whisk or hand mixer until foamy. Add milk, melted butter, vanilla and salt, and beat briefly. Add the flour, a little at a time, beating between additions, and beat until just smooth. Set the batter aside to rest for a few minutes. Heat a 10-inch cast-iron or other heavy skillet over medium heat until fairly warm, then brush the bottom and sides with a little butter. Add the batter and bake 15 minutes. Reduce heat to 350°F and bake 12 to 15 minutes longer, or until pancake is golden with browned edges and very puffy. Dust with a little powdered sugar (put a tablespoon in a small wire strainer and shake it over the pancake), then bring pancake to the table immediately. Cut into quarters, and serve with toppings of your choice.

BAKED HAM AND CHEESE OMELET

4 to 6 servings

Nothing could be easier than this oven-baked omelet. It's very rich, and needs only toast or muffins, and some fresh fruit, to make a perfect brunch. It's also great as a light supper; heat a loaf of bread and toss a green salad accented with apples and a tangy vinaigrette dressing, to accompany.

6 eggs
½ teaspoon baking powder
¼ teaspoon Tabasco sauce
¼ teaspoon salt
¼ cup flour
1 to 1¼ cups diced cooked ham (3 to 4 ounces)
1 cup cottage cheese with chives* (reduced-fat works fine)
8 ounces shredded cheddar cheese (about 2 cups)
1 tablespoon butter or margarine, melted

Heat oven to 400°F; spray an 8-inch-square baking dish, or a shallow 2-quart casserole, with nonstick spray, or butter lightly. In a large mixing bowl, beat eggs, baking powder, Tabasco sauce and salt with a whisk or fork until foamy. Add flour, and beat gently until just combined. Add ham, cottage cheese, cheddar cheese and melted butter; stir until well mixed. Pour into prepared baking dish. Bake 15 minutes, then reduce heat to 350°F and bake 15 minutes longer; the top should be golden brown and puffy.

*Feel free to substitute plain cottage cheese if that's what you have; you can add about 2 teaspoons snipped fresh chives if you have them.

Overnight Caramel Rolls

9 rolls

Fresh-baked caramel rolls are one of the best morning treats there is, but the idea of getting up at the crack of dawn to rise the dough is not appealing. In this easy recipe, frozen bread dough is thawed and formed into rolls the night before; after resting overnight in the refrigerator, the rolls get a quick rise on the countertop before baking.

1 loaf (1 pound) frozen white bread dough, or equivalent in homemade dough
2⁄3 cup packed brown sugar
1⁄2 cup powdered sugar
1⁄2 cup heavy cream
1 teaspoon vanilla extract
1 1⁄4 cups chopped pecans or other nuts, optional
A little flour for dusting
2 tablespoons butter or stick margarine, softened
2 tablespoons white sugar
1⁄2 teaspoon cinnamon

The evening before: Place frozen bread dough into a loaf pan that has been lightly coated with nonstick spray, butter or margarine. Cover with a towel and let thaw at room temperature 4 or 5 hours (if using homemade dough, mix and allow to rise once before proceeding). When the dough is thawed, spray an 8-inch-square baking pan with cooking spray, or butter lightly. Add brown and powdered sugars to dish. Combine cream and vanilla in a measuring cup, then pour over the sugars in the baking dish. Stir well to blend. Sprinkle half the nuts over the sugar-cream mixture; set aside. On a lightly floured board, roll the dough out to approximately an 11-inch square. Spread the softened butter over the dough. In a small bowl, mix the white sugar and cinnamon, then sprinkle evenly over the buttered dough. Sprinkle remaining nuts over all, then roll dough up jelly-roll style. Cut into 9 evenly sized pieces, each about 1¼ inches wide. Arrange evenly in prepared baking dish, laying them with a cut (spiral) side up. There will be a fair amount of space between the rolls. Cover the dish with plastic wrap or foil; refrigerate overnight.

In the morning: Let the covered rolls stand on the counter at room temperature for an hour, or even a little longer. When ready to bake, heat oven to 375°F. Uncover rolls and bake 30 minutes; cover dish with foil during last 10 minutes of baking if rolls are browning too quickly. Remove from oven, and remove foil if used. Let rolls cool for about 5 minutes, then cover with foil, bringing it down the sides of the dish. Place a large plate or baking sheet over the dish, and quickly but carefully flip everything over together. Remove the baking dish; spoon any caramel mixture remaining in the dish over the rolls. Let cool at least 10 minutes before eating; best served warm and fresh.

Variations:

- Substitute ¼ cup maple syrup for the powdered sugar. Increase brown sugar to ¾ cup. Omit the vanilla.
- To cut a few calories, substitute canned evaporated skim milk for the cream

MAPLE-STEWED APPLES

2 servings per apple

Serve this with pancakes or waffles, or as a breakfast side dish on its own. It's also great to top hot cereal.

1 Granny Smith or other firm, tart apple
1 tablespoon maple syrup
1 teaspoon butter or margarine
A good dash of cinnamon or nutmeg

Peel the apple if you like, or if you prefer, leave the peel on. Cut the apple into quarters and remove the core. Slice the quarters into ⅛-inch-thick slices the long way, then cut each slice into inch-wide pieces.

Combine the apple, syrup, butter, cinnamon and 3 tablespoons water in small saucepan. Cook over medium-low heat, stirring gently occasionally, until the apple is tender; if the mixture gets too dry before the apple is tender, add a bit more water. Serve warm.

Variation:

Add 2 tablespoons raisins per apple to the mixture when you begin the cooking; increase the water to ¼ cup.

Light Meals, Lunch Dishes and Soup

QUESADILLAS WITH VARIATIONS

Each quesadilla serves 2 as an appetizer or light snack

Everyone loves these easy, quick-to-make snacks—including the cook! Make a simple cheese-only version, or fill them with a variety of tasty tidbits including small bits of leftover cooked meat, raw or cooked vegetables, or leftover refried beans. These are good served with salsa and sour cream.

For each quesadilla, you'll need these basic ingredients:

2 flour tortillas (any size will work; recipe was tested with 8-inch tortillas)
½ cup shredded cheese, such as Monterey Jack or a blend using Jack and cheddar (finely shredded works best, but is not essential)
1 to 2 tablespoons prepared salsa, optional

Optional: *Choose* ***one or two*** *of the following additions:*

- 1 green onion, chopped or thinly sliced
- 1 or 2 tablespoons diced onion
- 2 tablespoons diced raw red or green bell pepper
- 2 tablespoons diced tomato
- 2 or 3 tablespoons chopped cooked bell peppers or other vegetables
- 1 tablespoon sliced ripe olives or chopped pimiento-stuffed olives
- 1 tablespoon diced pickled or fresh jalapeño peppers, or to taste
- A scant ¼ cup diced or shredded cooked turkey or chicken (smoked is good)
- A scant ¼ cup cooked, seasoned taco meat
- A scant ¼ cup cooked, crumbled pork sausage
- A scant ¼ cup cooked pinto or refried beans
- 1 or 2 slices crisp cooked bacon, crumbled

The best utensil for cooking quesadillas is a cast-iron griddle or large skillet, but any heavy griddle or skillet will work. You can also cook quesadillas on a charcoal or gas grill; simply place the assembled quesadilla(s) on a double layer of heavy-duty foil.

For each quesadilla: If you are using refried beans, spread them evenly over 1 tortilla before the cheese; otherwise, proceed by sprinkling the cheese evenly over 1 tortilla, spreading it not quite to the edge. If using salsa, dab it evenly over the cheese. Sprinkle with the optional toppings. (Hint: Don't use more than 1 type of meat.) Top with remaining tortilla.

Heat griddle or skillet over medium-high heat. When hot, carefully place the assembled quesadilla on the griddle. Cook until the bottom tortilla begins to get crusty brown spots (use a spatula to lift the edge of the tortilla so you can see how it is cooking). The cheese should begin to melt by this time, which will help hold the quesadilla together for flipping. When the bottom is nicely spotted, carefully flip the entire quesadilla with a spatula. Cook until the second side is crusty and lightly browned. Total cooking time should be about 5 minutes. Cooked quesadillas can be kept in a 250°F oven while you prepare additional quesadillas. To serve, cut into 6 wedges.

MARINATED ROAST BEEF FOR SANDWICHES

4 servings; easily increased

Sliced deli roast beef turns into a tasty Italian-flavored sandwich with this easy recipe. Fresh herbs are far superior to dried herbs for this recipe, although dried herbs can be used if that's all you have. If you can't get fresh parsley, however, leave it out of the recipe; dried parsley has a poor flavor for this dish.

2 tablespoons chopped fresh basil leaves, or 1 teaspoon dried
2 tablespoons minced fresh parsley (do not substitute dried)
2 teaspoons chopped fresh oregano leaves, or ¼ teaspoon dried
2 tablespoons olive oil
2 tablespoons dry white wine or water
1 tablespoons freshly squeezed lemon juice
½ teaspoon Dijon mustard
1 small clove garlic
1 anchovy fillet, drained and patted dry, optional
½ pound sliced roast beef from the deli
French bread, hard rolls or other bread of your choice
Lettuce leaves and thinly sliced red onion

In blender or food processor container, combine basil, parsley, oregano, olive oil, white wine, lemon juice, mustard, garlic and anchovy; process until creamy. Add to a mixing bowl with the roast beef, and toss gently together with your hands, separating the slices of the beef so all are coated lightly with the marinade. Cover and refrigerate 1 hour or longer.

To serve, cut French bread or rolls into halves; cut French bread into serving-sized lengths (usually 4 to 6 inches long, depending on the bread). Layer each sandwich with lettuce leaves, roast beef and thinly sliced red onions.

Chili Birdnests

Per serving; make as many as you need

The potato sticks become softer during cooking; if you want more crunch, spread them out to the sides of the dish so they are not covered with chili. Kids who enjoy eggs love these fun-looking individual dishes.

¾ cup french-fried potato strings (sold in the snack aisle; sometimes called shoe string potatoes)
⅔ cup prepared chili (leftover homemade or canned, as you prefer)
1 egg
Parsley or cilantro leaves for garnish, optional

Heat oven to 425°F. Lightly spray individual oven-safe serving dishes (I use shallow bowls that are about 6½ inches across and 2 inches deep) with nonstick spray, or grease lightly. Place potato strings in dish. Top with chili (if the chili is leftover and has been refrigerated, warm it briefly before assembling the dish). Make a small depression in the center of the chili, and carefully break the egg into the depression. Salt and pepper the egg to taste. Bake until egg white is opaque but yolk is still runny, about 15 minutes; if you prefer hard yolks, baking time will be 18 to 20 minutes. Garnish with parsley or cilantro leaves.

Wrap It Up

It's always interesting to study food trends. Often, you'll find that a "hot new food" actually has been around for a long time in a particular ethnic cuisine. Fondue, which swept the nation in the late '60s and early '70s (and made a comeback in the latter '90s) has been served in French and Swiss homes for generations. Quiche, another traditional French food, was reinvented in the '80s (and traditional French cooks will say that the dish has been destroyed by all the tinkering). Wraps, one of the biggest food crazes of the late '90s, are a reinterpretation of a staple dish in many cultures, the most common of which is the Mexican burrito.

A wrap is simply a piece of soft, flat bread—like a flour tortilla—that is filled with various ingredients and rolled up. They can be served whole as a single serving, or sliced into appetizer-sized portions. Wraps make ideal picnic food, because they can be prepared in advance and toted in a cooler. Some can even be frozen, and reheated (or simply thawed) at serving time. They're also ideal for using up small bits of leftovers. You might be surprised at how good something like leftover beef stew works in a wrap.

The foundation for any wrap is the bread. Eight-inch flour tortillas are probably the most common bread used for homemade wraps, but you can substitute any thin, soft, easily rolled bread you can find. Here are some options.

- Flour tortillas, 8 to 10 inches across ("burrito size")
- Lefse (Scandinavian potato flatbread, available in large sheets)
- Soft lavash breads (thin Mideastern flatbread)
- Mountain bread
- Mandarin pancakes (a very thin pancake used to make Chinese dishes such as Mu Shu Pork)
- Specially made "wrap" breads being marketed to take advantage of the wrap craze

Most wraps also use a spread of some kind—mayonnaise, soft cream cheese, or creamy dressing are common choices—to help hold the roll together, and also to provide flavor and moistness. If the wrap filling is bound with salad dressing or mayonnaise (like tuna salad), no additional spread is needed.

Cold wraps can be served immediately after they're made, or can be tightly rolled in plastic wrap and refrigerated for as long as 8 hours. The bread will soften somewhat during this time, which helps hold the wrap together and makes slicing easier. Some wraps are better if heated briefly in an oven, toaster oven or microwave.

The basic wrapping procedure is as follows:

1. Soften the bread, if necessary. Refrigerator-temperature tortillas and other flatbreads can be hard to roll, especially if they are a few days old. To soften, choose one of the following methods:
   - Microwave the bread for about 10 seconds (soften one piece at a time, then fill and roll it before softening another)
   - Wrap the bread in foil and place in a warm oven for 5 to 10 minutes
   - Steam the bread over a pot of simmering water for a minute or two
   - Heat a large skillet over medium-high heat. Sprinkle a few drops of water into the skillet, then add one piece of bread and sprinkle with a few more drops of water. Cook about 10 seconds, or until the bread is softened but not browned.
   - Keep the softened bread covered after it is warmed, and don't warm up more bread than you plan to use immediately, because it will harden again as soon as it is cool.
2. If using mayonnaise, cream cheese or a thick dressing, spread it evenly but thinly over the entire piece of bread (one side only).
3. If you're using thinly sliced meats or cheese as part of the filling, lay them flat on the bread, leaving a 1-inch margin at the edge of the wrap farthest away from you (this will help hold the wrap together when it is rolled). If the filling is loose, such as salad mixtures or chopped ingredients, pile it on the half of the bread that is nearest to you, leaving the back half clear.
4. Roll the bread up tightly to enclose the filling, starting with the filled side that is nearest to you. If you're making wraps to be served whole, you may want to tuck the sides of the bread in as you roll; this prevents the filling from coming out when the wrap is eaten.
5. Serve immediately, or wrap tightly in plastic wrap or foil and refrigerate up to 8 hours. For appetizers, slice the wrap into spirals at a slight angle; generally, you'll want the pieces to be about an inch wide.

On pages 248-251 are a few wrap suggestions, but feel free to experiment with your own variations! Each of these variations, except two, give ingredients for a single wrap, so increase as needed.

continued

Cold Wraps

COBB SALAD WRAP

1 tablespoon mayonnaise or salad dressing
¼ cup coarsely shredded romaine or head lettuce
1 slice bacon, cooked crisp, drained and crumbled
2 tablespoons chopped ripe tomato
3 tablespoons diced cooked turkey or chicken
2 tablespoons diced ham or Canadian bacon, optional
1 tablespoon crumbled blue cheese

Spread mayonnaise over bread. Pile remaining ingredients on half of bread.

CAESAR TURKEY WRAP

1 tablespoon prepared creamy Caesar dressing
2 small leaves bibb or romaine lettuce (remove the thick rib if necessary)
2 ounces thin deli-style sliced turkey
1 or 2 strips roasted red bell pepper (purchased, or made as described on page 299)
2 teaspoons grated Parmesan cheese

Spread dressing on bread. Lay lettuce flat on bread; top with turkey slices and bell pepper strips. Sprinkle Parmesan evenly over all.

HAM AND CHEESE WRAP

1 generous tablespoon garlic-chive cream cheese spread
2 ounces thin deli-style sliced ham
2 sandwich-size slices Colby or other cheese
1 tablespoon sliced or chopped pimento-stuffed green olives

Spread cream cheese on bread. Lay ham and cheese on bread, pressing into cream cheese. Sprinkle evenly with olives.

Chicken Salad Wrap with Apples and Walnuts

2 small leaves bibb or romaine lettuce (remove the thick rib if necessary)
⅓ cup Bare-Bones Chicken Salad (page 34)
2 thin slices apple
1 tablespoon chopped walnuts

Arrange lettuce on bread, leaving a 1-inch margin at the edge of the wrap farthest away from you. Spread chicken salad on the half of the bread nearest you. Top with apple slice, placing apples parallel to the edge of your work surface. Sprinkle walnuts evenly over the entire wrap.

Mideastern Wrap

1 tablespoon tahini (sesame paste)
2 small leaves bibb or romaine lettuce (remove the thick rib if necessary)
⅓ cup Tabbouleh Salad (page 40)
3 tablespoons cooked or drained canned garbanzo beans
A little thinly sliced red onion

Spread tahini on bread. Lay lettuce flat on bread. Spread tabbouleh on the half of the bread nearest you; top tabbouleh with garbanzo beans. Sprinkle onions evenly over the entire wrap.

Smoked Salmon Wrap

2 tablespoons cream cheese, softened
2 teaspoons mayonnaise or sour cream
1 teaspoon finely minced green onion
2 or 3 ounces thinly sliced smoked salmon, or flaked smoked salmon
3 very thin slices cucumber
1½ teaspoons chopped fresh dill leaves, optional

In mixing bowl, blend together cream cheese and sour cream. Spread on bread. Sprinkle evenly with minced onion. Arrange salmon evenly over cream cheese, pressing down gently. Top with cucumber; sprinkle with dill.

Hot Wraps

Heating instructions for hot wraps (except Mini-Wrap Crab Bites): Heat one or two wraps at a time in a microwave at REHEAT/80% for 1½ to 2 minutes; or, place as many wraps as you like in a covered dish or wrap in foil and bake in 350°F oven 15 to 20 minutes. Note: Wraps may be prepared in advance and rolled in foil or plastic wrap, then refrigerated before heating.

HOT TUNA WRAP

Makes enough filling for 2 or 3 wraps

1 can (6 ounces) tuna packed in water, drained and flaked
⅓ cup shredded cheddar cheese
2 tablespoons mayonnaise or salad dressing
2 tablespoons diced celery
2 tablespoons diced onion
½ teaspoon seasoned salt or plain salt

In mixing bowl, combine all ingredients. Spread the mixture evenly over 2 pieces bread, leaving a 1-inch margin at the edge of the wrap farthest away from you. Roll gently to prevent filling from squishing out, folding sides in as you roll.

CHICAGO DOG WRAP WITH CHEESE

½ teaspoon yellow mustard
3 tablespoons shredded Colby cheese
1 all-beef hot dog, preferably kosher
1 pickled hot "sport" pepper, seeds and stem removed, sliced into strips
1 tablespoon chopped tomato
2 teaspoons finely chopped onion
½ teaspoon pickle relish

Spread bread with mustard. Sprinkle cheese evenly over bread. Place hot dog on the edge of bread nearest you, parallel to the edge of your work surface. Tuck hot pepper strips next to hot dog. Sprinkle tomato, onion and pickle relish over hot dog. Roll fairly tightly, folding sides in as you roll.

REUBEN WRAP

2 tablespoons Thousand Island dressing
¼ cup shredded Swiss cheese
2 ounces thin deli-style sliced corned beef
2 tablespoons sauerkraut, drained and squeezed dry before measuring

Spread dressing on bread. Sprinkle cheese evenly over bread. Lay corned beef on the bread. Spread sauerkraut in a line on the side of the corned beef nearest you. Roll up tightly, folding sides in as you roll.

MINI-WRAP CRAB BITES

Makes enough to stuff two 8-inch flatbreads; 12 appetizers total

3 ounces cream cheese, softened
¼ cup shredded Monterey Jack or Gruyère cheese
3 tablespoons finely chopped red and/or green bell pepper
1 tablespoon snipped fresh chives, optional (or use chive cream cheese)
A few dashes of Tabasco sauce
1 can (6 ounces) lump crabmeat, drained and picked over; or 1 cup shredded frozen crabmeat (thawed) or imitation crab sticks

In mixing bowl, combine cream cheese, Monterey Jack cheese, bell pepper, chives and Tabasco sauce; mix well. Add crabmeat and stir gently to combine. Divide mixture evenly between 2 tortillas or other bread, and spread evenly; roll up tightly. Slice into ¾-inch-thick spirals and place on greased baking sheet. Bake at 375°F 14 to 18 minutes, or until cheese melts and begins to turn light brown. Serve warm.

CORNBREAD SALAD

4 servings

Leftover cornbread turns into a refreshing lunch dish in this easy recipe.

2 cups cubed day-old cornbread (broken into ¾-inch pieces before measuring)
1 cup canned or frozen corn kernels, drained or thawed
1 cup cubed ham or cooked chicken (about 3 ounces; cut into ½-inch cubes before measuring)
½ cup diced green or red bell pepper
½ cup diced cucumber
3 green onions, sliced ⅛ inch thick, or ¼ cup diced red or sweet white onion
1 tomato, peeled and cut into ½-inch pieces
1 hard-cooked egg, chopped, optional
Celery salt, garlic salt or plain salt
Creamy salad dressing such as ranch, blue cheese, or creamy Caesar

Combine all ingredients except salt and dressing in a large bowl. Sprinkle lightly with salt; stir gently to mix. Add dressing to taste, starting out with about ½ cup and adding more until the salad is as "dressed" as you like. I prefer to serve this immediately, but some people like to refrigerate it an hour or two before serving so the cornbread softens.

CARROT-PEANUT BUTTER SANDWICH SPREAD

2 servings; easily increased

Known and loved by campers all over, this vegetarian spread makes a great quick lunch. For even more nutritional punch, pack the mixture into whole-wheat pita breads, or roll it up in a whole-wheat tortilla. Raisin bagels also go well with this spread.

For each 2 servings, you'll need:

1 cup shredded carrot (about 1 large carrot)
3 tablespoons peanut butter (chunky peanut butter is best)
1 generous tablespoon honey, or to taste
Pita bread, toasted or untoasted bagels, flour tortillas or other bread

Combine all ingredients and blend together with a fork. Spread into pita or bread of your choice. That's it!

Optional add-in ingredients:

- 1 or 2 tablespoons roasted, salted sunflower nuts
- 2 tablespoons raisins or currants, or diced dried apricots or apples
- Half of a small apple, shredded
- 1 tablespoon wheat germ
- 1 stalk celery, diced or thinly sliced

SMOKY MUSHROOM AND WILD RICE SOUP

4 servings

When you're grilling a main course, take advantage of the free heat to make this excellent soup; you can prepare the soup for the same meal, or refrigerate the cooked mushrooms until the next day. This also makes a delicious part of a vegetarian meal; round it out with some grilled vegetables or a salad, wedges of sharp cheddar or creamy Brie cheese, and a loaf of crusty bread.

8 ounces fresh mushrooms (medium or larger), cleaned to remove soil
2 tablespoons olive oil or vegetable oil, divided
1 cup vegetable broth or chicken broth
¼ cup diced onion
1 tablespoon butter or margarine
1 tablespoon flour
1 cup cooked wild rice
1 cup cream or half-and-half
2 tablespoons snipped fresh chives

Prepare medium-hot grill. In mixing bowl, toss together the mushrooms and 1 tablespoon of the oil; sprinkle generously with salt and pepper, add the remaining tablespoon oil and toss again. Place the mushrooms on the grate over the coals; cover the grill and cook, turning and rotating the mushrooms every few minutes, until the mushrooms are tender and nicely browned, about 10 minutes. Return mushrooms to the mixing bowl.

Transfer half the mushrooms to a blender or food processor container. Add the broth and process until smooth. Add the remaining mushrooms and pulse on and off a few times, until the mushrooms are coarsely chopped; set aside. In a large saucepan, sauté onion in butter over medium heat until tender. Sprinkle the flour over the onion, stirring constantly to prevent lumps; cook, stirring constantly, until mixture thickens and bubbles. Add the mushroom mixture and the wild rice. Heat to boiling, stirring frequently; reduce heat and simmer 3 or 4 minutes. Add the cream and chives and cook, stirring frequently, until hot but not boiling. Taste for seasoning and add salt and pepper as needed. Serve hot.

CURRIED PUMPKIN SOUP

4 servings

Pumpkin usually makes its appearance only in the Thanksgiving pie, which is too bad because it also makes delicious soup. Try this autumn-in-a-bowl recipe and see if you don't agree.

2 cups chicken broth or vegetable broth
1 carrot, diced
Half of a medium onion, diced
1 bay leaf, optional
½ teaspoon crumbled dried thyme leaves
1 can (16 ounces) solid-pack pumpkin
½ teaspoon curry powder blend
½ teaspoon salt
⅛ teaspoon pepper
1 cup cream, half-and-half or canned evaporated milk
Sour cream and fresh chives for garnish, optional

In a large saucepan, combine chicken broth, carrot, onion, bay leaf and thyme. Heat to boiling, then reduce heat and cook at a very gentle boil until vegetables are tender, about 15 minutes. Remove from heat and set aside to cool slightly; remove and discard bay leaf. Transfer cooled broth mixture to blender container, and process until smooth. Return broth mixture to the saucepan and add pumpkin, curry powder, salt and pepper. Heat just to boiling over medium heat, then reduce heat and simmer 5 to 10 minutes, stirring occasionally. Add cream and continue cooking until cream is heated through. Garnish individual servings with a dollop of sour cream and a few snipped fresh chives.

Creamy Peanut Soup

4 servings

Although it may sound strange to someone who was not raised with it, peanut soup is a traditional first course in the South. It's very quick-and-easy to make, and opens up nicely for a dinner featuring grilled meats, baked ham or fried chicken. Keep serving sizes small, as the soup is quite rich.

2 cups chicken broth
⅔ cup smooth peanut butter
⅛ teaspoon celery salt
A pinch of onion powder
A pinch of sugar
A dash of Tabasco sauce
1 cup heavy cream or evaporated milk
¼ cup sour cream
1 tablespoon plus 1 teaspoon coarsely chopped cocktail peanuts

In a large saucepan, heat chicken broth to boiling over medium heat. Add peanut butter, celery salt, onion powder, sugar and Tabasco sauce, stirring until smooth. Heat until mixture just comes to a boil. Add cream and heat until hot but not boiling. Ladle into individual serving bowls; top each serving with a tablespoon sour cream and 1 teaspoon chopped peanuts.

Appetizers and Snacks

SOUTH-OF-THE-BORDER WONTONS

About 30 appetizers

Homemade wontons are really easy to make if you have a deep-fat fryer (and access to ready-made wonton skins, usually found in the dairy case). This version uses canned green chiles to add a delicious flair.

½ pound ground beef
2 cloves garlic, pressed or minced
1 teaspoon chili powder blend
¼ cup thick and chunky salsa, plus additional for serving
1 can (4 ounces) peeled whole green chiles, drained
30 wonton skins (or, 8 eggroll skins, cut into quarters)
1¼ cups shredded Monterey Jack cheese (about 5 ounces)
Vegetable oil for deep frying

In large skillet, brown ground beef over medium heat, stirring to break up. Drain excess grease. Add garlic and chili powder; cook, stirring occasionally, for 2 or 3 minutes. Stir in salsa and cook about 5 minutes longer. Remove from heat and set aside to cool slightly.

While the meat is cooling, cut chiles to yield 30 pieces. Place 1 piece chile in the center of a wonton skin. Add a heaping teaspoon of the cooked meat, and a heaping teaspoon of the shredded cheese. Moisten edges of the wonton skin lightly with cold water. Fold wonton skin diagonally over filling and press edges very well to seal. Moisten 1 pointy corner of the folded wonton, then bring the 2 corners together and overlap; press well to seal together. Place wrapped wonton on a baking sheet; repeat with remaining ingredients.

Heat oil in deep-fat fryer to 400°F. Cook wontons, a few at a time, until deep golden brown. Drain on paper-towl-lined plate and keep warm while you fry remaining wontons. Serve with additional salsa for dipping.

SAVORY TRIANGLE PIES

4 servings; easily doubled

For a quick snack or light lunch, assemble the triangles in advance and refrigerate, covered with plastic wrap, until you're ready to bake them. You may also refrigerate or freeze cooked triangles, then warm them in the oven before serving.

1 tube (8 ounces/8 rolls) refrigerated crescent rolls
¼ pound thinly sliced deli meat such as corned beef, roast beef or salami
Half of an 8-ounce container chive-and-onion or other flavored cream cheese spread, softened slightly

Heat oven to 375°F (if you are making the triangles in advance, heat the oven just before you are ready to bake). Separate the rolls into 4 squares (2 triangles each); pinch together the diagonal seam between the triangles to seal. Slice meat into ¼-inch-wide strips. Mix well with cream cheese. Divide the meat mixture evenly among the roll squares, keeping the filling away from the edges. Fold each square to form a triangle, stretching dough lightly as needed; press edges together very well. Arrange on an ungreased cookie sheet. Bake 12 to 15 minutes, or until golden brown. Cool slightly before serving, as the filling will be quite hot.

SWEET AND SNAPPY SNACK MIX

About 14 cups

This is a little different from the usual party mix. Feel free to substitute other cereals or crackers.

¼ cup butter or margarine (half of a stick)
¼ cup packed brown sugar
1 tablespoon honey or corn syrup
1 teaspoon garlic salt
½ to 1 teaspoon Tabasco sauce
4 cups Crispix or other multi-grain waffle-weave cereal
4 cups Golden Grahams or other sweetened graham squares
3 cups tiny pretzel twists
1 bag (6 ounces) goldfish crackers, cheddar or other flavor of your choice
1 can (11½ ounces) mixed nuts

Heat oven to 300°F (see below for a non-baked version). In microwave on LOW/10% power, or saucepan over low heat, heat butter, brown sugar, honey, garlic salt and Tabasco sauce until butter melts and brown sugar dissolves, stirring frequently.

Combine cereals, pretzels, goldfish crackers and nuts in 10x15x2-inch baking dish or large roaster. Pour butter-sugar mixture over cereal mixture, stirring with a wooden spoon to coat all pieces. Bake 45 minutes, stirring every 10 minutes. For browner, crispier mix, increase oven to 375°F and bake 8 to 10 minutes longer, stirring once. Remove from oven and cool, stirring frequently to break up clumps, before placing in storage containers.

Variation:

No-Bake Sweet and Snappy Snack Mix: Follow recipe above, cooking butter-sugar mixture as directed. When butter melts and sugar has dissolved, continue cooking 2 minutes longer, stirring frequently. Pour mixture over combined cereal mixture, stirring constantly. Stir constantly until mixture is cooled. This variation will not be as crispy as the baked mixture, and will also be a little more sticky, but is excellent nonetheless and perfect if your cabin doesn't have an oven.

"Pickle Dogs"

4 appetizer pieces per pickle wedge; make as many as you wish

This old standby recipe still is a real crowd-pleaser (put out a platter of mixed snacks, and see if these don't disappear first!). These—or something very similar—are sold at the Minnesota State Fair under the name "Pickle Dogs" (or Pickel Dogs, as I think they have it); if you're in Minneapolis-St. Paul at the end of August, visit their booth by the Midway.

For each dog, you'll need:

1 large, thin slice of corned beef (from the deli)
1 tablespoon softened cream cheese, or a little more
1 dill pickle wedge (if the pickles are large, cut them into quarters; if they're smaller, you can cut them into halves)

Spread the corned beef on one side with the cream cheese, spreading the cheese all the way to the edge of the meat. Lay the pickle wedge on one end of the meat, then roll up tightly. For appetizer servings, cut each "dog" into 4 slices; you could also serve the whole "dog" as an out-of-hand snack (especially appreciated by kids; this is how they serve them at the State Fair).

ARTICHOKE DIP, HOT OR COLD

8 to 10 servings

Hot artichoke dip is a perennial favorite at many restaurants … but the big surprise is, it's also fabulous served cold! This recipe makes a large batch, so you may want to serve half of it warm, reserving the other half to serve cold the next day. Microwaving is easy, and your kitchen won't get heated up in warm weather; however, you can also bake the dish in a conventional oven if you prefer.

½ cup regular mayonnaise (do not use salad dressing or reduced-fat mayo)
1 container (8 ounces) plain cream cheese, softened
¼ cup shredded Romano or Parmesan cheese
½ teaspoon celery salt or plain salt
½ teaspoon minced garlic
¼ teaspoon Tabasco sauce
1 can (14 ounces) artichoke hearts, drained and coarsely chopped
1 tablespoon chopped fresh basil leaves, or ¾ teaspoon dried
Crackers, Italian bread, pita crisps or toast points for dipping

In mixing bowl, combine mayonnaise, cream cheese, Romano, celery salt, garlic and Tabasco sauce; mix well. Add artichoke hearts and basil; stir gently to combine. Transfer to microwave-safe casserole or baking dish. Microwave on REHEAT/80% for 6 minutes, rotating and stirring every minute, or until mixture is hot and bubbly. Serve warm; or, allow to cool to room temperature, then cover and refrigerate until cold before serving.

Oven-baked variation:

Place mixture in a lightly greased oven-safe casserole or baking dish, and bake at 350°F until bubbling, 20 to 25 minutes; do not stir during baking. If you like, you can also top the dish with ¼ cup grated mozzarella cheese before oven baking; for an extra-browned crust, pop the dish under the broiler for a minute or two after baking.

TOASTED PUMPKIN SEEDS

After you've carved the jack-o-lantern (or made a pumpkin pie), turn the seeds into a tasty snack with this simple recipe; enlist the help of the kids to clean the seeds of the stringy pulp. Feel free to add additional seasonings as it pleases you; try chili powder for pumpkin seeds with a kick.

Seeds from a fresh pumpkin
Vegetable oil (you'll need about 2 tablespoons for each 2 cups of cleaned seeds)
Salt, garlic salt or seasoned salt

Separate stringy fibers from seeds; this is easiest if you put a quantity of the seed mass into a large bowl of cold water, then "squirt" the seeds away from the fibers and pulp (or, place the seeds in a colander and run water over them). Wash seeds and let dry completely on paper towels. When seeds are dry, heat oven to 250°F and place the seeds on a baking sheet. Sprinkle with oil, stirring to coat each seed; sprinkle generously with salt and any other seasonings you are using. Bake until seeds turn light golden brown, stirring occasionally, 30 to 45 minutes. Transfer seeds to paper towels to cool; store in airtight container.

Main Dishes

OVEN-CRISP BUTTERMILK CHICKEN

4 to 6 servings

Serve this chicken hot out of the oven, or make ahead to eat cold at a picnic.

1 cup buttermilk
½ teaspoon Tabasco or habañero pepper sauce, optional
1 cut-up chicken, or 3 to 4 pounds chicken pieces, skin-on or skinless
About ¾ of a 6-ounce package ranch-style croutons, or your favorite flavor
3 to 4 tablespoons butter or margarine, melted

In nonaluminum baking dish, bowl or casserole, combine buttermilk and Tabasco sauce; mix well. Add chicken pieces, turning to coat. Let stand 5 to 10 minutes, or cover and refrigerate up to 4 hours, turning occasionally. Meanwhile, crush croutons in blender or food processor until mixture is coarse crumbs (or place in zip-top plastic bag and crush very well with a rolling pin, can of corn or whatever is handy).

When you're ready to bake the chicken, heat the oven to 400°F. Remove chicken from buttermilk and coat each piece well with the crouton crumbs; discard buttermilk and excess crumbs. Place chicken pieces in a single layer in a baking dish. Drizzle melted butter evenly over the chicken pieces. Bake 45 to 55 minutes, or until coating is crispy and juices run clear when chicken is pricked with a small knife at the thickest part.

Variation:

Substitute 1½ cups corn flake crumbs, mixed with ½ cup flour and an envelope (1 ounce) ranch or other dry dressing mix, for the crushed croutons.

SEASONED CHICKEN WITH VEGETABLE PASTA

4 servings

Pretty enough for company, but easy enough for everyday, this dish provides meat, starch and vegetables all in one. You could also substitute turkey breast slices, or pork loin slices, for the chicken breasts.

4 smaller boneless, skinless chicken breasts (about 4 ounces each)
1 packet (.65 ounce) dry Italian salad dressing mix
2 carrots, scrubbed well or peeled
1 small zucchini
6 to 8 ounces wide egg noodles (uncooked)
1 tablespoon olive oil or vegetable oil
1 tablespoon white wine vinegar
1 cup chicken broth

Pound chicken breasts lightly with a meat mallet or the side of a sturdy plate until thickness is even. Sprinkle half of the dressing mix over the chicken and pound in lightly; reserve remaining dressing mix. Place chicken on a plate and refrigerate about 30 minutes if you have the time; otherwise, you may proceed immediately with the rest of the recipe.

Cut the carrots and zucchini into ⅛-inch-thick strips that are 2 inches long and about ⅛ inch wide. Place the zucchini in a large colander (you will use this in a minute to drain the pasta water, and the zucchini will get all the cooking it needs when the boiling water is poured over it during draining).

Heat a large pot of salted water to boiling over high heat. Add the noodles, stirring to prevent sticking. Cook, stirring frequently at first, until noodles are not quite done, then add the carrots. Cook until noodles are just cooked and carrots are tender-crisp. Drain the noodles and carrots into the colander with the zucchini, and rinse briefly. Return the noodle mixture to the cooking pot; cover to keep warm and set aside.

In a large skillet, heat the oil over medium heat. Add seasoned chicken and cook until golden brown on both sides and just cooked through; do not overcook, or the chicken will be tough. Transfer to a plate and keep warm. Add the vinegar, chicken broth and remaining dressing mix to the skillet, stirring to loosen any browned bits. Raise heat to high and cook until liquid is reduced to about half. Add the chicken broth mixture to the noodle mixture and toss to combine; if necessary, heat briefly to re-warm the noodles. Serve the noodles with the chicken.

Crock Pot BBQ Beef Brisket

6 to 8 servings

Easy and very delicious! If your crock pot has a removable inner crock (and you have lots of room in your refrigerator), place the beef and marinade ingredients directly into the crock, then cover and refrigerate overnight.

1 beef brisket, 3 to 3½ pounds
Celery salt
Garlic or onion salt
Freshly ground black pepper
¼ cup Worcestershire sauce
2 tablespoons Liquid Smoke
1 small onion, cut in half from top to bottom and sliced into ⅛-inch-thick half-rings
1 cup barbecue sauce

Cut the brisket into 2 portions that will fit in your crock pot. Season the brisket generously with celery salt, garlic or onion salt, and pepper. Place in a large ceramic bowl or glass baking dish, or large zipper-style plastic bag (if using a plastic bag, place the bag with the meat in a baking dish before proceeding). Combine Worcestershire sauce and Liquid Smoke in measuring cup, then pour over meat, turning to coat. Cover bowl or dish, or seal bag, and refrigerate overnight.

The next morning, transfer meat and marinade to crock pot; scatter onions over the meat. Cook on HIGH heat 1 hour, then reduce heat to LOW and cook 6 to 7 hours longer. Transfer meat to plate and allow to cool about 30 minutes. Slice thinly across the grain and return to the crock pot. Add barbecue sauce to crock pot. Cook on LOW for about 1 hour longer.

REUBEN CASSEROLE

4 servings

The taste of the sandwich in a quick-and-easy casserole.

½ cup sour cream (reduced-fat works fine)
2 teaspoons dry mustard powder, or 1 tablespoon prepared mustard
4 cups frozen O'Brien potatoes* (half of a 28-ounce bag), thawed
10 ounces sliced corned beef, cut into ¼ x 1½-inch strips
1 pound (2 cups) sauerkraut, drained and rinsed briefly
1½ cups shredded Swiss cheese (about 6 ounces)

Heat oven to 375°F. Spray a 9-inch-square baking dish, or 2-quart casserole, with nonstick spray, or grease lightly. In a large mixing bowl, blend sour cream with mustard. Add potatoes, stirring to combine. Transfer potato mixture to prepared baking dish. Top with corned beef, then with sauerkraut. Cover dish with foil or lid, and bake 30 minutes. Remove foil and sprinkle evenly with the shredded cheese. Bake, uncovered, 25 minutes longer, or until cheese melts and edges of casserole are bubbly.

*Pre-packaged frozen O'Brien potatoes have a bit of bell pepper and onion mixed with diced potatoes. If you prefer, use fresh potatoes, cut into ¼-inch dice, with some bell pepper and onion mixed in.

Variation:

Kielbasa Casserole: Substitute 8 to 10 ounces smoked kielbasa sausage, cut into ½-inch chunks, for the corned beef.

OLD WEST BURGERS

3 servings; easily doubled

I've traveled in Wyoming quite a bit, and often wondered why the burgers there were so tasty. The excellent range-fed beef contributes a ton of flavor, but that isn't easily found elsewhere in the country. After some experimentation, I've come up with this method that produces incredibly juicy, flavorful burgers similar in taste to those I've enjoyed so much out West. A note: These burgers may not please kids, so plan on having some hot dogs or other kid-friendly food for the younger cowpokes.

1 pound lean ground beef
½ cup finely crumbled blue cheese (about 2 ounces)
½ teaspoon chopped garlic
½ teaspoon coarsely ground or crushed black pepper
½ teaspoon salt
¼ cup brandy
3 whole wheat hamburger buns

Combine the ground beef, blue cheese, garlic, pepper and salt; mix very well with your hands. Divide into 3 even portions, and shape each into a patty about 4½ inches across and ⅝ inch thick.

Heat a cast-iron skillet over medium-high heat for about 5 minutes (your kitchen needs to be well-ventilated to cook these indoors; you may also cook them on an outdoor range or hot plate). Add the burgers in a single layer. Cook 4 minutes on the first side. Reduce the heat slightly and flip the burgers; cook 4 to 5 minutes on the second side. Carefully add the brandy; the alcohol will cook off immediately, but be careful since there is a slight chance it will flame up. Cook until the brandy has completely cooked away; this will happen quite quickly. Serve the burgers on the buns; ketchup, sliced ripe tomatoes, thinly sliced onions or other condiments may be used, but are not really necessary since the burgers are extremely flavorful.

TORTILLA CHIP CASSEROLE

4 to 6 servings

If you're in the mood for something fast, tasty and comforting, with a little bit of kick to it, this easy casserole will fit the bill. I guarantee that you can find all the ingredients you need at even a small-town convenience store!

1 pound ground beef
1 cup chopped onion
1 envelope (1.25 ounces) taco seasoning mix
2½ cups crushed tortilla snack chips,* crushed into 1-inch pieces before measuring, divided
1 can (10¾ ounces) condensed cheddar cheese soup
½ cup salsa

Heat oven to 350°F. Lightly spray an 8- or 9-inch-square baking dish, or a wide, flat 2-quart casserole, with nonstick spray, or grease lightly; set aside. In medium skillet, brown ground beef over medium heat, stirring to break up. Add onion and cook, stirring occasionally, until onion is just tender. Drain excess grease if necessary. Add taco seasoning mix and ¾ cup water. Cook, stirring occasionally, about 5 minutes.

Sprinkle 2 cups of the crushed tortilla chips into the prepared baking dish. Top with the meat mixture. In mixing bowl or large measuring cup, combine condensed soup and salsa, stirring to blend. Spoon evenly over the meat mixture, spreading gently with the back of spoon to even out. Top with remaining ½ cup crushed tortilla chips. Bake, uncovered, until bubbly, about 40 minutes.

*This is about half of a 16-ounce bag; I use plain salted chips, but feel free to experiment with flavored chips if you like.

Optional add-ins for more flavor: *Add **one or two** of the following, as noted (some will also increase serving yield):*

- Sliced ripe or green olives, sprinkled over the meat mixture (before the cheese sauce)
- Sliced pickled jalapeño peppers, sprinkled over the meat mixture
- 1 can (15 ounces) drained black beans, sprinkled over the meat mixture
- 1½ cups thawed frozen or drained canned corn, sprinkled over the meat mixture
- ½ cup diced tomato (fresh, or drained canned), sprinkled over the cheese sauce
- 1 cup diced roasted red bell peppers (from a jar), sprinkled over the sauce

TIN CAN STEW

6 servings

It's hard to believe that such a tasty mix comes largely out of cans! If you can't find butter beans, feel free to substitute any canned white bean, or even lima beans. If you have any leftovers, you'll probably need to add a bit of water before reheating.

1 pound lean ground beef
¾ cup diced onion
1 can (16 ounces) baked beans
1 can (15½ ounces) butter beans, drained and lightly rinsed
1 can (14½ ounces) diced tomatoes with garlic and onion, undrained
1 cup water
¾ cup macaroni or small shell noodles (uncooked)
2 teaspoon chili powder blend
Shredded cheese for garnish, optional

In a small Dutch oven or large pot, cook ground beef and onion until meat is no longer pink and onion is tender, stirring frequently to break up. Drain if necessary. Add remaining ingredients except cheese, stirring well. Reduce heat to simmer and cover; cook, stirring occasionally, until macaroni is tender, about 25 minutes. Sprinkle with cheese before serving.

SLOW-SMOKED RIBS

2 or 3 servings per rack; can be doubled

This recipe requires some advance preparation, and you also must dedicate the better part of an afternoon to cooking the ribs. For barbecue fans, though, all the time spent is worth it for these succulent, toothsome ribs. A water smoker works best for this, but you can also use a covered kettle grill; see instructions below.

2 quarts apple cider, divided
¼ cup cider vinegar
½ cup packed brown sugar
2 tablespoons mixed pickling spices (from the spice aisle)
1 rack pork spareribs (about 3 pounds)

Dry rub:
3 tablespoons packed brown sugar
2 tablespoons freshly ground black pepper
2 tablespoons paprika
1 tablespoons salt
1 teaspoon onion powder
½ teaspoon garlic powder

In quart measuring cup or large bowl, combine about 3 cups of the cider with the vinegar, brown sugar and pickling spices. Stir until sugar is completely dissolved. Pour into a glass baking dish or bowl that is large enough to hold the ribs; add remaining cider and stir. Add ribs; cover and refrigerate about 24 hours, turning ribs several times.

The next day, remove ribs from the cider mixture; discard cider mixture. Rinse and dry the baking dish. Pat ribs dry with paper towels. Combine all dry-rub ingredients in bowl and mix very well. Sprinkle half the mixture over the ribs and rub in with your fingers; reserve remaining rub. Place ribs in the baking dish; cover and refrigerate about 24 hours.

On cooking day, soak a handful of hardwood or fruitwood chunks in a bucket of water for 2 or 3 hours. Prepare smoker (see page 271 for kettle grill instructions). Sprinkle remaining dry rub over ribs and rub in with your fingers. Toss several wood chunks onto the coals and place the ribs on the smoker rack. Cook 2½ to 3 hours, keeping smoker temperature at about 250°F (clip a candy thermometer into a wooden clothespin and put the tip into the vent hole at the top of the smoker if there isn't a built-in thermometer); add wood and additional coals every hour, or as needed. When done, ribs should be rich mahogany in color, and the meat should be pulling slightly away from the tips of the bones.

To smoke ribs in a covered kettle grill: This won't work with the mini kettle grills; you need a regular or oversized kettle grill to smoke a rack of ribs. Start a relatively small pile of charcoal briquets—perhaps 20 or 25 briquets—on one side of the grill, and let burn until they are covered with ash. Adjust the vents on the bottom so they are three-quarters closed. Position a disposable foil pan on the opposite side of the bottom of the grill, and fill it with water or beer. Toss several wood chunks onto the charcoal, then position the grate so the hole by the handle is directly above the pile of coals (this makes it easier to add additional wood and coals during cooking). Place the ribs on the grate over the water pan—in other words, away from the coals. Cover the grill, positioning the cover so the top vent is over the meat. Cook as directed above, adding additional charcoal and wood chunks as needed; it's best to light the additional briquets in a separate grill or chimney starter and let them burn until covered with ash before adding them to the main pile of briquets. Use a long-handled tongs to put the lit coals into the main grill, slipping them through the hole by the handle of the grate.

PICADILLO: CUBAN MEAT HASH

3 or 4 servings

This Cuban dish is fantastic with black beans and rice, or as the filling for warm, soft flour tortillas. For a truly authentic feast, fry up some slices of ripe plantain (a banana-like starchy fruit, commonly used as a side dish in Cuba).

¾ cup diced onion
1 green bell pepper, cored and diced
1 tablespoon lard or vegetable oil
1 pound ground or coarsely ground beef
1 teaspoon minced garlic
1 can (14½ ounces) whole tomatoes, undrained
1 teaspoon paprika
½ teaspoon crumbled dried oregano leaves
½ teaspoon ground cumin
½ cup chopped pimiento-stuffed Spanish green olives
2 tablespoons chopped raisins
2 tablespoons red wine vinegar

In large skillet, sauté onion and bell pepper in lard over medium heat, stirring frequently, until tender. Add ground beef and garlic; cook, stirring to break up meat, until meat is no longer pink. Crush the tomatoes into small pieces with your hands as you add them to the skillet. Add paprika, oregano and cumin. Cook, stirring frequently, until most of the liquid has cooked away but mixture is still moist, about 15 minutes. Add olives, raisins and vinegar to the skillet. Reduce heat to low and cook 15 minutes, stirring occasionally. Serve over hot cooked rice, with black beans on the side.

Grilled Pork Chops with Apple-Curry Topping

2 servings; easily doubled or tripled

Different and delicious! You may prepare the applesauce topping in advance and keep refrigerated until you're ready to grill; allow to sit at room temperature while you prepare the grill.

½ cup chopped onion
1 teaspoon curry powder blend
1 teaspoon butter or stick margarine
¼ cup applesauce (a single-serve container is just right)
1 tablespoon honey
2 boneless pork loin chops, about 1 inch thick
About 1 teaspoon soy sauce

In a small heavy-bottomed saucepan, cook onion and curry powder in the butter over medium heat, stirring frequently, until the onion is tender-crisp. Stir in applesauce; reduce heat to low and cook about 5 minutes, stirring frequently. Remove from heat; stir in honey.

Prepare medium-hot grill. Brush both sides of the pork chops with soy sauce, and place on grate over coals. Cook until first side is nicely marked, about 4 minutes. Turn chops and top each with equal portions of the applesauce mixture. Cover grill and cook until chops are just cooked through, 8 to 10 minutes longer.

HAM STEAK WITH FRUIT-MUSTARD GLAZE

2 or 3 servings

Look for pre-sliced ham steaks in the meat case. They're usually vacuum wrapped, so they're great for taking to the cabin because the wrap keeps them fresh for days, and prevents a mess in the cooler on the way to the cabin.

2 tablespoons peach or apricot preserves (the new "all-fruit" preserves are very good)
1 tablespoon Dijon mustard
1 teaspoon vegetable oil
¼ teaspoon minced fresh gingerroot, optional
1 ham steak, 1 to 1½ pounds

In a small bowl, combine the preserves, mustard, oil and gingerroot; mix well. Make small cuts at 1-inch intervals around the outer rind of the ham to prevent curling.

To cook in the broiler: Heat broiler; set rack about 6 inches from the heat. Place ham on broiling pan; broil about 3 minutes. Turn ham steak; broil about 3 minutes longer. Brush half the preserve mixture over the ham; broil about 3 minutes longer. Turn ham steak and brush with remaining preserve mixture. Broil 3 to 5 minutes longer, or until heated through and glazed.

To cook on the grill: Prepare medium-hot grill. Place ham steak on grate; cook about 4 minutes. Turn ham steak and brush half the preserve mixture over the ham. Cook about 4 minutes on second side, then turn ham steak and brush with remaining preserve mixture. Cook about 3 minutes longer, then turn and cook 3 to 5 minutes longer, or until heated through.

MIDWESTERN CRAB CAKES

6 servings

If your vacation spot isn't near the coast, it's pretty hard to get lump crabmeat except in cans, and that doesn't make good crab cakes. But imitation crab bits, also known as surimi, are easy to find in the refrigerator or freezer case at most supermarkets; they work surprisingly well in this easy recipe.

⅓ cup mayonnaise (reduced-fat works fine)
1 egg
½ teaspoon celery salt
A few drops of Tabasco sauce
1 pound imitation crab tidbits or sticks
1 cup fine bread crumbs, divided
½ cup finely chopped green pepper (about half of a medium pepper)
½ cup finely chopped onion (about a quarter of a medium onion)
¼ cup butter or stick margarine (half of a stick)

In mixing bowl, combine mayonnaise, egg, celery salt and Tabasco sauce; blend well with a fork. Use your fingers to shred the imitation crab into the mixing bowl; leave some crab in fairly large shreds, but the majority of the shreds should be about ⅛ inch wide (about the consistency of carrots or potatoes shredded on a standard box grater). Add ½ cup of the bread crumbs, and the green pepper and onion. Mix gently but thoroughly with your hands. Cover and refrigerate ½ hour.

Heat oven to 425°F. Place the butter into an 11x7x2-inch or 13x9x2-inch baking dish. Place the dish into the oven until the butter is melted and bubbly. Meanwhile, divide the crab mixture into 6 equal portions, then shape each into a patty 3 to 3½ inches across. Dip both sides into the remaining ½ cup bread crumbs. Arrange the crab cakes in the baking dish. Bake, uncovered, 10 minutes. Remove dish from oven and carefully flip each cake over. Return to the oven until crab cakes are nicely browned, about 5 minutes longer.

GRILLED FISH TACOS

4 servings; easily increased

I first had Fish Tacos at the landmark Seattle fish restaurant, Anthony's HomePort. They are served at many restaurants and tacquerias *along the West coast, all the way down to Mexico. This version is based on the one served at Anthony's. If this looks like a bit of work, don't worry; these are so delicious that it's absolutely worth it.*

Marinade:
½ cup dry white wine
3 tablespoons olive oil or vegetable oil
2 tablespoons freshly squeezed lemon juice (from about half of a lemon)
2 tablespoons minced fresh parsley
1 tablespoon snipped fresh chives
2 cloves garlic, coarsely chopped

1 pound boneless, skinless halibut or other firm fish steaks or fillets about ¾ inch thick, cut into 4 strips
¼ cup mayonnaise (not salad dressing)
¼ cup tomato-based salsa
1 cup thinly shredded mixed red and green cabbage, or packaged coleslaw mix
1 teaspoon salt
1 teaspoon cider or other vinegar
4 flour tortillas (10-inch diameter)
2 green onions, thinly sliced
2 tablespoons coarsely chopped cilantro leaves

In nonaluminum dish, combine all marinade ingredients and mix well. Add fish strips, turning to coat. Cover and refrigerate 1 to 2 hours (but no longer, or the texture of the fish will be affected), turning fish occasionally. Meanwhile, combine mayonnaise and salsa in a small bowl; stir to blend and refrigerate until needed. In medium mixing bowl, combine cabbage with salt and vinegar; stir gently. Let stand at room temperature 30 minutes, then drain, rinse briefly with cold water, and drain again. Keep refrigerated until needed.

Prepare medium-hot grill. Grill fish until nicely marked and just cooked through,* 3 to 4 minutes per side. To assemble tacos, place one piece of fish in the center of a flour tortilla. Top with one-quarter of the cabbage mixture and one-quarter of the salsa mixture. Sprinkle with green onion and cilantro, then roll up in the usual fashion.

*To hold the fish strips together during grilling, I place them on an inexpensive cake-cooling rack, which I top with another cake-cooling rack of the same size. I secure the edges together with wire twist-ties, and then place the entire rack on the grate of the grill for cooking.

Vegetables, Starches and Side Dishes

GRILLED MUSHROOMS ON BRUSCHETTA

4 servings

You can make this dish with regular white button mushrooms, which can be had at even most small-town grocery stores. But this dish is so delicious with specialty mushrooms that it's worth the effort needed to use them—even if it means porting them in the cooler from the big city. This mushroom dish is also excellent served without the bruschetta, as a side vegetable.

8 ounces mixed specialty mushrooms such as cremini, oyster, portabella or shiitake (use at least 2 varieties)
6 large fresh basil leaves, or ½ teaspoon crumbled dried
3 tablespoons olive oil
2 teaspoons freshly squeezed lemon juice
½ teaspoon kosher salt (tiny flakes), or ¼ teaspoon regular salt
A few grindings of black peper
A wedge of Parmesan or Romano cheese (not pre-shredded)
Piece of foil, 12 x 24 inches*
Bruschetta (page 279), without tomato topping

Clean mushrooms with damp paper towels. Quarter smaller mushrooms such as cremini or baby portabellas; cut larger mushrooms into similar-sized pieces. Place mushrooms in a large bowl. Roll up basil leaves into long cylinders, then slice thinly (this is called a chiffonade). Add basil strips, olive oil and lemon juice to the bowl with the mushrooms. Sprinkle with the salt and some freshly ground black pepper. Toss to mix, and let marinate at room temperature 15 to 30 minutes. While mushrooms marinate, use a vegetable peeler to shave about 3 tablespoons large shreds from the Parmesan; set aside.

Prepare medium-hot grill so it is ready at the end of the marinating time. Fold the foil in half, shiny side in, so you have a piece that is 12 x 12 inches. Roll up the edges slightly to form a small rim. Place the foil on the grate over the prepared coals. Transfer the mushroom mixture and juices to the foil. Cover the grill and cook, stirring the mushrooms occasionally, until mushrooms are tender, about 15 minutes. Spoon the mushrooms into a serving dish, then lift the foil from the grate and pour any remaining juices over the mushrooms. Cover and keep warm while you grill the bruschetta. When bruschetta are ready, toss the shaved Parmesan with the mushrooms, and spoon the mushroom mixture evenly over the bruschetta.

***Even easier:** Instead of making a grilling pan out of foil, use a disposable foil pie tin.

Bruschetta

Variable servings; easily tailored to make as much as you wish

Bruschetta has become rather trendy in the last few years, and there are many versions of it that are little more than bad toast dripping with oil. The method below is the classic way of preparing bruschetta. Try it once, and you'll be hooked. Note: Do not try to make this with soft-textured bread; it would fall apart during the application of the garlic. Chewy, rustic, country-style bread is what you want for this dish.

Firm-textured Italian or French bread, sliced about ¾ inch thick
Fresh peeled garlic cloves, cut in half (2 halves for every 2 slices of bread)
Extra-virgin olive oil (about ½ teaspoon per slice of bread)
Coarse kosher or sea salt (preferably), or plain salt

Arrange the bread in a single layer on a baking sheet, and allow it to dry out for an hour or so, turning once or twice; if the bread is slightly stale, you can skip this step.

Prepare medium grill. If you are grilling meat or another dish, cook that first, then grill the bruschetta when the meat is done. Charcoal will probably be about the right temperature by this point; if using propane, simply reduce the temperature a bit and allow the grill to cool slightly. Place the bread on the grate over the coals and grill until both sides are golden brown with a few char marks. Watch the bread carefully, as it can burn very quickly. When the bread is done, transfer it to a platter. Quickly rub each side of the bread with the cut side of the garlic. Brush each side lightly with olive oil (if you have one of those oil sprayers, it works great for bruschetta). Sprinkle lightly with salt, and serve hot.

Fresh Tomato Topping

Enough topping for 3 or 4 pieces of bruschetta; easily increased

1 medium-large vine-ripened tomato (don't bother making this with winter tomatoes, as they just do not have the flavor needed for this dish; instead, wait until late summer, when local tomatoes are at their best)
1 tablespoon chopped fresh basil leaves (not dried)
2 tablespoons extra-virgin olive oil

Remove seeds from a vine-ripe tomato (peel the tomato first if the skin is thick), then cut the tomato into ⅜-inch dice. Place in a mixing bowl. Roll up basil leaves into long cylinders, then slice thinly. Add basil strips and olive oil to tomatoes, stirring gently to combine. Let marinate at room temperature for about an hour. Sprinkle with salt and freshly ground black pepper to taste. Spoon over hot bruschetta and serve immediately.

OVEN-BROASTED POTATOES AND SQUASH

4 servings as written; easily adapted for any number of servings

These delicious vegetables are easy to tailor for the size of the crowd you're feeding and the meal that you're serving. Serve with roasted or grilled meats, or with a hearty salad and whole wheat bread for a vegetarian meal.

1½ pounds winter squash such as butternut or acorn
1¼ pounds potatoes (3 medium Yukon gold potatoes, or 2 large Idaho potatoes)
2 tablespoons olive oil or vegetable oil

Heat oven to 375°F. Peel squash; remove and discard seeds and soft center pulp. Cut into 2-inch chunks. Peel potatoes and cut into 2-inch chunks (for medium-sized potatoes, this will mean quartering the potatoes; larger baking potatoes may need to be cut into 6 or 8 pieces each). Place squash and potatoes in a single layer in a large baking pan. Drizzle with the oil, then toss well with a spoon to coat each piece with oil. If using a seasoning variation below, sprinkle the vegetables with the seasoning and toss well; otherwise, sprinkle generously with salt and pepper. Bake until the vegetables are almost tender when pierced with a fork, 35 to 45 minutes, stirring every 10 or 15 minutes with a large spoon. Raise oven temperature to 425°F and continue cooking an additional 15 minutes, or until potatoes are browned and crusty.

Variations:

- After tossing potatoes and squash with oil, season with one of the following:
  - -A generous tablespoon dry salad-dressing mix, such as Italian, cheese and garlic, or ranch flavor; don't add any additional salt or pepper
  - -½ teaspoon curry powder blend
  - -1 teaspoon Cajun-blend seasoning or other spicy seasoning blend
  - -1 teaspoon celery salt and ½ teaspoon onion or garlic salt; no additional salt or pepper
- Replace the potatoes with sweet potatoes or yams, peeled and cut into 2-inch chunks
- Add 8 to 10 whole, peeled cloves of garlic to the pan before putting into the oven (this works in combination with any of the other variations here)
- Just before removing from oven, sprinkle with ¼ cup grated Parmesan cheese, toss well with spoon and bake an additional 5 minutes
- Add 1 or 2 bell peppers, cored and cut into quarters, during the last 30 minutes of cooking

WISCONSIN SUNSHINE BROCCOLI SALAD

6 to 8 servings

You'll often see variations of this broccoli salad at deli counters, but it doesn't keep well enough to transport to the cabin. This is an easy-to-make version with a twist: Dried cranberries, or "craisins," are substituted for the more common raisins, adding a delightful tangy dimension to the salad. Also, the broccoli is briefly blanched, providing a nicer texture and color than the totally raw broccoli that is usually used.

8 cups fresh small broccoli florets (about 1 pound)
8 ounces sliced bacon, cut into ½-inch pieces
1 small red onion, very thinly sliced then cut into quarters
¾ cup roasted, salted sunflower nuts
¾ cup craisins (dried cranberries)

Dressing:

1 cup mayonnaise (reduced-fat mayo works fine, but don't use salad dressing)
¼ cup sugar
2 tablespoons vinegar

Heat a large pot of salted water to a vigorous boil. Add broccoli; when water returns to boiling, cook 30 seconds, then drain immediately and shower with cold water until completely cool (if you can, plunge the broccoli into a pot of ice water after draining and rinsing). Drain the broccoli very well in a colander for 15 minutes or so.

While the broccoli cools, combine dressing ingredients in a small bowl; set aside. Cook bacon over medium heat until crisp, stirring frequently. Drain well, discarding bacon drippings. Combine cooked bacon, onion, sunflower nuts and craisins in a very large bowl. When the broccoli has drained well, add to the bacon mixture and combine gently with your hands or a wooden spoon. Add the dressing mixture, stirring gently to combine. Cover and refrigerate 1 hour before serving.

Other substitution options or additions:

- Substitute ½ cup purchased pre-cooked crumbled bacon (from a jar, or sometimes found in the freezer case) for the fresh bacon
- Substitute slivered blanched almonds for the sunflower nuts
- Substitute raisins or chopped dried apricots for the craisins
- Add ½ to ¾ cup coarsely shredded cheddar cheese to the mixture before dressing
- Top with canned French-fried onions

MAKE-AHEAD LAYERED SALAD

4 to 6 servings

Assemble this easy salad early in the day and let it sit in the refrigerator; when suppertime rolls around, simply toss and serve. You can also assemble it the evening before, for a noon-time picnic.

Dressing:
⅓ cup mayonnaise or salad dressing (reduced-fat works fine)
⅓ cup sour cream (reduced-fat works fine)
2 teaspoons prepared mustard
¾ teaspoon seasoned salt or celery salt
2 teaspoons sugar if you are using mayonnaise for the dressing (don't add this if using salad dressing, which is sweeter than mayonnaise)

⅓ cup sliced celery (about 1 stalk)
3 or 4 green onions, sliced ⅛ inch thick
1 cup frozen peas, thawed
4 to 5 cups cut-up head lettuce (cut into 1-inch pieces before measuring)
1 cup shredded cheddar cheese (about 4 ounces)
¼ pound sliced bacon (about regular 6 slices), cooked crisp, drained and crumbled
2 small tomatoes, cut into ¾-inch pieces

In a large mixing or salad bowl, combine all dressing ingredients; mix very well with a fork (if using a clear glass bowl, the salad will be prettier if you mix the dressing in a separate bowl and then pour it into the bottom of the glass bowl). Layer celery, onion and peas over the dressing in the order given. Top with lettuce. Sprinkle the cheese evenly over the lettuce, then sprinkle with the bacon pieces. Arrange tomatoes attractively over the top. Cover tightly with plastic wrap or foil, and refrigerate 4 to 16 hours. Toss just before serving.

Variations:

- Add one or two of the following, in the position noted:
  - -⅓ cup sliced salad olives (stuffed green olives that have been sliced or cut up) or 1 drained can (2¼ ounces) sliced ripe olives; layer on top of the celery
  - -1 drained can (8 ounces) sliced water chestnuts; layer on top of the celery
  - -¼ cup diced green or red bell pepper; layer on top of the celery
  - -2 hard-cooked eggs, finely chopped; sprinkle over the lettuce
  - -½ cup roasted, salted sunflower nuts; sprinkle over the cheese

- Substitute 8 or 10 cherry tomatoes, cut in half, for the cut-up small tomatoes
- Add ½ teaspoon chopped fresh dill leaves to the dressing
- For a different presentation, arrange shredded cheese, bacon, tomatoes, and sliced ripe olives or chopped egg (if using), in 3 or 4 "stripes" across the top of the salad, rather than sprinkling them evenly over the top (or layering them into the salad)

MUSHROOMS IN FOIL

4 or 5 servings

Cook these on the grill, or bake in the oven, for an easy-and-delicious side dish.

1 pound fresh whole white mushrooms
A large piece of heavy-duty foil, or 2 pieces of regular foil*
1 tablespoon finely chopped garlic
1 tablespoon chopped fresh chives or parsley, optional
1 tablespoon butter, stick margarine or olive oil
1 teaspoon soy sauce or teriyaki sauce

If cooking on the grill, prepare medium grill; if baking, heat oven to 375°F. Wash mushrooms to remove any soil, and drain well; pat dry with paper towels. Place mushrooms in the center of the foil, shiny-side up. Sprinkle with the garlic and chives. Cut the butter into small pieces and dot evenly over the mushrooms (if using oil, drizzle it evenly over the mushrooms). Sprinkle the soy sauce evenly over the mushrooms. Seal the packet, using the "Drugstore Wrap" technique (page 284). Grill over medium coals, or bake in preheated oven, until mushrooms are very soft, 45 minutes to 1 hour; turn the packet over several times if grilling. Serve mushrooms with the cooking juices.

*16-inch-wide foil works best; you'll need a 16-inch square. If all you have is 12-inch-wide foil, use a piece that is about 22 inches long.

GRILLED ONIONS

Per 2 servings; easily doubled or tripled

Onions become sweet and tender when cooked with this method. These are great served with Perfect Grilled Chicken (page 154); place the onions on the hot side of the grill while the chicken is on the non-heated area; then, when you move the chicken to the hot area of the grill, transfer the onions to the non-heated area (timing for the onions isn't critical, so don't fuss too much about that).

1 large Spanish or Bermuda onion
2 pieces heavy-duty foil (12x16 inches each), or two 12x32-inch pieces of regular foil folded in half
1 tablespoon butter or margarine, softened
1 teaspoon beef or chicken bouillon granules
1 teaspoon crumbled dried basil or oregano leaves

Peel onion and cut off a bit of the root and blossom ends so each end is flat. Cut onion in half across the equator (not from top to bottom). Pull out a small amount of the center of the onion to form a small cup about 1 inch across; you may need to use a paring knife or grapefruit spoon to free the center of the onion. Place each onion in the center of a foil square (shiny-side up). Rub half the softened butter over the cut surface of each onion, letting any excess butter accumulate in the center cup. Divide the bouillon granules and oregano evenly between the 2 center cups.

Fold the foil together, using the following "Drugstore Wrap" technique:

1. Bring 2 edges of the foil together over the onion.
2. Fold the 2 edges together to make a channel about ½ inch wide.
3. Roll-and-fold the channel tightly until it is tight to the top of the onion.
4. Roll in each end tightly, making sure each end has at least 3 folds.

These can be prepared to this point in advance; refrigerate until you're ready to grill.

Prepare medium-hot grill. When ready, place onions, cut-side up, on the grate. Cook about 30 minutes, turning the foil packet over several times. To determine if the onions are done, press the sides in (use a potholder or oven mitt to protect your hand) as though squeezing an orange to check for ripeness; the onions should yield and feel slightly soft.

Tangy Sweet Potatoes with Bacon

3 or 4 servings

This is a change of pace from the usual candied sweet potatoes, and cooks in less than 45 minutes on the stovetop. It's great with grilled or roasted meat. You may substitute yams for the sweet potatoes.

1 pound sweet potatoes (about 2 medium)
¼ pound bacon (about 6 regular slices)
3 green onions, sliced ¼ inch thick
3 tablespoons cider vinegar
½ teaspoon salt
¼ teaspoon dry mustard powder, or ½ teaspoon prepared mustard
A pinch of crumbled dried thyme leaves, optional
Chopped fresh parsley for garnish, optional

Have ready a large pot of salted water. Peel potatoes and cut into quarters; cut each quarter into ¼-inch slices, adding to the pot of water as you slice (the potatoes will discolor if they sit on the cutting board after being sliced). When all potatoes have been added to the pot, heat to boiling and cook until potatoes are just tender.

While potatoes are cooking, cook the bacon in large nonaluminum skillet over medium heat until crisp. Transfer bacon to paper-towl-lined plate, and drain off all but 1 tablespoon drippings from the skillet. When potatoes are tender, drain well. Reheat the bacon drippings in the skillet over medium heat; add the drained potatoes and the green onion. Cook, stirring occasionally, until potatoes are lightly browned, about 5 minutes. Add vinegar, salt, mustard and thyme; crumble bacon and add to skillet. Cook until heated through, stirring frequently. Garnish with fresh chopped parsley.

WILD RICE SKILLET FRITTERS

4 fritters per cup of wild rice; make as much as you wish

This easy recipe can be altered to suit what you have on hand; some suggestions are listed below.

1 egg
2 tablespoons flour
1 tablespoon cream cheese-based dip or dressing, optional
¼ teaspoon salt
1 cup cooked, cooled wild rice
Vegetable oil for frying

In mixing bowl, beat together egg, flour, cream cheese and salt until smooth. Add wild rice and stir well to combine. Heat a scant ⅛ inch oil in a large skillet over medium-high heat. Spoon about ¼ cup of the rice mixture into the hot skillet, spreading out gently with a spoon to form a 3-inch patty. Repeat with remaining rice mixture, or until skillet is full; do not overcrowd. Cook until crispy and golden brown, then carefully flip and cook the second side. Transfer to paper-towl-lined plate and keep warm while you cook remaining fritters.

Variations:

- Stir 2 teaspoons grated onion or celery into the mixture with the wild rice
- Use a tablespoon or two of cold, leftover Artichoke Dip (page 261) in place of the cream cheese … excellent!
- Substitute bacon drippings for the vegetable oil, and/or add a bit of crumbled, crisp bacon to the mixture before frying
- Substitute celery salt or garlic salt for the plain salt
- Add ¼ teaspoon dry mustard powder to the egg mixture

EASY MUSHROOM RISOTTO

4 or 5 servings

For the most flavor, use cremini, oyster, portabella or other specialty mushrooms; however, the humble white button mushroom also works fine.

5 to 6 ounces fresh mushrooms, such as cremini
¼ cup butter (half of a stick), divided
3 tablespoons minced green onions (about 2 green onions)
2 to 2½ cups vegetable broth or chicken broth
¾ cup arborio rice*
½ cup dry sherry
3 tablespoons half-and-half or light cream
1 teaspoon salt

Clean and slice the mushrooms. In heavy-bottomed medium saucepan, melt 2 tablespoons of the butter over medium heat. Add the green onions and cook, stirring frequently, about 2 minutes. Add sliced mushrooms and cook, stirring occasionally, until mushrooms are tender, about 3 minutes longer. Transfer mushroom mixture, including any juices, to a bowl; set aside. In a separate pan, heat the broth to a gentle simmer; reduce heat and keep broth barely simmering throughout the cooking.

Return the mushroom saucepan to the heat to dry. Add remaining 2 tablespoons butter and melt over medium heat. Add rice and cook, stirring frequently, until rice is beginning to turn golden brown, about 3 minutes. Carefully add the sherry (it will steam vigorously, and could burn you if you are not ready for this); cook, stirring constantly, until the sherry has been absorbed by the rice. Add mushroom mixture and all juices to the rice; cook, stirring constantly, until the mushroom liquid has cooked away. Add broth one-half cup at a time, stirring constantly; cook until the liquid has been completely absorbed before adding more liquid. Continue cooking in this manner until the rice is tender with a slightly firm center; total cooking time will be about 20 minutes from the time you add the first batch of broth. When the rice is ready, stir in the half-and-half and salt, and cook 2 minutes longer.

*Arborio rice is a special short-grain rice used for risotto. You may substitute the short-grain rice used for paella (sometimes called paella rice), but do not use regular long-grain rice; it will not cook correctly in this dish.

Pasta Carbonara (with Bacon)

4 to 6 servings

Use top-quality durum pasta for this traditional, quick-cooking Italian dish; less-expensive brands get mushy. The eggs are cooked only by the heat of the pasta; if you are concerned about possible dangers of underdone egg, substitute 1/2 cup pasteurized egg product (like Egg Beaters) for the fresh eggs.

1 pound spaghetti, linguini or fettuccini (uncooked)
¼ pound thick-sliced bacon, cut into ½-inch lengths
2 eggs, lightly beaten; or ½ cup pasteurized egg substitute such as Egg Beaters
⅔ cup grated Romano or Parmesan cheese, plus additional for serving
A good grinding of black pepper

Heat a very large pot of salted water to boiling. Add pasta slowly, stirring constantly to prevent sticking. Cook, stirring very frequently at first and less often after a while, until the pasta is tender yet still has a firm bite. While the pasta is cooking, cook the bacon in a medium skillet over medium heat, stirring frequently, until crisp; set aside and keep warm.

When pasta is cooked, drain and quickly return the pasta to the pot. Add the eggs, and the bacon and drippings, stirring to coat the pasta evenly and set the egg. Stir in the Romano cheese; grind a good quantity of black pepper over the pasta and stir again. Serve with additional grated Romano.

GRILLED FLATBREAD

Variable servings; make as many as you wish

These slightly puffy breads are similar to a pita bread but without the pocket and are great warm or cold. This recipe is based on one developed by the good folks who make Rhodes frozen bread dough. The rolls can be thawed in a microwave in less than a minute, so this is a great last-minute recipe when you're grilling.

Rhodes frozen Texas Rolls*
A little olive oil or vegetable oil
Salt and pepper, optional

Thaw the rolls according to package directions. Rub a small amount of oil on a cutting board, plate or other work surface. Place one thawed roll on the cutting board and pat out with your fingers to form a 5-inch circle. Rub the top side lightly with a little more oil, then sprinkle lightly with salt and pepper if you wish. Place bread on a large plate, and repeat with remaining rolls.

Grill over medium heat, turning and rotating frequently, until breads are golden brown and nicely marked, about 5 minutes total. Watch carefully, as bread burns easily on the grill.

Variation:

Use a loaf of Rhodes frozen bread dough instead of the Texas Rolls. Thaw as directed (the loaf takes much longer to thaw, so this is not a quick recipe; however, it can be thawed unattended in the refrigerator or at room temperature). Cut the loaf into 8 equal pieces, and roll each into a smooth ball. Proceed as directed. This variation makes 8 flatbreads.

*You could, of course, also use homemade bread dough! Rise the dough once, then cut into 2-ounce pieces and proceed as directed.

GARLIC MASHED POTATOES

4 servings; easily increased

I like to boil the potatoes in their jackets, then peel them afterwards (or leave the peels on, depending on the texture I want). I think they come out less waterlogged this way. However, for faster cooking, cut the potatoes up—peeled, if you wish—into large chunks before boiling.

2 pounds small russet or Idaho potatoes
(you may also use Yukon gold, but do not use red potatoes)
1 cup whole milk
10 to 15 cloves garlic, peeled
3 tablespoons butter or margarine

Scrub potatoes well. Heat a large pot of water to boiling (there should be enough water to cover the potatoes by an inch). Add the potatoes and cook until just tender when poked with a fork, 20 to 30 minutes depending on size. In the meantime, combine the milk and garlic cloves in a small saucepan and heat just to boiling; reduce heat to very low and simmer 15 to 20 minutes, or until garlic is tender. Mash garlic in the milk with a potato masher; set aside. When potatoes are tender, drain and refresh with cold water. Slip off skins, or leave them on if you prefer. Mash to medium consistency with potato masher. Add butter, mashing to mix in. Add garlic-milk mixture and stir or mash until combined (if mixture is too dry, add a little more milk). Add salt and pepper to taste.

FRY BREAD

4 servings; easily increased or decreased

Traditional Native American fry bread is yeast bread dough that is flattened and fried, then eaten plain or topped with honey, powdered sugar or whatever you desire. This easy version uses frozen uncooked yeast rolls, and can be whipped up in less than 20 minutes, freezer to table, if you have a microwave to thaw the frozen dough. You can also thaw the frozen dough on the countertop, but it takes a bit longer.

4 pieces Rhodes frozen Texas Rolls,* or as many as you need
Vegetable oil for frying (about ¼ cup to start)

Thaw the rolls according to package directions. Rub a small amount of oil on a cutting board, plate or other work surface. Place one thawed roll on the cutting board and pat out with your fingers to form a 6- to 7-inch circle; form a ¾-inch hole in the center of the bread. Rub the top side lightly with a little more oil, then sprinkle lightly with salt if you wish. Place bread on a large plate, and repeat with remaining rolls.

Heat ¼ inch oil in heavy-bottomed skillet over barely medium heat until hot but not smoking. Add one dough round and fry until golden brown, about 45 seconds per side; if bread is cooking too quickly, reduce heat for subsequent pieces. Transfer to a paper-towl-lined plate and repeat with remaining dough rounds. Sprinkle with salt if serving with meats or vegetables; for a sweet breakfast treat, drizzle with honey or sprinkle with powdered sugar.

Variation:

Use a loaf of Rhodes frozen bread dough instead of the Texas Rolls. Thaw as directed (the loaf takes much longer to thaw, so this is not a quick recipe; however, it can be thawed unattended in the refrigerator or at room temperature). Cut the loaf into 8 equal pieces, and roll each into a smooth ball. Proceed as directed. This variation makes 8 fry breads.

*You could, of course, also use homemade bread dough! Rise the dough once, then cut into 2-ounce pieces and proceed as directed.

Desserts and Sweets

CROCK POT CARAMEL APPLES

4 servings

Serve these on a cool fall evening for dessert. Because all of the work is done in advance, they're great for the end of a hectic day.

4 large Granny Smith or other firm, tart apples (don't use Delicious apples)
¼ cup packed brown sugar
¼ cup raisins, optional
¼ cup butter or margarine (half of a stick)
8 individual square caramel candies, unwrapped
½ cup apple juice
Whipped cream or ice cream for serving, optional

Remove the core of each apple, leaving a layer at the bottom to serve as a cup. Pare off the peel on about the top half-inch of each apple. Place the apples in a crock pot. Into each cavity, place 1 tablespoon brown sugar, 1 tablespoon raisins, 1 tablespoon butter and 2 caramel candies. Pour the apple juice over the apples. Cover and cook on LOW heat 4 to 6 hours, or until the apples are tender. To serve, place an apple in a serving dish, spooning the juices from the crock pot evenly over the 4 apples; top with whipped cream, or place a scoop of ice cream alongside.

MONSTER COOKIES

About 48 3-inch cookies, or 24 6-inch cookies

Look in the typical community cookbook published recently, or on most internet cooking sites, and you'll find a version of this recipe. I have no idea where the original came from, unfortunately; all I can tell you is that the proportions below are supposedly one-quarter of the original. I have adapted the quantities and the method slightly, to bring it more in line with common kitchen measurements and practices. There is no flour in this recipe; this is not a mistake in printing!

½ cup butter or stick margarine (1 stick), softened
1 cup packed brown sugar
1 cup white sugar
3 eggs
1 jar (1 pound, 2 ounces) peanut butter, or about 2 cups; I use chunky peanut butter
2 teaspoons baking soda
1 teaspoon corn syrup
¼ teaspoon vanilla extract
4½ cups rolled oats (I use the regular variety, not the "one-minute" type; this amount is the majority of a 1-pound, 2-ounce box)
1 cup plain M&M's candies
1 cup chocolate chips

Heat oven to 350°F; lightly grease as many baking sheets as you have because you'll need all of them. In a large mixing bowl (and I do mean large), cream butter until light and fluffy. Add sugars and beat until well incorporated. Add eggs, peanut butter, baking soda, corn syrup and vanilla; beat well. Add rolled oats, M&M's and chocolate chips; stir with a wooden spoon just until well mixed.

Use an ice cream scoop to drop dough onto cookie sheets, pressing the scoop firmly against the side of the bowl to pack the dough firmly; keep 2 inches between scoops on the sheets (if you don't have an ice cream scoop, figure out something else that will give you about ¼ cup of dough at a time). Or, for a truly "monster" cookie, use ½ cup dough. Flatten the ball of dough slightly; the larger cookies should be flattened quite deliberately until the cookie is about 4½ or 5 inches across. Bake 12 to 15 minutes, or until edges are golden brown and the tops are beginning to color; centers will still be slightly soft. Cool 5 minutes on baking sheets, then transfer to wire racks to cool completely. If you don't want to bake all of this at once—it will take a number of batches—you may refrigerate some of the dough for a few days until you're ready to bake more.

Spiced Honey Pineapple Sundaes

4 servings

Definitely an adult dessert! The curry powder lends a sweet warmness that is a fabulous contrast to the cold ice cream; the slight tang of the dark rum really points up the mix of flavors.

1 can (8 ounces) pineapple slices packed in juice
1 tablespoon butter or margarine
⅓ cup honey
2 teaspoons curry powder blend
Pinch of salt
¼ cup dark rum
1 pint French vanilla ice cream
8 crisp ginger cookies

Drain pineapple juice, reserving 2 tablespoons; cut pineapple into 1-inch-wide chunks and set aside. In heavy-bottomed medium saucepan, melt the butter over medium-low heat. Add the honey, curry powder, salt and reserved pineapple juice; stir well to blend. Heat just to boiling; reduce heat and add pineapple chunks. Cook, stirring frequently, for about 5 minutes (you can do this in advance and set it aside at room temperature for an hour or so; heat gently before proceeding with the rest of the recipe). Remove the pan from the heat.

Place the rum in a small saucepan and heat gently over medium heat. Using a long-handled match and commonsense precautions, ignite rum and allow to burn until flames die out. Stir rum into warm pineapple mixture. Scoop ice cream into 4 individual serving dishes; divide pineapples and sauce evenly over ice cream (the sauce is soupy, and will start melting the ice cream; this is normal). Place 2 cookies alongside each mound of ice cream.

FRUIT JUBILEE

4 servings

Cherries Jubilee is an old-fashioned dessert that is as easy and delicious as ever. For the classic recipe, fresh Bing cherries are used. But fresh peaches or apricots are just as good. You may substitute canned dark cherries for the fresh Bing cherries, but don't try to make this with canned peaches or apricots; they are too soft.

1 pound fresh Bing cherries, peaches or apricots; or, 1 can (15½ ounces) pitted dark cherries in syrup
¼ cup complementary liqueur or cordial (Kirsch, cherry or other fruit cordial, etc.)
2 tablespoons butter
¼ to ⅓ cup sugar, depending on the sweetness of the fruit
1 tablespoon lemon, orange or other juice
¼ cup brandy, lemon-flavored rum or other 80-proof flavored liquor to complement the fruit (brandy, or Kirsch, is traditional)
1 pint French vanilla ice cream

Pit the fruit and cut up; cherries should be cut into halves, while peaches or apricots should be cut into wedges, then into 1-inch chunks. Combine fruit and liqueur in mixing bowl, stirring gently to combine. Cover and let stand at room temperature 30 minutes to several hours, stirring occasionally.

When you're ready to serve, melt the butter in a medium saucepan over low heat. Stir in sugar and lemon juice and cook over medium heat, stirring constantly, until sugar dissolves. Add fruit and liquid and cook, stirring frequently, until the mixture is syrupy, about 5 minutes. Place the brandy in a small saucepan and heat gently over medium heat. Using a long-handled match and commonsense precautions, ignite brandy and allow to burn until flames die out. Stir rum into warm fruit mixture. Scoop ice cream into 4 individual serving dishes; divide fruit and sauce evenly over ice cream. Serve immediately.

COOKIES-AND-CREAM FUDGE

36 pieces

Make a pan of this easy fudge on a rainy day when you're stuck indoors. Unlike traditional fudge, which requires a lot of tedious beating, this version uses marshmallows to provide the proper texture; the basic recipe comes from the folks at Carnation milk. I substituted cookies-and-cream candy bars for chocolate chips to make a unique, delicious white fudge.

2 tablespoons butter or stick margarine, plus additional for greasing pan
1 can (5 ounces) Carnation evaporated milk (not sweetened condensed)
1½ cups sugar
⅛ teaspoon salt
10½ ounces (1½ large bars) Hershey's Cookies-and-Cream bars, broken up
2 cups miniature marshmallows
½ cup chopped walnuts or pecans, optional

Butter an 8-inch-square baking dish; set aside. In a heavy-bottomed large saucepan, combine the 2 tablespoons butter with the evaporated milk, sugar and salt. Heat to a rolling boil over medium heat, stirring constantly. Boil about 5 minutes, stirring constantly; remove from heat. Stir in the cookies-and-cream bars and marshmallows. Continue stirring until the candy and marshmallows have completely melted and are well incorporated, about 1 minute. Stir in the walnuts. Pour into the prepared pan. Let cool 2 hours (if the weather is hot, cool the fudge in the refrigerator), then cut into 36 squares. Store in a covered container.

Beverages and Miscellaneous

HOT WINE PUNCH

6 to 8 servings

This recipe is from a hand-written recipe journal I've kept since my college days; when someone would give me a good recipe, I'd jot it down in the book. The original title I wrote on this one is "Bill's We've-Been-Skiing-All-Day-And-We're-Tired Hot Wine." I got it from a friend who later ended up becoming a professional chef.

2 cups cold water
3 Earl Grey or other tea bags
1 whole cinnamon stick
3 whole cloves
3 cups dry red wine such as burgundy or merlot
1 cup dark rum
1 small can (6 ounces) frozen orange juice concentrate, thawed
½ cup sugar

In large nonaluminum saucepan, heat water to boiling. Add tea bags, cinnamon and cloves and immediately remove from heat. Steep 5 minutes, then remove and discard tea bags. Add remaining ingredients, and heat over low heat about 15 minutes, stirring to dissolve sugar. Remove and discard cinnamon and cloves.

"RUSSIAN" TEA

About 30 servings

I have no idea why this tea is called Russian, but it's been that way since this recipe started being passed around in the '70s. It's good hot or iced.

1 cup instant tea (unsweetened)
1/3 cup powdered orange-flavored breakfast drink such as Tang
1/4 cup powdered lemonade mix
1/4 cup sugar
1/2 teaspoon cinnamon
1/4 teaspoon ground cloves

Combine all ingredients in a pint glass jar; cover tightly and shake to blend. For each serving, add a tablespoon (more or less to taste) to 1 cup boiling water or cold water. Stir well.

Make-Your-Own

Even though commercial versions are readily available for many of these, sometimes it's fun to experiment with making your own sauces and spice blends. Here are a few recipes you may enjoy trying. Some of these are best made at home, in advance, because they use hard-to-find ingredients; others can be made at the cabin on the spur of the moment, using ingredients that are readily available at even small-town markets.

SPIKED BARBECUE SAUCE

About 1 cup

½ cup tomato sauce
¼ cup bourbon
¼ cup soy sauce
2 tablespoons packed brown sugar
2 tablespoons orange juice concentrate, thawed
2 tablespoons Dijon mustard
2 tablespoons honey
1 tablespoon Worcestershire sauce

In small nonaluminum saucepan, combine all ingredients. Heat just to boiling over medium heat, then reduce heat and boil very gently for about 10 minutes, stirring occasionally. Cool and refrigerate until ready to use.

ROASTED PEPPERS

Roasted bell peppers—particularly red bell peppers—are used in Mediterranean cooking quite a bit. You can buy them in jars at large supermarkets, but they can be hard to find in small towns. Luckily, they're easy to make with these directions.

Place whole, washed peppers (bell or chili, any color you have) over the burner on a gas stove, or on a grate above hot coals. Roast until the skin is completely blackened, turning as necessary. Transfer to a paper bag, seal and let stand about 10 minutes; then, scrape off the charred skin, remove the stem and core, and cut up as desired. If you have an electric stove, char the peppers under the broiler, or pierce the stem end with a long-handled fork and toast them over a very hot burner.

South Carolina Mustard-Based Barbecue Sauce

About 1¼ cups

½ cup cider vinegar
⅓ cup yellow mustard
¼ cup white sugar
2 tablespoons packed brown sugar
1 teaspoon black pepper
½ teaspoon salt
¼ teaspoon Tabasco sauce
A good pinch of cayenne pepper
1 tablespoon butter or margarine

In small nonaluminum saucepan, combine vinegar, mustard, white sugar, brown sugar, black pepper, salt, Tabasco sauce and cayenne pepper. Heat just to boiling; reduce heat and simmer about 10 minutes, stirring occasionally. Remove from heat and stir in butter. Cool and refrigerate until ready to use.

Blackened Seasoning Mix

About ¼ cup

1 tablespoon paprika
2 teaspoons salt
2 teaspoons freshly ground black pepper
2 teaspoons dry mustard powder
2 teaspoons ground fennel seeds
1 teaspoon cayenne pepper
1 teaspoon onion powder
½ teaspoon garlic powder
½ teaspoon finely crumbled dried thyme leaves
½ teaspoon finely crumbled dried oregano leaves

Combine all ingredients, shaking or stirring to blend. Keep in a sealed glass jar.

SWEET-AND-SOUR SAUCE

About 1½ cups

¼ cup ketchup
¼ cup peanut oil
¼ cup seasoned rice vinegar*
3 tablespoons packed brown sugar
1 tablespoon light soy sauce
1 clove garlic, pressed or minced
½ cup pineapple juice
1 tablespoon cornstarch

In medium nonaluminum saucepan, combine ketchup, oil, vinegar, brown sugar, soy sauce and garlic. Heat to boiling over medium heat. Meanwhile, blend together pineapple juice and cornstarch in measuring cup or a small bowl. When ketchup mixture is boiling, add pineapple-juice mixture in a thin stream, stirring constantly. Cook, stirring constantly, until thickened and translucent. Cool and refrigerate until ready to use.

*Rice vinegar is found with the Asian specialty foods at large supermarkets. If you can't find it, substitute 1 tablespoon plus 1 teaspoon white vinegar, 2 teaspoons water and ¼ teaspoon sugar.

HOMEMADE OR SUBSTITUTE TERIYAKI SAUCE

About 1½ cups

1 cup soy sauce
¼ cup honey
2 tablespoons freshly squeezed lemon juice (from about half of a lemon)
½ teaspoon pressed or finely minced garlic

Combine all ingredients. Refrigerate for storage.

Winter

Table of Contents

Appetizers and Snacks

Main Dishes

Vegetables, Starches and Side Dishes

Maple Syrup: Sweet Water from the Earth

Ininaatig. The Ojibwa word for the maple tree sounds at once both simple and lyrical. It's an appropriate name for the tree that produces one of the world's simplest, yet finest, sugar products: maple syrup.

The Ojibwa (or Chippewa, as some say), and other indigenous peoples of the north central and northeastern U. S., learned many years before the coming of the white man to harvest the sap that flowed through maple trees in late winter. Lacking iron kettles, they boiled the sap in birchbark, clay or wood containers, or reduced it by placing hot rocks in with the sap. Alternately, they allowed the collected sap to partially freeze, repeatedly casting off the ice (which contains little sugar) until the mixture was concentrated enough to use. Whether refined by fire or by ice, the resulting maple sugar was precious fare; a family would process hundreds of pounds each year, packing it into molds for storage and transport.

Taken fresh from the tree, raw maple sap has a cleanness of taste that is remarkable. As the tree drinks from the earth, it filters the water through living wood, cleansing the water and imparting a subtly sweet, fresh taste (think of the sweet tang of freshly sawn lumber, mixed with the pure, fresh air of a springtime thaw). To approximate the taste, buy a pint of the finest natural spring water you can find. Mix a generous teaspoon of pure maple syrup with the water, and chill it until to about 35 degrees. Now, to fully appreciate the flavor of this brew, go outside on a crisp late-winter morning and chop a cartful of wood, then haul a few sloshing gallons of water a quarter-mile through the forest. When you're hot and thirsty, pull your maple water from the cooler and enjoy a long draught. That is what it's like to work in a sugarbush.

Sugaring is hard work. A maple tree of the proper variety will average about a gallon of sap per day during the sugaring season. It takes about 40 gallons of sap to make one gallon of finished maple syrup. If you had just one tree, it would take about a month and a half to gather enough sap for a gallon of syrup. Obviously, sugarers collect from many trees, not just one, but it still takes a great deal of effort and time to make a decent-sized batch of maple syrup.

Although there are over one hundred varieties of maple tree, only a handful produce the proper type and quantity of sap for serious harvesting. Prime among these is the aptly named sugar maple (*Acer saccharum*), whose leaves turn hot-poker-orange in the fall. The black maple (*Acer nigrum*) is also prized for the sugar content of its sap. Softer maples, such as the common silver maple (*Acer saccharinum*) and the red maple (*Acer rubrum*), yield sap with a lower sugar content, so it takes as much as 75 gallons of sap to produce a gallon of finished maple syrup.

Identifying these trees in the winter, when they are barren and leafless, is a skill that sugarers quickly develop. They look at the texture and color of the bark, and also study the growth habits of the trees. Side branches of a maple fork off the main branch in pairs, one directly opposite another, while other trees branch in a stairstep or staggered manner. Of course, another clue for the sugarer is to look for trees in the sugarbush which have been previously drilled, although this is not always infallible. I have some friends who have a sugarbush, and one year, someone mistakenly tapped a tree that was not a maple. Of course, it didn't produce, and they soon removed the tap. But the hole still remains to confuse them when they are going through the woods placing the taps each winter (and when they have friends helping them with the tapping chores, it is a sure bet that one of these well-meaning folks will tap into this tree "because it's been tapped before").

Modern-day metal taps (photo at left) are more efficient than the original cedar spouts used by the Indians, although these were surprisingly effective. Drills work better than primitive blades for making the hole where the spout will be pushed into the tree, and today's plastic collection bags keep out dirt, sticks and animals, making for an easier and cleaner harvest.

One aspect of sugaring hasn't changed much in the last hundred years: the boiling of the sap, which with few exceptions is still done over large, open-air fires. When the Indians received the first iron kettles from Europeans, they quickly replaced the birchbark containers and clay pots with the new *akik,* the trade kettle. Unlike the previous vessels, these could be put over a hot flame for the time required to reduce the sap. Similar large kettles are still in use today by many smaller sugarers, although some producers use specially constructed wide, stainless-steel troughs, which encourage more rapid reduction. In contrast, large commercial operations use gas-heated boiling vats with sophisticated controls.

Timing on the sap run varies somewhat from year to year, but it generally begins in late March. Indians used to watch for bald eagles, whose return to the North coincides with the beginning of the sap flow. Ideal conditions have days in the 40s, with nighttimes dropping to below-freezing.

Interestingly, sap doesn't flow on an extremely windy day; I've been told that this is a self-defense mechanism for the trees, ensuring that sap won't bleed out of a branch that may be broken in a big wind.

Once the trees are tapped, a collection device is placed below each tap. Buckets or cans are traditional, but modern sugarers often use sturdy plastic bags that attach to a metal hanger. Large-scale operations have that beat; they string a pipeline of flexible plastic tubing from tree to tree, with the tubing eventually emptying directly into the cooking vats. Smaller operations and individual producers, though, have the drudgery of moving from tree to tree, emptying the collected sap into a larger bucket, and moving to the next tree. The large buckets are then hauled through the woods to the fire area, where they will eventually be emptied into the boiling container.

I have pleasant memories from my college days of trudging through the Wisconsin woods helping friends who had a sugarbush. When an active boil is going on, the woods are filled with a sweet, fragrant haze of smoke, reminding me of pleasant times around a campfire (to be specific, it reminds me of frying bacon for a hearty camping breakfast). Friends are spread out through the forest, but since there are no leaves it's easy to catch a glimpse of the brightly colored parka of someone who is off chopping wood, or hauling a bucket. Work starts early in the day, so everyone is ready for a noontime hot dog roast, then it's back to work. It takes a lot of wood and many hours to boil the sap; this often goes on through the night and into the next morning. But it's a pleasant sort of work, as the stars wink through the clear night sky and the red eyes of curious nocturnal animals peer out from the woods.

Sap turns to syrup when its volume has been reduced sufficiently to form two beads at the same time off a metal spoon; if the beads drip alternately, the sap is not yet ready. As the sap reduces during cooking, it is transferred to smaller kettles to avoid burning. For the final transfer, the sap needs to be strained through thick felt pads, to remove the surprising amount of ash and other detritus that ends up in the sap as it cooks. Many small-volume sugarers do the final boiling on the kitchen stove, using stockpots.

If you have a few maple trees in your yard and want to try syruping on a very small scale, it's surprisingly easy to do. You'll need a tap and collection device for each tree. Perhaps you can beg or borrow a few from someone who has a good supply. You can also contact a sugar-supply house (try the Reynolds Sugar Bush company in Aniwa, Wisconsin 55408). Since a handful of trees will take a while to produce enough sap to cook, you'll have to store the sap until you've accumulated enough. A well-scrubbed 5-gallon food-grade pail works well for this. Keep it on the back porch or in an unheated garage until you're ready to boil.

Plan on doing the majority of the cooking outside over a propane burner or sturdy electric hot plate, unless you are also planning to remodel your kitchen afterward. Boiling this amount of sap releases a tremendous amount of water vapor into the air, and this can peel off wallpaper, stain painted walls and the ceiling, and add an undesirable amount of humidity to the entire house. A large stockpot works well for the first stages of boiling. I have one that holds three gallons, and this amount will make about a cup and a half of finished syrup. Once the sap has been reduced to about one-twelfth volume (in other words, three gallons of sap has been reduced to about one quart), you can transfer the sap to a heavy-bottomed saucepan and move it inside. You probably won't have impurities such as ash and wood chips in your "suburban sap," but you can strain it through several layers of cheesecloth as you transfer it to the saucepan to catch any small particles. Continue boiling the sap in the saucepan until it passes the spoon test (page 308). Once it's done, pour it into a sterilized glass canning jar. Let cool, keep it refrigerated, and enjoy it until it's all gone.

Here are a few suggestions for cooking with raw sap, as well as some full recipes that use finished syrup.

MAPLE-SWEETENED RICE

Substitute raw maple sap for the water when cooking white or brown rice. The rice will have a subtle maple flavor that is almost indefinable.

MAPLE-SAP TEA

Use raw maple sap to make hot tea. I prefer milder teas, such as Darjeeling, to stronger teas such as Irish Breakfast, which overwhelm the subtle maple flavor.

MAPLE-STEWED DUMPLINGS

If you're actually boiling maple sap for syrup, you can use the partially cooked sap to make these; otherwise, use finished syrup and dilute as indicated.

2 cups buttermilk baking mix such as Bisquick
⅔ cup milk
2 cups finished maple syrup, or 4 cups partially reduced maple sap
2 tablespoons butter
Heavy cream or whipped cream for serving, optional

To make the dumpling batter, combine biscuit mix and milk in a mixing bowl; stir until just combined.

To use finished syrup: In large saucepan, combine syrup, butter and 2 cups water and heat to boiling over medium heat. Drop the dumpling batter by spoonfuls into the boiling liquid. Cook at a gentle boil 5 minutes, then reduce heat, cover the pan and simmer 10 minutes longer. Serve warm, topped with a tablespoon or two of heavy cream or whipped cream.

To use partially reduced sap: When the sap is about half reduced, draw off 4 cups and strain if necessary. Heat the sap and butter to boiling in large saucepan over medium heat. Drop the dumpling batter by spoonfuls into the boiling sap. Cook at a gentle boil 5 minutes, then reduce heat, cover the pan and simmer 10 minutes longer. Serve warm, topped with a tablespoon or two of heavy cream or whipped cream.

Creamy Maple Breakfast Bake

6 to 8 servings

A friend told me about this easy breakfast dish, which is assembled the night before. It's similar to the breakfast casseroles on page 313, but it is sweet, not savory, because it contains no meat or vegetables.

1 loaf (1 pound) French or Italian bread, cut into ½-inch cubes, divided
8 ounces regular cream cheese, cut into ½-inch cubes
8 eggs, or equivalent in egg substitute such as Egg Beaters
2½ cups half-and-half or whole milk
½ cup real maple syrup
½ teaspoon salt
¼ cup sugar
1 teaspoon cinnamon

Spray a 9 x 13-inch baking dish with nonstick spray, or butter lightly. Distribute half the bread cubes in the dish. Top with the cream cheese cubes, distributing evenly; top the cream cheese evenly with the remaining bread. In large mixing bowl, beat together the eggs, half-and-half, maple syrup and salt until smooth. Pour the mixture evenly over the bread. Cover and refrigerate overnight.

Heat oven to 350°F. Combine sugar and cinnamon, then sprinkle over the bread. Bake until the top is golden brown and the center is set, 35 to 45 minutes. Let stand 10 minutes before serving.

FROZEN MAPLE MOUSSE

8 servings

It's hard to imagine that three ingredients make such a delicious dessert—and it's so easy to make! I don't know where the original recipe came from; it appeared in the Minneapolis Star-Tribune *in an article about "old recipe clippings" that we all save, and the author of the article didn't remember the source of the original clipping. In any case, it's a fabulous cabin dessert, and keeps for several days in the freezer.*

¾ cup real maple syrup
1 egg white
1 cup heavy cream

Chill a 1-quart mixing bowl in the freezer for 15 minutes. Heat the maple syrup in the microwave or on the stovetop until very hot but not boiling; keep warm. In a 2-quart mixing bowl, beat the egg white with an electric hand mixer until it begins to thicken. Slowly add the hot maple syrup, beating continuously; continue beating until the mixture is thick and shiny like a meringue, about 4 minutes.

Quickly rinse and dry the beaters. In the chilled bowl, beat the cream until stiff, incorporating as much air as possible while you whip; this will take 3 or 4 minutes. Gently fold the whipped cream into the egg-white mixture. Pour into a 1-quart mold (or, rinse and dry the mixing bowl you used for the cream, and pour the mixture into that) and freeze for at least 2 hours. Top with fruit, if desired.

Topping ideas:

The original clipping didn't say anything about this, but I find this dessert is delicious when topped with fresh fruit in a natural syrup (mix raspberries, blueberries, cut-up peaches or other soft fruit with a little sugar and maybe a splash of orange juice or sherry, then let stand for 30 minutes, stirring occasionally). I bet it would also be good with some sort of brandy-nut sauce, maybe heated and drizzled over the top or spooned over the plate before scooping the mousse on top. Use your imagination, and take advantage of the items in your pantry, to experiment with this simple dessert.

Breakfast and Brunch Dishes

LAYERED BREAKFAST CASSEROLE

8 to 12 servings

Assemble this the night before you need it, then refrigerate overnight. The next day, pop it in the oven for about an hour, and serve with fresh fruit for a perfect breakfast or brunch. Some folks serve this for an informal supper also; in that case, assemble the dish in the morning and refrigerate until an hour before suppertime.

This recipe is very versatile, and will work almost no matter what you put in it. The key is the egg-milk mixture, which holds everything together. The base layer should be some sort of starch; feel free to use bread, potatoes, English muffins or whatever you like (the list below gives you some suggestions). Don't worry about the bread getting soggy overnight; when it's baked, it's delicious.

Base layer: *Choose **one** of the following:*

- 6 to 8 slices bread (stale bread is fine), cut into 1-inch cubes or left whole
- 4 to 5 cups salad croutons or bread stuffing cubes, any flavor (about a 6-ounce package)
- 1 bag (2 pounds) frozen shredded or cubed hashbrowns
- 4 or 5 cups cooked rice (try brown-and-wild rice for a change)
- 4 English muffins, split into halves
- 4 to 5 cups cubed cooked potatoes

Spray a 9x13-inch dish with nonstick cooking spray, or butter lightly. Distribute the base layer evenly in the dish; if using bread slices or English muffins, arrange in even rows.

Meat and vegetable layer: *Choose **one meat** and **one or two vegetables** (if you prefer a meatless dish, simply add another vegetable):*

Meat:

- 12 ounces bulk sausage, such as Jimmy Dean's
- 12 ounces bacon, cut into ½-inch pieces
- 1 pound lean ground beef or turkey
- 8 ounces chopped shrimp or tiny shrimp
- 6 to 8 ounces flaked smoked salmon or other firm fish

continued

- 8 ounces shredded imitation crabmeat, or real crabmeat
- 2 cups diced ham, or cooked turkey or chicken
- 2 cups diced ring bologna or other cooked sausage

Vegetables:

- 8 ounces sliced fresh mushrooms, or 1 can (13¼ ounces) sliced mushrooms, drained
- 1 onion, coarsely chopped
- 2 stalks celery, thinly sliced
- 1 large green or red bell pepper, cored, then chopped
- 1½ cups leftover cooked broccoli or green beans
- 1 package (10 ounces) frozen chopped spinach, thawed and drained

In large skillet, cook sausage, bacon or ground meat over medium heat until cooked through; if using sausage or ground meat, stir frequently to break up. Drain excess fat if necessary. (If using crabmeat or another already-cooked meat, don't re-cook it; after the vegetables are cooked and scattered on the base layer, sprinkle the seafood or meat over the top, then proceed with the egg-milk mixture and the cheese.) Add any uncooked vegetables you are using to the skillet with the just-fried meat, and cook until vegetables are tender; canned or cooked leftover vegetables can simply be stirred in without further cooking. Sprinkle meat and vegetables evenly over base layer.

Egg-milk mixture: *Beat together in mixing bowl:*

6 eggs, or equivalent in egg substitute such as Egg Beaters
2 cups milk or half-and-half (or any combination you like of milk, skim milk, canned evaporated milk, half-and-half or cream)
½ teaspoon dry mustard powder or mixed herb blend, optional
1 teaspoon plain salt or seasoned salt

Pour the egg-milk mixture evenly over the meat and vegetables. Top evenly with ***one*** of the following:

- 8 ounces shredded cheese (about 2 cups)
- 8 ounces Velveeta cheese, cubed or sliced
- 6 ounces cheese "singles" slices (generally 8 slices)
- 1 can (10½ ounces) cheddar cheese soup, undiluted
- 1 jar (8 ounces) pasteurized process cheese sauce such as Cheez Whiz
- 1 can (10½ ounces) condensed cream of mushroom soup
- 1 package plain or flavored cream cheese (8 ounces), cubed

Cover baking dish with foil; refrigerate overnight or from 4 to 12 hours. When ready to bake, heat oven to 350°F (325°F for glass dish). Bake covered dish 45 minutes, then remove foil and continue baking until the cheese is melted and the edges are bubbly, about 15 minutes longer. Let stand 5 minutes before cutting into squares to serve.

For a smaller batch:

Use an 8 - or 9-inch-square baking dish, or a 2-quart casserole. Use about two-thirds of the ingredients listed above; here are typical measurements for a smaller recipe.

3 cups salad croutons or bread stuffing cubes
8 ounces bacon, cut into ½-inch pieces
½ large onion, chopped
1 can (7 ounces) sliced mushrooms, drained
4 eggs
1⅓ cups half-and-half
6 ounces shredded cheese (about 1½ cups)

CORNED BEEF OR OTHER HASH

4 servings

Use leftover corned beef, roast beef or smoked turkey to make a hearty breakfast, brunch or light supper dish. I like to serve a fried egg on top, and have plenty of ketchup, horseradish and Tabasco sauce on hand to dress it up.

4 pounds potatoes (about 2 medium russet potatoes, or about 5 red potatoes)
About 1 tablespoon vegetable oil
2 cups chopped or finely diced leftover corned beef or other meat (about ¾ pound)
1 small onion, diced
¼ cup chicken broth or water
1 teaspoon grainy mustard or Dijon mustard, or ½ teaspoon dry mustard powder
½ teaspoon crumbled dried thyme leaves, optional
3 eggs, optional
Ketchup, horseradish, Tabasco sauce for serving, optional

Peel and dice potatoes. In large cast-iron or other heavy-bottomed skillet, heat oil over medium heat; add potatoes and cook, stirring occasionally, until potatoes are golden brown on all sides. Don't rush this step; it usually takes me about 15 minutes to do this. If you turn the potatoes before they've had the chance to brown, they will stick to the pan; however, if they stick to the pan even after they are browned, add a little more oil. When potatoes are nicely browned, add the meat and onion; cook, stirring occasionally, until onions are just tender. Stir together the broth, mustard and thyme; pour into the skillet, stirring to loosen any crusty bits from the bottom of the skillet. Let the hash cook until it is beginning to crisp up on the bottom, then stir and continue cooking until the bottom becomes crispy again. Just before the hash is ready, fry the eggs over-easy. Salt and pepper the hash generously, divide among 4 plates, and top each portion with a fried egg. Serve with ketchup, horseradish and Tabasco sauce on the side.

DOUBLE-DECKER OVEN OMELETTE

2 or 4 servings per omelette

Serve this fancy omelette for a special breakfast or brunch, or a light supper. It's easier to make than a traditional stovetop omelette, but does require a bit of dexterity for the rolling. Word to the wise: Even if it doesn't roll up perfectly, it will still taste great!

Ingredient	2-person omelette	4-person omelette
Nonstick spray or other fat	As needed	As needed
Eggs	3	5
Flour	1 teaspoon	2 teaspoons
Filling from list below	½ to ⅔ cup	¾ to 1 cup
Starch from list below	⅔ cup	1 cup
Shredded cheese	½ cup	1 cup
Baking dish*	11 x 7 x 1½ inch	13 x 9 x 2-inch

*Quality nonstick, pyrex or heavyweight stainless-steel dishes work best. If you use a thin aluminum dish, it may warp in the oven and cause the eggs to be uneven.

Note: The filling and starch need to be hot when you assemble the omelette. If you're frying potatoes from scratch for this dish, cook them just before you put the eggs in the oven, and keep them warm until ready to stuff the omelette; already-cooked ingredients or leftovers can be reheated while the eggs are baking. If you're making a quick vegetable-and-ham filling (see page 318), you will have enough time to sauté these ingredients while the eggs are baking. See a few suggestions below the filling and starch lists (page 318) to give you ideas, but feel free to use whatever you have in the refrigerator; this is a great way to use up dabs of leftovers.

Heat oven to 350°F. Spray baking dish generously with nonstick spray, or grease liberally with butter, margarine or oil. In mixing bowl, combine eggs, flour, and salt and pepper to taste, and beat very well. Pour egg mixture into pan. Bake until eggs are just set, about 10 minutes. While the eggs are baking, heat the chosen filling and starch ingredients.

When eggs are set, place the dish on hot pads with one of the narrow ends facing you. Mentally divide the eggs into 4 sections parallel to the short end; don't actually cut the eggs, just visualize four

continued

equal strips. Working quickly, spread the heated filling evenly in the second section away from you, keeping the first section clear. Spread the heated starch over the third section, leaving a ½-inch gap between the filling and the starch. Sprinkle the cheese evenly over the filling and starch. Use 2 spatulas to gently lift and roll the first section of egg over onto the second section, covering the filling; press it gently to compact. Lift and roll the stuffed section onto the third section (there will be a layer of egg between the filling and the starch), then lift and roll one more time so the stuffed sections end up on top of the fourth section, which is just plain egg.

If you like, you may sprinkle appropriate garnish (chopped parsley, heated salsa or hot cheese sauce are a few ideas) over the folded omelette. To serve, cut the rolled omelette into sections as though slicing a jelly roll.

Filling ideas: *Choose **one** of the following:*

- Canned or homemade chili
- Leftover seasoned meat used for tacos or burritos
- Leftover stir-fry (if pieces are large, cut into ½-inch or smaller chunks)
- Quick vegetable-and-ham filling: sauté ¼ cup (2-person omelette) or ⅓ cup (4-person omelette) each chopped onion, bell pepper and diced ham in a little butter or margarine until vegetables are tender
- Leftover sloppy joe mix or similar meat mixture
- Leftover creamed chicken or à la king-type mixture

Starch ideas: *Choose **one** of the following:*

- Hashbrowns or fried diced potatoes
- Leftover scalloped or au gratin potatoes (use only half the amount of cheese called for above, and sprinkle it only over the filling, if using au gratin potatoes)
- Leftover Spanish-style rice
- Leftover Chinese-style fried rice
- Leftover black or pinto beans, partially mashed (not completely puréed; best if there is a fair amount of texture)

CHILI-AND-POTATO OMELETTE

Use chili for the stuffing, and hashbrowns or fried diced potatoes for the starch. Monterey/Colby blend cheese is a good choice for this omelette.

CHINESE OMELETTE

Use leftover stir-fry (one with a fair amount of bean sprouts is particularly good) for the filling, and leftover fried rice for the starch. Top with some heated sweet-and-sour sauce if you have some.

MEXICAN-STYLE OMELETTE

Use leftover seasoned taco meat for the filling, and Spanish rice or partially mashed black or pinto beans. Top with heated salsa and a bit more shredded cheese or sour cream.

CORN PANCAKES

4 to 6 servings

For a change of pace at brunch, try these corn pancakes instead of the usual. They're great with Honey Butter (page 33).

1½ cups milk
2 eggs
3 tablespoons butter or margarine, melted
1½ cups buttermilk baking mix such as Bisquick
½ cup cornmeal
1 can (8 ounces) "fiesta" corn (with red and green peppers) or plain corn, drained
Vegetable oil for greasing griddle or skillet

In mixing bowl, beat together milk and eggs with a fork. Stir in melted butter. Add biscuit mix and cornmeal; stir gently until well mixed. Stir in drained corn. Heat a griddle or heavy-bottomed large skillet until a drop of water dances on the surface (if you're using an electric, temperature-controlled griddle or skillet, heat to 375°F). When griddle is hot, grease lightly; stir the batter to distribute the corn evenly and ladle the batter onto the skillet to form pancakes; each pancake should use just under ¼ cup batter. Cook until the top side bubbles and the edges are firm, then flip and cook the second side until golden brown. Keep warm while you fry the remaining pancakes.

Southern Country-Style Breakfast

4 to 6 servings

Talk about good! This hearty breakfast pairs cornmeal mush, or Couch-Couch, as it is called in Louisiana, with fried ham and Red-Eye Gravy. It's a full breakfast or brunch that is sure to get your day off to a good start.

Couch-Couch

1½ cups cornmeal, preferably stone-ground
¾ teaspoon salt
½ teaspoon baking powder
1½ cups milk (2% or skim milk work fine)
¼ cup bacon drippings, butter, margarine or vegetable oil

In a mixing bowl, combine cornmeal, salt and baking powder, stirring to mix well. Add the milk and stir well to combine. In a large heavy-bottomed skillet, heat the bacon drippings over medium heat until hot but not smoking. Add the cornmeal mixture and cook until a nice crust forms on the bottom, about 5 minutes. Stir well and reduce the heat to medium-low. Cover and cook, stirring often, for 15 to 20 minutes longer. This is traditionally served with cane syrup, or milk and sugar; in this version, it is served with Red-Eye Gravy (below).

Fried Ham with Red-Eye Gravy

Country-style ham, which is very salty and has a unique flavor, is the ham traditionally used for this treatment, but you may use slices of high-quality "real" smoked ham in its place. Do not, however, use processed or water-added ham; it doesn't have enough flavor, and also leaks too much water during cooking.

Thickly sliced ham for 4 to 6 people
2 tablespoons butter or margarine
2 tablespoons packed brown sugar
½ cup strong black coffee

In large skillet, fry the ham in the butter over medium heat until it is nicely browned, turning several times. Remove ham from pan, reserving drippings; set ham aside and keep warm. Reduce heat to low and add brown sugar to drippings in skillet, stirring constantly until sugar melts. Add coffee; simmer 5 minutes, stirring occasionally. Spoon gravy over the Couch-Couch; accompany with fried ham (and a fried egg, if you wish).

INDIVIDUAL QUICHE CUPS

10 servings

Perfect brunch fare; toss together some fresh fruit salad or melon wedges and beverages, and let the people help themselves.

1 small tube (10.8 ounces/5 biscuits) large refrigerated flaky biscuits, such as Pillsbury Grands!
1 cup whole milk
3 eggs
½ teaspoon salt
1 cup shredded cheddar or other cheese

Heat oven to 375°F. Spray a 12-cup muffin pan (or two 6-cup muffin pans) with nonstick spray. Cut each biscuit into 2 thinner rounds using a serrated knife. Gently stretch and pat each round into a slightly larger circle, then press evenly in the bottom and up the sides of a muffin cup.

In mixing bowl, beat milk, eggs and salt together until smooth. Divide the milk mixture evenly between the muffin cups, filling about three-quarters full. Divide cheese evenly among cups, sprinkling it on top of the egg mixture; each cup will get about a tablespoon of cheese. Fill each of the 2 empty cups half-full with water to prevent scorching. Bake until egg is just set and biscuit edges are rich golden brown, 25 to 30 minutes. Cool 10 minutes before serving.

Variations:

Prepare one of the following, and then sprinkle it in the bottom of the biscuit-lined muffin cups before adding the egg mixture (divide the mixture evenly among the cups):

- 3 strips bacon, cooked crisp, drained and crumbled
- ½ cup diced or thinly sliced mushrooms, sautéed in a little butter until tender
- ½ cup thinly sliced or chopped green onion

CREAMY PEACH MUFFIN CUPS

10 servings

These are similar to the quiche cups on the facing page, but feature a creamy, slightly sweet cheese mixture instead of the custard.

1 small tube (10.8 ounces/5 biscuits) large refrigerated flaky biscuits, such as Pillsbury Grands!
1 can (8½ ounce "snack size") sliced peaches in heavy syrup
1 container (8 ounces) honey-nut cream cheese
1 egg

Heat oven to 375°F. Spray a 12-cup muffin pan (or two 6-cup muffin pans) with nonstick spray. Cut each biscuit into 2 thinner rounds using a serrated knife. Gently stretch and pat each round into a slightly larger circle, then press evenly in the bottom and up the sides of a muffin cup.

With fork, transfer peach slices to a plate and cut into ¾-inch chunks; reserve syrup in can. Divide peaches evenly among biscuit-lined muffin cups. In mixing bowl, beat cream cheese and egg with electric mixer or crank-operated eggbeater until creamy (you could use a fork in a pinch; just be sure to beat thoroughly so egg is well incorporated into the cream cheese). Spoon 2 tablespoons cream-cheese mixture into muffin cups, covering peach slices completely. Drizzle ½ teaspoon reserved peach syrup over the mixture in each muffin cup. Fill each of the 2 empty muffin cups half-full with water to prevent scorching. Bake until cream-cheese mixture is cracked and just firm to the touch, and muffin edges are rich golden brown, 15 to 20 minutes. Cool 15 minutes before serving.

Variation:

Substitute a container of plain cream cheese for the honey-nut cream cheese. Add 1 tablespoon reserved peach syrup to the cream cheese when beating with the egg.

Light Meals, Lunch Dishes and Soup

MEXICAN STACKED PIZZA

2 servings; easily doubled or tripled

If you like, you can make up a big batch of this seasoned meat mixture and keep it in the refrigerator for quick burritos or tacos.

Seasoning mix:
2 tablespoons flour
1 tablespoon chili powder blend
1 teaspoon sugar
½ teaspoon crumbled dried oregano leaves, optional
¼ teaspoon salt
¼ teaspoon garlic powder, optional

½ pound lean ground beef
½ cup refried beans (about half of a 16-ounce can)
Oil or shortening for frying (about ½ cup)
4 flour tortillas (8-inch diameter)
1 cup shredded colby-Jack cheese
¼ cup salsa
3 to 4 tablespoons sliced ripe olives
2 green onions, thinly sliced, or 2 tablespoons chopped red or yellow onion
1 small tomato, diced, optional
½ cup shredded lettuce
Sour cream or yogurt for garnish, optional

Combine seasoning mix in large mixing bowl. Add ground beef and a tablespoon cold water, then mix very well with your hands. Set aside for about 15 minutes, unless you're really in a hurry. Meanwhile, heat oven to 375°F. Heat the refried beans in microwave or on the stovetop, adding a little water if they are too thick. Keep warm.

Line a cookie sheet with paper towels. Heat about ¼ inch oil in a large skillet over medium-high heat. Carefully add 1 tortilla and cook about 15 seconds per side, poking any large bubbles in the tortilla and pressing with a spatula. Transfer the fried tortilla to the cookie sheet while you fry the remaining tortillas one at a time.

Drain off all but a tablespoon or so of the oil from the skillet. Add the seasoned ground beef and cook over medium heat, stirring frequently to break up as small as possible.

Spread half the refried beans on each of 2 tortillas, placing them on the cookie sheet (remove the paper towels first!). Top each with half the meat mixture, then sprinkle each with about 2 tablespoons shredded cheese. Top each with another fried tortilla. Spread each evenly with 2 tablespoons salsa. Divide the olives and green onions over the 2 pizzas, then divide the remaining cheese evenly over both. Top each pizza with half the tomato. Bake about 10 minutes, or until hot and the cheese is melted. Top with shredded lettuce, and sour cream if using, before serving.

Even easier: Substitute ½ of a package (1.25 ounces) taco seasoning mix for the homemade seasoning mix in the recipe.

BAKED ITALIAN SANDWICH LOAF (STROMBOLI)

5 to 7 servings

This takes a bit of time to make, but most of it is rising or baking time. The stromboli is great served hot; add a side salad and fresh fruit for a complete meal. Wrap the cooled stromboli in foil and refrigerate; snackers can easily cut off a strip to eat cold or quickly warm in a toaster oven or microwave.

1 loaf (1 pound) frozen yeast bread dough, or equivalent in homemade dough
8 ounces sliced mushrooms
1 cup mixed sliced bell peppers and onion (you can buy frozen stir-fry peppers–yellow, red and green bell peppers with onions; or, cut up your own)
1 teaspoon minced garlic
2 teaspoons olive oil or vegetable oil
¼ cup prepared pesto, or 4 teaspoons olive oil mixed with 1 tablespoon crumbled dried basil leaves
4 to 5 ounces thinly sliced ham
1 cup (4 ounces) shredded mozzarella cheese
2 ounces thinly sliced pepperoni
Prepared spaghetti sauce for dipping, optional

Thaw bread dough and allow to rise once as directed on wrapper; this usually takes 5 to 7 hours at room temperature. When dough is ready, punch it down and let it rest while you prepare the vegetables. Sauté mushrooms, pepper/onion mixture and garlic in oil over medium heat until tender, stirring frequently. Set aside to cool. While vegetables are cooling, roll the bread dough on a lightly floured board to a 10x14-inch rectangle, with one of the wide edges facing you. Spread the pesto evenly over the bread, keeping 1 inch on each of the sides and 3 inches at the long back edge clear of pesto. Arrange the ham slices evenly over the pesto, keeping the sides and back edge clear as you did with the pesto. Sprinkle the cheese evenly over the ham; top the cheese evenly with the pepperoni. Spread the cooled vegetables over the pepperoni, always keeping the sides and back edge clear. Roll the covered bread up, starting with the long edge that is facing you. When the loaf is completely rolled up, tuck any stray vegetables back into the center so the sides and back edge are clear, then pinch the back edge together very well to seal. Pinch the sides together as well, and place the roll, seam-side down, on a lightly greased baking sheet. Cover with a clean towel and allow to rise about 1½ hours, or until nearly double. Bake at 350°F for 45 minutes; loaf should be nicely browned. Cool at least 15 minutes before slicing into serving pieces. If you like, have a bowl of warmed spaghetti sauce to dip the slices into. Refrigerate leftover loaf.

Sandwich Buffet

When you've got a crowd to feed, a Sandwich Bbuffet is an easy solution. A quick trip to the deli counter will provide most of the ingredients, and even finicky eaters can put together a concoction to suit their tastes, if you offer a good variety of items.

You'll need a couple of big platters (maybe you can borrow one from the neighbors), a big basket for bread, several bowls and serving spoons for side salads, and individual plates. A pair of tongs is nice for lifting slices of meat or cheese from the trays, but you can provide a few forks for that purpose instead. Cutting boards also work well in place of platters. For a less-fancy presentation, press baking sheets into service as platters; or, you could even cover pieces of corrugated cardboard or wood with foil. If you have room in your refrigerator, prepare the platters in advance and cover with plastic wrap; keep refrigerated until serving time.

All the fixings should be ready to go. You don't want individuals to be slicing cheese or other foods at the buffet. Arrange the buffet in a logical order. The first thing the diner needs is a plate, so start the line there. Next to that, put a big basket of bread (for a nice touch, line the basket with a pretty napkin) so they can start building the sandwich from the base up. Condiments such as mustard are next in line, followed by the meats, cheeses and any other fillings. If you're offering vegetable toppers, they are the next order of business, along with pickles, olives and other preserved vegetables. Potato salad or other accompaniments are added to the plate after the sandwich is built, and the last things in line are forks and napkins. To save space, place the forks in a large, heavy glass, or for a fun accent, use an old-fashioned canning jar.

As a rough guide, plan on 3 ounces of meat, 1 ounce of cheese, and 3 slices of bread (or equivalent in non-sliced bread, such as buns or pitas) per person. A pound of potato or macaroni salad should provide 4 servings; if you're serving a tossed salad, plan on ¾ cup per person. Paper plates and plastic forks make for easy cleanup. One last note: Don't leave the ingredients out on the counter for more than an hour. You don't want to serve up a dose of food poisoning along with your sandwiches!

Here are some items to consider for your Sandwich Buffet, in the order they should be arranged. Choose as many as you like to suit your tastes and the number of guests.

Breads

- White, wheat, pumpernickel, sourdough, etc., slices
- Croissants, sliced horizontally into halves
- Hamburger-type buns or hoagy buns

continued

- French or Italian bread, sliced horizontally into halves, then cut into 3-inch lengths
- Bagels, sliced horizontally into halves
- Pita breads, cut into halves and carefully opened

Condiments

- Yellow mustard, plus Dijon or grainy mustard for variety
- Mayonnaise or salad dressing such as Miracle Whip
- Sandwich spread (sold in jars by the mustard; it is basically salad dressing with pickle relish mixed in)
- Softened butter or margarine, or tub margarine
- Vinaigrette, if you are offering French bread as one of the choices
- Prepared pesto

Thinly sliced meats

- Ham
- Chicken or turkey
- Corned beef or pastrami
- Roast beef
- Tongue
- Salami
- Mortadella (authentic Italian bologna), or regular bologna if kids are present

Thinly sliced cheeses

- Monterey Jack, pepper-Jack or Muenster cheese
- Cheddar
- American
- Colby or Colby-Jack

Other fillings

- Chicken salad (pages 34–37)
- Tuna salad or ham salad
- Hummus spread

Vegetables

- Pickle slices or spears (dill and sweet, if you can)

- Black or green olives
- Pickled peppers or pepperoncini peppers
- Sliced pickled jalapeño peppers or banana peppers
- Sliced bell pepper rings (remove the seeds)
- Thinly sliced red onion
- Thinly sliced tomatoes
- Crisp lettuce, shredded or broken into bread-sized pieces

Salads and side dishes

- Potato salad (pages 187–192)
- Macaroni salad
- Coleslaw (pages 80, 365)
- Mixed marinated vegetables (pages 77, 362)
- Tabbouleh Salad (page 40)
- Potato chips, corn chips

ITALIAN BEEF SANDWICHES WITH DELI BEEF

4 or 5 servings

Sliced roast beef from the deli makes this a hassle-free recipe.

1 small onion, cut in half from top to bottom and thinly sliced
1 red or green bell pepper, cored and cut into strips (for color and flavor, use half red and half green bell pepper)
1 stalk celery, thinly sliced (about ⅓ cup), optional
4 cloves garlic, thinly sliced
2 cans (10½ ounces each) condensed beef broth or consommé
1 tablespoon dried Italian herb blend (or make your own mix from oregano, basil, marjoram, rosemary and thyme)
¼ teaspoon crushed dried hot red pepper flakes
1 pound thinly sliced roast beef
Individual-sized sub-type rolls
¼ pound sliced provolone or other mild cheese

This version is written for a crock pot, but you can also prepare this on the stovetop; see the variation below. Combine onion, bell pepper, celery, garlic, undiluted beef broth, herb blend and hot pepper flakes in crock pot; stir well. If roast beef slices are large, cut them in half. Separate roast beef slices and add them to the pot; stir well. Cover crock pot and turn to HIGH. Cook 1 hour, then stir well. Re-cover and continue cooking on HIGH for 1 hour longer. At this point, the meat is ready to serve; if you like, you may turn the crock pot to LOW and leave it for up to 5 hours. (You may also cook entirely on the LOW setting; allow 6 to 8 hours total cooking time.)

When ready to serve, slit the rolls almost in half and pull out some of the soft interior; reserve this soft bread for other uses such as bread crumbs or croutons. For extra crispiness, place the opened rolls on a baking sheet and bake at 375°F for 5 to 10 minutes; this step may be omitted, but the sandwiches will be softer. For each serving, spoon sliced meat, vegetables and juices over a roll; top with sliced cheese.

Variation:

To cook this on the stovetop, combine ingredients as noted above in large pot. Cover and heat just to boiling over medium-high heat. Reduce heat to a gentle simmer and cook, stirring occasionally, for 2 hours; if too much liquid cooks away, add a bit of water or additional beef broth as needed to come about halfway up the beef. Assemble sandwiches as directed.

Cobb Salad

4 servings

For an even prettier presentation, make individual Cobb salads by arranging the ingredients as listed on individual serving plates. A hearty vinaigrette dressing is traditional with Cobb salad, but some people prefer chunky blue cheese dressing.

1 head romaine lettuce, washed, dried and torn into bite-sized pieces
1½ cups cubed boneless smoked turkey (cut into ¾-inch cubes before measuring)
1½ cups cubed ham (cut into ¾-inch cubes before measuring)
3 ounces crumbled blue cheese (about ¾ cup)
¼ pound bacon (about 6 slices), cooked crisp, drained and crumbled
2 hard-cooked eggs, cut into small dice
2 ripe tomatoes, cut into ½-inch cubes
1 ripe avocado, peeled and diced, optional
Vinaigrette or blue cheese dressing, homemade (pages 98-99) or purchased

Place lettuce in large salad bowl. Arrange remaining ingredients except dressing attractively on top of greens; the salad will look very pretty if you arrange each ingredient in a separate "stripe" across the top of the salad. Serve with dressing on the side, allowing each person to add as much as desired.

BAKED REUBEN SANDWICHES FOR A CROWD

8 sandwiches

This recipe is great for a party, because you can prepare the sandwiches in advance and bake them when you need them. Be sure to layer the ingredients in the order given; this helps prevent the sandwiches from getting soggy.

3 tablespoons butter or margarine, softened*
16 slices rye or pumpernickel bread
3/8 cup Thousand Island or Russian dressing
3 tablespoons yellow mustard
1½ pounds thinly sliced corned beef
2 cups sauerkraut, rinsed and drained very well
8 bread-sized slices Swiss cheese

Spread about ½ teaspoon softened butter on 1 side of each slice of bread. Spread the non-buttered side of 8 slices of the bread with 2 teaspoons of the dressing; spread remaining 8 slices of the bread with 2 teaspoons mustard (on the non-buttered side). Place the bread that has the dressing in a single layer, dressing-side up, on 10½ x 15-inch baking sheet (standard cookie sheet). Top each piece of bread with 3 ounces corned beef. Top corned beef with ¼ cup sauerkraut, then a piece of Swiss cheese. Place remaining bread on top of cheese so the mustard side faces the cheese. Cover well with plastic wrap or foil, and refrigerate until 45 minutes before you want to serve the sandwiches.

About 45 minutes before you're ready to serve the sandwiches, remove the baking sheet from the refrigerator; heat oven to 350°F. Uncover sandwiches and place baking sheet in oven. Bake until sandwiches are heated through and cheese melts, about 35 minutes.

*For a lower-fat version, omit the butter; spray 1 side of each bread slice with nonstick spray (butter-flavored spray works well). Proceed as directed.

Chicken Club Salad Sandwiches

2 servings as written; easily doubled

The taste of a club sandwich, in a different new way! This is a breeze to make with the already-cooked chicken that's sold in markets everywhere; cooked leftover turkey is great also.

1 small tomato
¾ cup diced cooked chicken meat (½-inch or slightly smaller dice; remove bones and skin before dicing and measuring)
½ cup shredded or chopped Swiss cheese
2 finely sliced green onions, or 3 tablespoons minced red or white onion
4 strips bacon, cooked until crisp, then drained and cut into ½-inch pieces
¼ cup mayonnaise (low-fat or no-fat works fine)
4 slices bread, or 2 English muffins or croissants
Lettuce for garnish, optional

Cut tomato in half through the equator. Remove and discard seeds. Sprinkle cut side of each tomato with salt; set in a dish cut-side down and allow to drain for 15 to 30 minutes. While tomato drains, combine chicken, cheese, green onions, bacon and mayonnaise in mixing bowl. Mix gently with spoon. Taste for seasoning, and add plain salt, celery salt or seasoned salt if necessary (depending on the bacon, salt may not be necessary). When tomato has drained, chop into ½-inch pieces. If you are preparing the salad in advance, cover and refrigerate the chicken mixture and tomatoes separately until ready to serve; if you mix them and then wait to serve, the salad may be too juicy. When ready to serve, toast bread or English muffins (croissants don't need to be toasted). Stir tomatoes gently into salad, discarding any additional juice that may have drained from the tomatoes. Divide salad evenly between the toast or croissants; top with lettuce if desired.

Chicken Club Salad in Tomato Cups

Substitute a large tomato for the small tomato. Cut tomato in half through the equator; scoop out the seeds and surrounding softer pulp (in the center of the tomato) to make a cup. Salt and drain as instructed above; discard seeds and pulp or use for another dish. Mix chicken salad as instructed above. Line 2 plates with lettuce leaves and top each with a drained tomato half. Divide the salad evenly between the tomato halves.

TORTELLINI SOUP WITH INFINITE POSSIBILITIES

4 to 6 servings, depending on additions

Pre-packaged tortellini (stuffed pasta pillows) is now available in the refrigerated or frozen case at most grocery stores, and gives you a head start in preparing a quick yet delicious meal. This recipe is designed for utmost flexibility so you can adapt it to use whatever you have in the refrigerator or pantry (or what is available at the local convenience store). Heat up some soft breadsticks, toss a green salad, and dinner's on the table!

The basic ingredients:

6 cups well-flavored chicken or turkey broth*
½ teaspoon minced fresh garlic, or a pinch of dried garlic flakes or powder (optional)
1 package (9 ounces) refrigerated or frozen prepared tortellini, any flavor
1 can (14½ ounces) diced Italian- or Mexican-flavored tomatoes, drained (or 1 large fresh tomato, peeled, seeded and diced)

*Choose **one** of the following seasonings:*

½ teaspoon dried Italian herb blend
¼ teaspoon each dried oregano and basil (or ½ teaspoon each of fresh herbs)
1 teaspoon dried parsley flakes, or 2 teaspoons fresh

Heat chicken broth, garlic and your choice of seasoning to boiling over medium-high heat. Add frozen or thawed tortellini. Cook as directed on package, generally 5 to 10 minutes depending on if the tortellini is frozen or thawed. Stir in the tomatoes, and your choice(s) from the list below.

*Stir in your choice of **one to three** of the following additions:*

¾ cup cooked or canned garbanzo beans (drained and rinsed if canned)
2 cups coarsely cut-up fresh spinach leaves, or ½ package (10-ounce package) frozen chopped spinach, thawed
1 cup frozen mixed vegetables
½ cup frozen peas and ½ cup frozen Italian-style green beans
¾ cup frozen diced potatoes, or cooked or canned diced potatoes
½ cup frozen pearl onions, cut into quarters before measuring
½ cup frozen or canned corn kernels and ½ cup frozen or canned carrot slices
1 cup frozen or cooked fresh small broccoli florets
½ cup frozen or cooked fresh small cauliflower florets
½ cup diced fresh zucchini or summer squash

¼ cup diced roasted red bell pepper (prepared as on page 299, or purchased)
½ cup diced cooked boneless chicken, turkey or ham; or, ½ cup crumbled or sliced cooked Italian sausage

Heat the soup just to boiling, then immediately reduce heat to simmer and cook 5 minutes, stirring occasionally. Taste for seasoning; if necessary, add salt and perhaps a dash of vinegar. Serve with one of the following garnishes:

Garnishes for Tortellini Soup:

Salad croutons
Shredded Parmesan or Romano cheese
Crumbled feta cheese

*It's important to have well-flavored stock for this dish. Homemade stock is the best, but if you don't have this, boil 8 cups (2 quarts) low-salt canned chicken broth until it is reduced to 6 cups (if you start with regular canned chicken broth and boil it down, it will be way too salty). Another option is to add 1 tablespoon chicken base (a type of chicken-stock paste) to 6 cups regular or low-salt canned chicken broth.

French Onion Soup

4 servings

The secret to this soup is the slow caramelization of the onions. The onions can be prepared in advance and kept refrigerated until you're ready to put the soup together.

2 tablespoons butter, preferably unsalted (do not use margarine)
3 tablespoons olive oil
4 large red onions, cut in half from top to bottom and thinly sliced
1 tablespoon sugar
4 cups rich beef broth*
4 slices day-old French bread
¼ cup grated Parmesan or Romano cheese (about 1 ounce)
1⅓ cups shredded Gruyère or mozzarella cheese (about 6 ounces)

In large skillet, melt butter in oil over medium heat. Add onions and sugar, stirring to coat. Reduce heat to medium-low and cook, stirring occasionally, until onions are very soft and a rich golden brown. Near the end of the onion cooking time, heat the beef broth; taste for seasoning and add salt and pepper if necessary. Heat oven to 375°F.

Place 4 oven-safe bowls or crocks on a baking sheet (this makes it easy to get them into and out of the oven). Divide the onions between the bowls. Pour stock into bowls. Float a bread slice in each bowl (if bread is larger than bowls, trim so the bread fits inside the bowls). Top each slice with 1 tablespoon Parmesan cheese and ⅓ cup Gruyère cheese. Bake until cheese melts; for a toastier cheese crust, place each bowl under the broiler briefly before serving.

*You need a rich, full-flavored beef broth for this recipe. If you're using canned broth, start with 5 or 6 cups, then boil it down to 4 cups before using. This will concentrate the flavor.

Appetizers and Snacks

MANHATTAN PORK CHUNKS

6 to 8 appetizer servings

The basic ingredients of a Manhattan cocktail turn pork cubes into an interesting appetizer. Not for kids!

2 pounds boneless pork loin chops, about 1 inch thick
2 tablespoons butter or stick margarine, divided
1 tablespoon vegetable oil
¾ cup bourbon or blended whiskey
⅜ cup sweet vermouth (3 ounces)
2 teaspoons sugar
1 teaspoon salt
4 generous dashes Angostura bitters (from liquor store, or in bar-mix area of a supermarket)
1 tablespoon cornstarch
15 maraschino cherries, stems removed, halved
1 tablespoon juice from the maraschino cherries

Trim and discard fat from pork. Cut pork into 1-inch chunks; salt generously. In medium skillet, melt 1 tablespoon butter in oil over medium heat. Add half the pork chunks; increase heat to medium-high and brown pork well on all sides. Transfer browned pork to a bowl; add remaining butter to skillet and brown remaining pork. Add bourbon, vermouth, sugar, salt and bitters; stir to loosen any browned bits. Return first batch of pork to skillet, along with any juices that have accumulated. Reduce heat to low and cook about 10 minutes, stirring occasionally. Blend cornstarch with ¼ cup cold water in a small bowl. Add cornstarch mixture to skillet; increase heat to medium and cook, stirring frequently, until sauce thickens. Stir in cherries and cherry juice. Cook, stirring frequently, about 1 minute longer. Serve warm, with cocktail forks or toothpicks.

Baked Brie with Caramelized Almonds

4 or 5 main-dish servings; 8 to 10 appetizer servings

If the Brie you use is larger than this, simply increase the toppings proportionally. You may also need to increase baking time slightly.

1 whole small wheel of Brie (8 ounces) with rind left on
¼ cup sour cream
2 tablespoons packed brown sugar
2 tablespoons sliced almonds
2 teaspoons butter or stick margarine
Accompaniments: sliced bread, crisp tart apple slices, assorted crackers

Heat oven to 350°F. Spray a small ovenproof dish with nonstick cooking spray. Place Brie in dish. Spread sour cream over Brie, as though frosting a cake. Sprinkle top with brown sugar, then with sliced almonds. Dot top with butter. Bake until cheese is very soft to the touch, 15 to 18 minutes. Increase heat to 425° and bake 5 minutes longer; Brie will be starting to melt at the bottom, and the sugar topping should be bubbly. Serve with bread, sliced apples, crackers, etc.

BAKED BRIE WITH PRESERVES

1 whole small wheel of Brie (8 ounces) with rind left on
2 teaspoons butter or stick margarine
3 tablespoons apricot or other preserves
Accompaniments: sliced bread, crisp tart apple slices, assorted crackers

Heat oven to 350°F. Spray a small ovenproof dish with nonstick cooking spray. Place Brie in dish. In small saucepan, melt butter over low heat; stir in preserves and cook, stirring constantly, until heated through (you can also do this in the microwave rather than on the stovetop). Brush sides and top of Brie lightly with preserve mixture; pour remaining over top of Brie. Bake until cheese is very soft to the touch and bottom is starting to melt, 15 to 18 minutes. Serve with bread, apples, crackers, etc.

Microwave instructions:

Follow recipe above, placing Brie in microwave-safe dish. Microwave on HIGH until cheese is very soft to the touch, 2 to 4 minutes. Let stand 5 minutes before serving.

Variations:

Baked Brie with Chutney: Follow recipe for Baked Brie with Preserves, substituting chutney for the preserves. Bake and serve as directed; pickled onions also make a nice accompaniment to chutney-topped Brie.

Baked Brie with Jalapeño Jelly: Follow recipe for Baked Brie with Preserves, substituting jalapeño jelly or preserves for the apricot preserves; sprinkle with 2 tablespoons chopped pecans before baking, if desired. Bake and serve as directed.

MARINATED MOZZARELLA

6 to 8 appetizer servings

Marinating adds a depth of flavor to plain-Jane mozzarella cheese in this easy recipe. If you have left-overs, use them to top pizzas, or toss into a mixed salad for an exciting touch.

8 to 10 fresh basil leaves, or 1 teaspoon crumbled dried basil
⅓ cup extra-virgin olive oil
1 tablespoon chopped fresh parsley
1 teaspoon chopped fresh oregano leaves, or ½ teaspoon crumbled dried
¼ teaspoon crushed dried hot red pepper flakes
2 sun-dried tomato halves, cut into fine dice (⅛ inch), optional
1 clove garlic, pressed or minced, optional
½ pound mozzarella cheese, cut into cubes slightly smaller than ½ inch

Roll up the fresh basil leaves and slice into thin ribbons (if using dried basil, you don't need to do anything other than add it to the oil with the other herbs). In mixing bowl, combine basil, olive oil, parsley, oregano, hot pepper flakes, diced tomato and garlic; stir to mix well. Add cubed mozzarella cheese. Cover and refrigerate at least 1 hour, and as long as overnight. Serve with toothpicks.

Rumaki

16 appetizers

These can be rolled as much as a day in advance, then cooked just before serving.

8 ounces chicken livers
2 tablespoons dry sherry, or brandy
1 tablespoon soy sauce
1 teaspoon sugar
8 green onions
8 slices bacon, each cut into 2 shorter halves (don't use thick-cut bacon; it doesn't stretch enough to wrap around fillings)
16 canned whole water chestnuts
16 wooden toothpicks
Sweet-and-sour sauce (purchased, or from recipe on page 301) and/or hot Chinese mustard for dipping

Drain chicken liver. Trim away and discard any fat or other non-appetizing material from the livers; cut up so you have a total of 16 pieces. In small mixing bowl, blend together the sherry, soy sauce and sugar. Add chicken livers, stirring to coat. Cover and refrigerate for an hour or two. While livers marinate, cut white end of green onion so it is 1½ inches long; discard green parts or save for another use. Slice each onion bulb in half lengthwise; set aside.

To assemble rumaki, drain chicken livers and pat dry. Lay a half-slice of bacon on work surface. Add 1 piece of the liver, 1 green onion half-bulb and 1 water chestnut on one end of the bacon. Wrap bacon tightly around everything and secure with toothpick, making sure the toothpick pierces the liver, onion and water chestnut. Repeat with remaining ingredients. If making in advance, cover and refrigerate until you're ready to cook.

Heat broiler. Arrange rumaki in a single layer on a broiler pan. Broil 3 inches from heating element until the bacon is crisp and the liver is just pink inside, about 10 minutes; turn once during cooking to crisp the second side. Serve warm, with sweet-and-sour sauce and hot Chinese mustard.

CARROT-PARMESAN PÂTÉ

6 to 8 appetizer servings; very easily adjusted

I can't recall who first told me about this unusual but tasty dish; the recipe is so easy to remember that it's the type of thing that gets verbally passed around at parties, office water coolers and the like. It's easy to make any quantity you wish, because you use equal amounts of three ingredients—that's it! Quantities of the optional chives and paprika are not critical.

1 cup shredded carrots, tightly packed in measuring cup
1 cup regular mayonnaise (not reduced-fat)
1 cup shredded Parmesan or Romano cheese
2 tablespoons snipped fresh chives, optional
Paprika
Crackers for accompaniment

Heat oven to 350°F. Combine carrots, mayonnaise, cheese and chives in a medium ovenproof bowl; smooth the top. Sprinkle with paprika. Bake until the edges are bubbly and the top is lightly browned, 30 to 40 minutes. Serve hot, with crackers for dipping.

Note: To adjust quantity, simply use equal measures of the 3 ingredients, stirring in a few chives if you like and sprinkling the top with paprika. Smaller amounts will cook more quickly, while a much larger batch needs a bit more baking time.

Main Dishes

OVEN-FRIED DEVILED CHICKEN

4 servings; easily adjusted to make more or less

Crispy, crunchy, buttery-tasting "fried" chicken, without all the mess!

3 tablespoons Dijon mustard
2 tablespoons sherry, white wine or chicken broth
1 tablespoon olive oil or vegetable oil
½ teaspoon paprika, optional
4 or 5 dashes of Tabasco sauce
2 boneless, skinless chicken breast halves* (about 1 pound total)
¾ cup finely crushed buttery crackers, such as Ritz (about 2 ounces)

Heat oven to 400°F. Use a dish that will hold the chicken in a single layer and spray it with nonstick cooking spray. In wide bowl, blend mustard, sherry, oil, paprika and Tabasco sauce. Cut breast halves in half so you have 2 almost-square portions per breast half. Dip each portion in the mustard sauce, shaking off excess. Coat well with crushed crackers. Arrange coated chicken in a single layer in baking dish. Bake until cooked through, 30 to 40 minutes; the juices should run clear when the chicken is pierced with a fork.

*You may use chicken thighs for part or all of the chicken, if you prefer. Boneless, skinless chicken thighs usually weigh under 2 ounces apiece, so you'll need 2 per portion. As an example, if two people prefer white meat and two prefer dark meat, you'll need one 8-ounce breast half (cut into 2 portions) and 4 thighs. Place 2 thighs together with smooth sides out, then tuck in small pieces to form a neat shape. Dip the pair into the mustard sauce and crumbs; pat into a regular shape when placing in the baking dish.

Extra-crispy variation: Use ¾ cup finely crushed buttery crackers and ¼ cup crushed potato chips. You may also top the crumbed chicken portions with small pats of butter, whether you're using the potato chips or not; this will make a more crisp and buttery surface.

Cheese-stuffed variation: Cut a shallow slit in the top of each chicken breast portion before coating with the mustard sauce, then turn the knife sideways to make a small pocket (don't cut all the way through the chicken); if using chicken thighs, do not make any cuts. Insert a small piece of cheese, such as Swiss, Gruyère or Brie, in the pocket, and close the chicken meat around the slit; if using thighs, place the cheese between the 2 thighs. Dip in mustard sauce and coat with crumbs as directed. Place chicken in dish slit-side up, and bake as directed.

QUICK CHICKEN WITH CURRY

4 servings

Take advantage of convenience ingredients—like pre-cooked chickens available at many delis and supermarkets—to whip up a quick and delicious American-style curry. It's not anything like the complex curries you'll find in true Indian cooking, but is tasty and easy, and enjoyed by most people.

1 small onion, diced
1 small apple, cored and diced
2 stalks celery, sliced ¼ inch thick
1 or 2 cloves garlic, pressed or minced
1 finely minced hot pepper, optional
1 tablespoon butter
3 tablespoons sherry, chicken broth, apple juice or water
1 can (14 ounces) unsweetened coconut milk, or heavy cream
2 tablespoons curry powder blend
¼ teaspoon salt
2 cups cut-up boneless cooked chicken*
Hot cooked rice
Garnishes of your choice: diced avocado, chopped peanuts or other nuts, raisins, chutney, shredded unsweetened coconut, halved seedless grapes, yogurt, sliced green onions, French-fried onions, chopped fresh cilantro leaves

In large skillet, sauté onion, apple, celery, garlic and hot pepper in butter over medium heat until celery is tender-crisp, stirring occasionally. Add sherry to skillet; cook, stirring frequently, until liquid has almost completely cooked away. Add coconut milk, curry powder and salt. Heat to boiling; reduce heat and simmer, stirring frequently, about 5 minutes. Stir in cooked chicken. Cover; reduce heat to low and cook, stirring occasionally, for 10 minutes. Serve with hot cooked rice and garnishes of your choice.

*Tyson is marketing cooked, frozen chicken breast meat in 9-ounce packages, and this is just right for this dish. Or, you may cut 10 ounces boneless, skinless raw chicken breast meat into ½-inch pieces and add it to the skillet with the vegetables at the beginning.

Variation:

Quick Shrimp with Curry: Substitute 1 pound raw shrimp for chicken. Shell and devein shrimp before cooking. Proceed as directed, adding the shrimp when directed for the chicken.

TEXICAN POT ROAST

4 to 6 servings

Beans, hominy, mild green chiles and Mexican-style stewed tomatoes combine to make a hearty meal; the crock pot makes it easy. A pan of cornbread and some coleslaw would go great with this dish; have a bottle of hot sauce ready for those who want to turn up the heat. If there are any leftovers, break up the meat into large stew-sized chunks and mix with the remaining ingredients for an easy one-dish meal.

1 large onion, coarsely chopped
1 can (15 ounces) pinto or great northern beans, drained, or 1½ cups cooked beans
1 can (15½ ounces) yellow or white hominy, drained (if unavailable, substitute a second can of beans)
2 cans (4 ounces each) chopped green chiles, or one 7-ounce can
1 blade or chuck pot roast (2 to 3 pounds)
1 can (14½ ounces) stewed tomatoes with Mexican seasonings*
1 tablespoon chili powder blend
½ cup beer, beef broth or water

Place onion, beans, hominy and green chiles in bottom of slow cooker; stir to mix. Salt and pepper both sides of roast, then place on top of bean mixture. Pour stewed tomatoes with their juices over the meat. Blend chili powder into beer, and pour into the slow cooker. Cover and cook on HIGH for 1 hour, then reduce heat to LOW and cook 7 to 9 hours longer, or until meat is very tender.

*If you can't find Mexican-flavored stewed tomatoes, substitute a can of onion-and-garlic diced tomatoes, or regular stewed tomatoes.

CHILI-STYLE STEAKS WITH CHEESE

4 servings

For a true chili-style meal, serve with pinto beans to sop up all the juices; rice or noodles also work well. Cornbread and a tossed green salad round out the meal.

1½ pounds top round steak, about ¾ inch thick
1 tablespoon chili powder blend
4 teaspoons flour
2 tablespoons vegetable oil
1 large onion, chopped
1 can (14½ ounces) stewed or diced tomatoes (Mexican-style or another flavor variation works)
1 cup shredded cheddar or pepper-Jack cheese (about 4 ounces)

Trim off excess fat and any gristle from round steak; cut into 4 pieces. Sprinkle half the chili powder and half the flour over the steaks; pound gently with a meat mallet or the edge of a heavy plate. Turn steaks and repeat on second side.

To cook in a crock pot: In large skillet, heat oil over medium-high heat and brown steaks well on both sides. While steaks are browning, scatter onion over the bottom of the crock pot. Transfer browned steaks to the crock pot, laying them on top of the onion. Salt and pepper generously (unless your chili powder blend is very salty). Drain and discard liquid from the tomatoes; pour the tomatoes over the steaks. Cover and cook on HIGH 1 hour, then reduce heat to LOW and cook about 8 hours, or until steaks are fork-tender. Sprinkle cheese over steaks and increase heat to HIGH; cook until cheese melts, about 15 minutes.

To cook on the stovetop: In Dutch oven, heat oil over medium-high heat and brown steaks well on both sides. Transfer browned steaks to a plate, then scatter the onion in the bottom of the Dutch oven and return steaks. Pour tomatoes, including juices, over the top. Heat to a gentle boil over medium heat. Cover and reduce heat; simmer 1½ hours, or until meat is fork-tender. Sprinkle cheese over the steaks; re-cover and cook until cheese melts, about 5 minutes.

Crock Pot Venison Swiss Steak

4 servings

This easy recipe is also fabulous with beef round steak.

1½ pounds venison round steak, about ½ inch thick
½ cup flour
¼ teaspoon mixed herbs, such as Bouquet Garni, Fines Herbes, or any herb blend
3 tablespoons vegetable oil, divided
1 medium onion, cut in half from top to bottom, then sliced ¼ inch thick
1 can (12 ounces) beer (flat beer is OK)
1 can (10½ ounces) condensed French onion soup
1 tablespoon plus 1½ teaspoons cornstarch

Trim any fat or gristle from steaks; sprinkle generously on both sides with salt and pepper. In flat dish, combine flour and herbs. Dip steaks into flour on both sides. Pound each steak lightly with a meat mallet or the edge of a sturdy plate; you are not trying to tenderize the steaks but to pound the flour into the meat.

Heat 2 tablespoons of the oil in a large skillet over medium-high heat. Add a single layer of steaks, and cook until nicely browned on both sides. Transfer browned steaks to crock pot. Add remaining oil to skillet, if necessary, and brown remaining steaks; transfer to crock pot. Scatter sliced onion over steaks. Add the beer to the skillet—watch out for steam and spattering—and stir well to loosen crusty bits from the bottom of the skillet. Heat to boiling, then reduce heat slightly and cook 5 minutes, stirring occasionally. Blend the condensed soup and ¼ cup water into the beer and heat to boiling. Pour beer mixture over onions and meat in crock pot. Cover crock pot and cook on LOW heat 6 to 7 hours. 30 minutes before serving, blend cornstarch into ¼ cup cold water. Stir into crock pot. Raise heat to HIGH and cook 30 minutes, or until gravy has thickened somewhat.

NO BEANS ABOUT IT: FOUR-PEPPER CHILI

6 servings

This recipe has several things that distinguish it from many other chili recipes. First, it has no beans in it (for a tasty chili that does include beans, see page 65). Second, it uses small cubes of meat, rather than ground meat. Third, it calls for a variety of peppers and spices, rather than using commercial chili powder blend which varies considerably from brand to brand.

1 jar (16 ounces) pickled hot cherry peppers (if you prefer very mild chili, substitute sweet pickled cherry peppers)
1 dried ancho chile, optional
1½ pounds boneless beef or venison chuck or sirloin
2 tablespoons lard or vegetable oil
1 green or red bell pepper, cored, diced
1 bottle (12 ounces) beer, or 1½ cups beef broth
1 can (4 ounces) diced green chiles, undrained
1 can (14½ ounces) diced tomatoes packed in juice, undrained
1 tablespoon sugar
1 large onion, peeled and cut into ¾-inch chunks
4 cloves garlic, peeled
2 tablespoons ground cumin
2 tablespoons crumbled dried oregano leaves
Shredded Monterey Jack cheese for garnish

Drain off and reserve ¼ cup pickling liquid from the cherry peppers. Remove the stems and seeds from the cherry peppers, then cut the peppers into ¾-inch chunks; set aside. Remove and discard the stem from the ancho chile, then break the chile open so you can shake out and discard the seeds (if you are sensitive to chile pepper oil, wear rubber gloves when handling the chile). You may have to break the chile into several pieces to get all the seeds out. Crumble the chili or cut it into thin strips (a small scissors works well for this); set aside.

Cut the meat into ½-inch cubes, trimming away any silverskin or gristle. Heat the lard in a Dutch oven over medium-high heat, then add the meat and cook, stirring occasionally, until the meat is no longer red on the outside. Add the bell pepper; cook, stirring occasionally, for about 5 minutes. Add the cut-up cherry peppers, reserved pickling liquid, ancho, beer, canned diced green chiles, diced tomatoes with their juice and sugar. Heat just to boiling, then reduce heat and simmer, uncovered, about 1½ hours. Meanwhile, prepare the onion and garlic.

Heat a cast-iron skillet over medium-high heat until hot, then add the onion and garlic. Cook over high heat, stirring occasionally, until the vegetables are moderately charred on all sides. Remove from heat; add the cumin and oregano leaves to the skillet and stir constantly until the pan has cooled down, about 5 minutes. Cut the garlic into slices. Set all aside.

When the chili has cooked about 1½ hours, add the charred vegetables and seasoning; if the chili is becoming dry, add water as needed. Continue cooking 30 to 45 minutes longer; the meat should be tender and the chili should be neither soupy nor dry. Serve chili with Monterey Jack cheese on the side, allowing each person to add some to his or her bowl of chili.

SPIRAL MEATLOAF

4 or 5 servings

Cheese and vegetables appear in a spiral design when you cut this meatloaf, making a very pretty presentation. You can also serve slices of this on buns, just like hamburgers; the round shape is perfect.

¼ cup diced onion
¼ cup diced green or red bell pepper
½ teaspoon minced garlic, optional
1 teaspoon vegetable oil
⅓ cup Italian-flavored or plain bread crumbs
1 egg
⅓ cup spaghetti sauce, barbecue sauce or ketchup, divided
½ to ¾ teaspoon garlic salt or plain salt
1 pound lean ground beef
¾ cup shredded Colby, Monterey Jack or other cheese
2 tablespoons shredded Parmesan or Romano cheese

Heat oven to 350°F. Sauté onion, bell pepper and garlic in oil over medium heat until just tender; set aside to cool slightly. In mixing bowl, combine bread crumbs, egg, 2 tablespoons spaghetti sauce and salt; blend with fork. Add ground beef and mix well with your hands.

On a sheet of waxed paper, shape the meat mixture into a 12 x 8-inch rectangle. Sprinkle cooked vegetables evenly over meat, keeping about 1 inch clear at the edges. Sprinkle shredded cheeses evenly over the vegetables. Starting with the short side, roll up tightly in jelly-roll fashion, peeling back the waxed paper as you roll. Pinch ends together and seal the seam well; place roll seam-side down in a baking dish that comfortably holds the roll. Push the ends in to make the roll more compact so it is 6½ to 7 inches wide; it will get slightly thicker around as you do this.

Bake for 1 hour, or until meat is firm and no longer pink; a meat thermometer should read 160°F. Spread remaining spaghetti sauce over the top, and bake 10 minutes longer. Let stand 10 minutes before slicing.

PORKETTA ROAST

4 to 6 servings

This flavorful roast makes excellent leftovers; try some in a crusty roll with sliced red onion, Dijon mustard and lettuce.

Seasoning mix (you may want to mix this up at home; carry it in a plastic bag):

1 tablespoon kosher or other coarse salt
1 tablespoon fennel seeds
1 tablespoon anise seeds
1 bay leaf, finely crumbled
1 tablespoon coarsely ground black pepper
1 tablespoon paprika
¾ teaspoon onion powder
¼ to ½ teaspoon crushed dried hot red pepper flakes

2½ to 3-pound pork roast (sirloin, loin or butt)
2 tablespoons olive oil or vegetable oil
6 to 8 cloves garlic, chopped

Combine salt, fennel seeds, anise seeds and bay leaf in mortar and pestle; crush coarsely. Combine with remaining seasoning mix ingredients (you may want to do this at home, then carry it to the cabin in a plastic bag). Rub pork roast all over with olive oil; place into large plastic food-storage bag. Combine seasoning mix with garlic. Sprinkle mix evenly over pork roast, then rub it in with your fingers. Let the roast stand at room temperature 1 hour, or up to 12 hours refrigerated.

Heat oven to 450°F. Place pork, fat-side up, in roasting pan; top with any loose seasonings remaining in plastic bag. Roast, uncovered, for 10 minutes. Reduce oven temperature to 300°F and continue roasting until the internal temperature of the meat reads 155°F on an instant-read thermometer; total roasting time will be 1 to 1½ hours. When pork is done, remove from oven and tent loosely with foil; let stand 15 minutes before carving.

SKILLET GLAZED PORK

2 servings; easily doubled

For a wonderful combination, serve this with Garlic Mashed Potatoes (page 290) and Crispy Green Beans (page 181).

2 pork chops, 1 inch thick (6 to 7 ounces each)
1 tablespoon sesame seeds
2 teaspoons butter or margarine
1 teaspoon Asian sesame seasoning oil
½ cup chicken broth
1 tablespoon honey
1 tablespoon red wine vinegar
2 teaspoons Dijon mustard
¼ teaspoon crumbled dried thyme leaves, or ½ teaspoon fresh

Sprinkle pork chops generously with salt and pepper. Sprinkle sesame seeds evenly over both sides, and press in with your fingers. In medium skillet, melt butter in oil over medium heat. Add pork chops; cook until nicely browned on both sides. Meanwhile, combine chicken broth, honey, vinegar, mustard and thyme in measuring cup or small bowl; stir to blend. When chops are browned, add chicken broth mixture to skillet. Cover skillet and reduce heat to low; cook 15 minutes, keeping heat low to prevent boiling. Uncover skillet and cook 15 minutes longer, or until chops are tender. If you would like a thicker sauce, transfer the chops to a heated serving plate and keep warm; increase heat under skillet and cook a few minutes, stirring frequently, until the sauce has reduced and thickened.

Crock Pot Pork Chops with Apples and Kraut

4 servings

The long, slow cooking in a crock pot produces tender chops. Browning the chops before putting them in the crock pot makes for a more attractive dish.

1 can (14 ounces) sauerkraut, drained (Bavarian sauerkraut is particularly good)
4 pork chops (each about ¾ inch thick)
2 tablespoons vegetable oil
1 medium onion
1 large firm green cooking apple, such as a Granny Smith
1 cup flat beer or chicken broth; or ½ cup water

Place sauerkraut in the crock pot. In a large skillet, brown the pork chops in the oil over medium heat. While the chops are browning, cut the onion in half, then slice ¼ inch thick. When chops are well browned, use tongs to transfer them to the crock pot, arranging them over the sauerkraut. Add the onion to the skillet and cook for about 5 minutes, stirring frequently. While onions are browning, core and slice the apple; scatter over the chops in the crock pot. When onions are richly colored, transfer them to the crock pot on top of the apples. Add the beer to the skillet and raise the heat to high. Stir well to loosen any browned bits and cook until liquid has reduced to about half volume, about 5 minutes (if using water, simply stir the water around to loosen browned bits and then pour into the crock pot; there's no need to reduce the water). Pour the liquid over the onions in the crock pot. Cover and turn crock pot to HIGH; cook 4 to 5 hours (or cook on LOW for 7 to 8 hours).

Variations:

- Substitute ½ cup dried apple slices for the green apple
- Substitute 1½ cups chunky-style applesauce for the green apple; use ⅓ cup water in place of beer or chicken broth

OVEN-BARBECUED RIBS

Servings depend on type of ribs used; see notes below

These tasty, fall-off-the-bone ribs are similar to those served in many restaurants (including some large rib chains). They're very different from the dry, smoky ribs that are cooked for hours in a smoker (see Slow-Smoked Ribs, page 270). But if you don't have a grill or smoker, or if the weather is too horrible to cook outdoors, give this easy recipe a try; many people prefer it to traditional pit-smoked ribs.

Pork baby back ribs or spareribs, as needed for number of servings*
1 cup barbecue sauce per rack, purchased or homemade (see recipe on page 299)
Additional sauce for final baste, about ¼ cup per rack, plus extra for serving if desired

Cut ribs between the bones into 2- or 3-rib portions. Arrange in baking dish, in a single or double layer. Pour barbecue sauce over, and turn ribs to coat well. If you have the time, marinate the ribs for a few hours in the barbecue sauce before cooking; otherwise, proceed directly to the cooking step. To marinate, cover the dish tightly with foil and refrigerate 1 to 8 hours, turning occasionally.

When you're ready to cook, heat oven to 300°F. Place the tightly covered dish in the oven and bake 2 to 2½ hours, until the ribs are very tender and the meat has pulled away from the bone tips. Remove the ribs from the oven; if you're not ready to eat at this point, simply keep the ribs covered and warm for up to 45 minutes.

When you're almost ready to eat, heat the broiler (or, if you have a barbecue grill going, you can finish the ribs on the grill). Arrange the ribs in a single layer on a broiler pan and brush with fresh barbecue sauce; if the ribs don't fit in a single layer, you'll have to cook them in batches. Broil the ribs for 5 to 10 minutes (baby backs need less time than spareribs), until they get a few browned, crispy spots; watch carefully so they don't burn. Serve with additional barbecue sauce for those who wish it.

Side-dish tip: Twice-Baked Potatoes (page 366) go great with these ribs, and it makes perfect sense to bake the potatoes during the long, slow cooking of the ribs. The potatoes need 1½ to 1¾ hours at 300°F to get done; when they're cooked through, remove them from the oven and let them cool enough to handle, then stuff them while the ribs finish cooking. Remove the ribs from the oven when they're tender and keep them warm, then re-bake the potatoes at 375°F as directed; remove the potatoes from the oven while you quickly finish the ribs under the broiler.

*• 2-pound rack of baby backs will serve 2, but not to excess; one rib fanatic could eat a whole rack
• 3-pound rack of spareribs will serve 2 or 3

ITALIAN LAYERED CASSEROLE

4 to 6 servings

Reminiscent of lasagna, this dish needs only some bread and perhaps a salad for a complete meal.

1 pound bulk Italian sausage (if you can't find it in bulk, buy uncooked Italian sausages and remove the casing)
½ cup diced onion
1 jar (14 ounces) ready-to-serve tomato-based pasta sauce with mushrooms
¼ cup Italian-flavored bread crumbs
¾ cup cottage cheese (reduced-fat works fine)
1 egg
1 package (10 ounces) frozen chopped spinach, thawed and drained
1 cup (4 ounces) shredded mozzarella cheese, divided

In large skillet, cook sausage over medium heat, stirring frequently to break up, until meat is no longer pink. Add onion and cook, stirring frequently, until onion is tender. Drain excess grease. Add tomato sauce and cook about 5 minutes longer, stirring occasionally. Remove from heat and stir in bread crumbs.

Heat oven to 350°F; spray 9-inch-square baking dish or 2-quart casserole with nonstick spray, or grease lightly. In mixing bowl, combine cottage cheese and egg, stirring with fork to blend. Squeeze excess moisture from spinach; add spinach and half of the mozzarella cheese to cottage cheese mixture. Stir gently to combine.

Spread half of the sausage mixture into prepared dish. Top with spinach mixture, then with remaining meat mixture. Sprinkle remaining mozzarella cheese on top. Bake until the cheese has some golden brown spots and the meat mixture is bubbly at the edges, 35 to 45 minutes. Let stand 10 minutes before cutting into serving portions.

WHITE BEANS AND GREENS WITH SAUSAGE

4 servings

This hearty yet easy Italian one-pot dish is great for a quick meal, especially in cold weather. Heat up a loaf of good bread, set the table and you're done fixing dinner. Since this dish is a cross between a soup and a casserole, it is best served in bowls.

1 package (12 ounces) pork-blend breakfast-style sausage, such as Jimmy Dean's, thawed ("light" sausage, which is a turkey-pork blend, works great)
½ cup diced onion
2 cloves garlic, chopped
1 can (19 ounces) cannellini or white kidney beans, drained and rinsed
1 package (1 pound) frozen chopped collard greens
1 cup chicken broth
½ teaspoon dried mixed herb blend, such as Fines Herbes or Herbs de Provence
¼ teaspoon crushed dried hot red pepper flakes or 1½ teaspoons Tabasco sauce, optional
Shredded Parmesan or Romano cheese for garnish

In Dutch oven, cook pork sausage, onion and garlic over medium heat until browned, stirring frequently to break meat up into bite-sized or smaller pieces. Drain excess fat if necessary. Add beans, greens, chicken broth, herbs and red pepper flakes. Heat to boiling; cover and reduce heat. Simmer about 15 minutes, stirring occasionally. Serve with Parmesan cheese on the side.

SPAGHETTI WITH CLAM SAUCE

3 or 4 servings

This is a delicious and quick "pantry dish," made from items you can easily keep on hand for those nights when you need something quick and satisfying for dinner. Toss together a green salad or fix some broccoli, and serve with a loaf of crusty bread and a bottle of crisp white wine for a fabulous feast. Traditionally, this dish is not accompanied with Parmesan cheese, but is served "as is."

⅓ cup finely chopped onion
1 teaspoon minced garlic
1 tablespoon butter, olive oil or margarine
¼ cup dry white wine, clam juice or chicken broth
1 can (6½ ounces) minced clams in clam juice, undrained
¼ teaspoon red wine vinegar (balsamic vinegar is best, but not essential)
Freshly ground black pepper to taste*
3 tablespoons chopped fresh parsley, optional**
Hot cooked spaghetti (8 to 10 ounces uncooked weight)

In large skillet, sauté onion and garlic in butter over medium heat for about 5 minutes, stirring occasionally. Add white wine; cook, stirring occasionally, until liquid has reduced almost completely away, about 5 minutes. Add clams with their juices, vinegar and black pepper. Rinse the clam can with about ¼ cup water and add that to the skillet also. Reduce heat to medium-low and cook, stirring occasionally, about 5 minutes; sauce should still be juicy but clams should not be swimming in liquid. Remove from heat and stir in the parsley. In large bowl, combine sauce with hot spaghetti, tossing well to mix.

*This dish is great with a fair dose of black pepper, so don't be shy—I recommend at least ½ teaspoon, unless you like really mild food. It is important that the pepper be freshly ground for this dish.

**You may substitute finely chopped greens such as watercress, arugula or other bitter greens for the parsley; add them to the sauce at the same time as the clams, rather than at the end of cooking.

Variation:

Spaghetti with Clam Sauce alla Diavola: Follow instructions above, adding ¼ to ½ teaspoon crushed dried hot red pepper flakes at the same time you add the black pepper. Continue as directed.

MUSHROOM RAGOUT

3 to 5 servings, depending on how it's served

This cooking method produces a rich and deeply flavored mushroom dish. Serve over Stuffed Polenta Squares (facing page), or hot biscuits, toast or rice; toss with wide pasta; or serve "as is" for a side dish.

8 ounces fresh mushrooms (a mix of two types is best; cremini, shiitake, portabella, oyster, morel or other specialty mushrooms are better than white mushrooms)
1 to 2 tablespoons olive oil or vegetable oil, divided
3 tablespoons sherry, brandy or apple juice
1 tablespoon butter or margarine
½ cup shredded carrot
¼ cup diced onion
2 cloves garlic, pressed or minced
1½ cups chicken or vegetable broth
1 teaspoon cornstarch
3 tablespoons snipped fresh chives or parsley

Clean the mushrooms (remove and discard stems from shiitakes), then slice ¼ inch thick. Heat a heavy-bottomed large skillet over medium heat. Add about a teaspoon and a half of the olive oil, and heat until the oil looks rippled. Add enough mushrooms to just cover the bottom of the skillet. Let them cook without stirring until they have begun to brown, then stir and continue cooking until both sides are nicely browned. Push the browned mushrooms off to the side of the pan, add a little more oil, and cook another batch of mushrooms until browned. You will probably have to cook the mushrooms in 3 batches like this (if you cook them all at once, they will not get properly browned, and they will release a lot of liquid). Once all the mushrooms are browned and any liquid has cooked away, add the sherry and stir well. Cook, stirring frequently, until the sherry has cooked almost completely away. Transfer the mushrooms to a bowl and set aside.

Add the butter to the skillet and heat over medium heat until the butter stops foaming. Add the carrot and onion to the skillet and cook, stirring occasionally, for about 5 minutes. Add the garlic and cook a few minutes longer. Add broth; stir well and cook about 5 minutes. Return the mushrooms and any juices to the skillet. Heat just to boiling, then reduce heat and cook at a gentle bubble for about 5 minutes. Meanwhile, blend the cornstarch into 3 tablespoons cold water in a cup. When the vegetable mixture has cooked about 5 minutes, add the cornstarch mixture to the skillet, stirring constantly to prevent lumps. Cook, stirring constantly, until mixture bubbles and thickens, about 3 minutes. Remove from heat and stir in the chives.

STUFFED POLENTA SQUARES

6 to 9 servings

Not your everyday cabin fare! This is a wonderful vegetarian main dish when topped with Mushroom Ragout (facing page). It's also delicious topped with a hearty pasta sauce. It has a fancy feeling to it, but is quite easy to prepare. The polenta may be prepared and layered as much as 2 days in advance and kept refrigerated before final baking.

2 teaspoons salt
1⅓ cups quick-cooking polenta
1½ cups shredded Gruyère, fontina or mozzarella cheese
Mushroom Ragout (facing page), or your favorite pasta sauce

Spray a 9-inch-square or 9-inch-round baking dish with nonstick spray, or butter lightly; set aside. Add salt to 2 quarts cold water and heat to boiling. Add polenta in a very thin stream, whisking constantly. Immediately reduce heat to low and cook, stirring constantly to break up lumps, until polenta is thick, 2 to 5 minutes. Remove from heat. Transfer polenta to the prepared baking dish; even out and smooth the top with a wet spatula. Let cool to room temperature, then cover and refrigerate at least 2 hours, or up to 2 days.

When you're ready to do the final cooking, heat oven to 350°F (see below for microwave instructions). Carefully flip the dish upside down to release the polenta onto a cutting board. Use a long serrated knife to slice the polenta into 2 layers by holding the knife parallel to the cutting board. Put 1 layer back into the baking dish. Top this layer with the shredded cheese, then carefully put the second layer on top of the cheese. Cover with foil and bake 40 minutes, or until hot. Cut into squares (or wedges if using a round pan) and transfer with a spatula to individual plates. Top with Mushroom Ragout or spaghetti sauce.

Microwave instructions: If you use a pyrex baking dish, the polenta can easily be reheated in the microwave rather than the oven. Slice and stuff polenta as directed, then cover the dish with plastic wrap, leaving a small corner open for a steam vent. Microwave on REHEAT/80% power for 12 to 15 minutes, or until hot, rotating dish occasionally.

Vegetables, Starches and Side Dishes

BRAISED RED CABBAGE WITH APPLES

4 servings

Cabbage is a wonderful vegetable to take to the cabin, because it keeps well for a long time. It's also usually available in even small-town grocery stores, so you can make this dish on the spur of the moment. You may substitute green cabbage, but the dish won't be as pretty.

2 tablespoons vegetable oil, or 1 tablespoon each butter and oil
3 cups thinly sliced red cabbage (about two-thirds of a small head)
1 Granny Smith or other tart apple
Half of a small onion, thinly sliced into half-rings
¼ cup chicken broth or dry red wine
2 tablespoons red wine vinegar or cider vinegar

In large nonaluminum skillet, heat oil over medium heat. Add cabbage and cook, stirring frequently, for about 3 minutes. Meanwhile, remove and discard the apple core, then cut the apple into ½-inch chunks. Add the apple and onion to the skillet; cook until the onion is tender-crisp, about 5 minutes. Stir in the chicken broth and vinegar. Cover and reduce heat; simmer about 10 minutes, stirring once or twice. Remove lid, increase heat to medium, and cook about 5 minutes longer. Season to taste with salt and pepper.

BAKED SCALLOPED CORN

6 servings

A natural accompaniment to ham or pork chops, scalloped corn is also good with fried chicken, meatloaf or fried fish. I like to reheat leftovers in the microwave the next morning and pour on a little extra milk, for a delicious breakfast.

2 cups frozen corn, thawed, or equivalent in fresh kernels cut from the cob
1 cup whole milk or half-and-half
⅓ cup minced onion
¼ cup minced red or green bell pepper, or roasted red bell pepper*
1 teaspoon celery salt or plain salt
1 teaspoon sugar
2 eggs, lightly beaten
½ cup cracker crumbs
Paprika, optional

Heat oven to 350°F. Spray an 8- or 9-inch-square baking dish with nonstick spray, or butter lightly; set aside. In saucepan, combine the corn, milk, onion, pepper, salt and sugar. Heat over medium heat just until tiny bubbles form around the edges. Remove from heat; stir in eggs and cracker crumbs. Pour into prepared baking dish; sprinkle with paprika. Bake until the mixture is golden brown and set in the center, 45 to 55 minutes.

*Roast as described on page 299, or purchase already-roasted peppers in a jar.

MIX-AND-MATCH MARINATED ITALIAN VEGETABLE SALAD

8 servings

Customize this colorful salad by choosing the ingredients you prefer from the "optional" list below. A note about the main vegetables: I prefer parboiled cauliflower and carrots in this salad; the tender-crisp texture seems more mellow than that of completely raw vegetables. Broccoli, unfortunately, turns a drab olive-green in color if it's cooked before marinating, so I use small uncooked florets, which don't seem as out-of-place as large uncooked florets. If you like really crunchy salad, skip the cooking step for the cauliflower and carrots.

½ pound fresh bite-sized cauliflower florets (about 3½ cups)
2 carrots, peeled and cut into ¼-inch-thick coins (about 1 cup)
½ pound fresh broccoli florets (about 4 cups), no larger than ¾ inch across
Half of a small red onion, sliced into ⅛-inch-thick half-rings
¾ to 1 cup Italian vinaigrette dressing, homemade (page 99) or purchased
¼ cup shredded Romano or Parmesan cheese

Optional ingredients: *Choose* ***two, three or four:***

- **1 jar (6½ ounces) marinated artichoke hearts, drained and cut into bite-sized pieces**
- **1 jar (8 ounces) pickled mushrooms, drained**
- **1 can (2¼ ounces) sliced ripe olives, drained**
- **1 green or red bell pepper, cored, cut into 1-inch chunks**
- **1 to 2 cups cooked or drained canned garbanzo beans**
- **1 cup sliced raw celery (sliced ¼ inch thick before measuring)**
- **1 package (10 ounces) frozen Italian flat green beans, thawed (these will turn drab olive in color after marinating; you may want to stir these in just before serving to preserve color)**

Add cauliflower and carrots to a large pot of rapidly boiling salted water. Return to a rapid boil and cook 2 minutes. Drain, and rinse with cold water until vegetables are no longer warm; allow to drain for about 10 minutes, shaking strainer occasionally.

Combine well-drained vegetables, raw broccoli, onion slices and optional ingredients in a large mixing bowl; stir to combine. Add dressing and shredded cheese and stir again. Cover and refrigerate at least 2 hours, or as long as 2 days, stirring occasionally.

Even easier: Substitute a 1-pound bag of frozen broccoli-cauliflower-carrot mix for the fresh vegetables; thaw before combining with other ingredients (no need to cook the frozen vegetables).

Note that the broccoli in this mixture will turn olive-drab in color; the salad will not be as attractive, but it will still taste good.

CREAMED SPINACH

4 servings

An easy, tasty side dish that goes well with almost any grilled or roast meat.

1 package (10 ounces) frozen chopped spinach, thawed*
⅓ cup minced onion
3 tablespoons butter or margarine
2 tablespoons flour
1 cup milk (skim or 2% milk works fine)
½ teaspoon sugar
½ teaspoon salt
A pinch of nutmeg, optional
½ cup shredded cheddar or Colby cheese
French-fried onions for garnish, optional

Place spinach in a colander and allow to drain while you prepare the other ingredients. In heavy-bottomed saucepan, sauté onion in butter over medium heat, stirring frequently, until just tender. Sprinkle flour over the onions and stir vigorously to blend. Heat until mixture is bubbly, then reduce heat to medium-low and cook, stirring frequently, 5 minutes.

Add milk, sugar, salt and nutmeg to onion mixture, stirring to prevent lumps. Increase heat to medium and cook, stirring frequently, until mixture is bubbly and thickened. Meanwhile, press on spinach in colander to extract excess moisture. When sauce has thickened, add spinach and reduce heat to medium-low. Cook 5 minutes, stirring occasionally. Stir in cheese; cover and remove from heat. Let stand about 3 minutes, then stir before serving. Top with French-fried onions, if you like.

*If you have fresh spinach, chop it coarsely and steam just until done; then proceed as directed above. A pound of fresh spinach is about the right amount for this dish.

Sweet and Tangy Refrigerator Carrots

4 to 6 servings

This easy vegetable dish keeps very well for several days in the refrigerator. It's a great counterpoint to grilled meats.

1 can (8 ounces) tomato sauce
¼ cup sugar
¼ cup vegetable oil
⅓ cup cider vinegar
1 pound mini carrots, or peeled regular carrots cut into ½-inch chunks
Half of a small red onion
1 green bell pepper, cored, cut into ½ x 2-inch strips
Chopped parsley for garnish, optional

In nonaluminum saucepan, heat tomato sauce, sugar, oil and vinegar to boiling, stirring to dissolve sugar. Remove from heat; set aside. Cook carrots in microwave, steamer or boiling water until tender-crisp. Drain and refresh briefly with cold water. Meanwhile, cut the red onion half into thin wedges from top to bottom, then cut each wedge if necessary into pieces no longer than 2 inches (if the onion you're using was cut in half from top to bottom, then you will need to cut the wedges in half; however, if the onion you're using was cut in half across the middle, the wedges will already be the correct length). Combine onions, carrots, bell pepper and tomato sauce mixture in large mixing bowl; stir gently to combine. Cover and refrigerate until completely cold, stirring several times (if you keep this in the refrigerator for several days, stir once or twice a day). Garnish with chopped parsley before serving.

24-HOUR COLESLAW

6 to 8 servings

Prepare this the afternoon or evening before you head off for vacation. It will be ready to eat when you get to your destination, and keeps well for several days.

½ cup cider vinegar
3 tablespoons packed brown sugar
¾ teaspoon mixed pickling spices
1 teaspoon dry mustard powder
1 teaspoon salt
½ cup vegetable oil
5 cups finely chopped green and/or red cabbage (about half of a medium cabbage, or 12 ounces; you can use a 12-ounce package of pre-shredded coleslaw mix if you like)
½ cup shredded carrot
Half of a small onion, minced

In medium nonaluminum saucepan, heat vinegar, brown sugar and pickling spices to boiling; or, combine in microwave-safe dish and heat to boiling on HIGH. Remove from heat and allow to cool completely. Strain out and discard pickling spices through a paper coffee filter or paper towel placed in a strainer. Blend in mustard powder, salt and oil with a whisk (or whir all together in the blender). Combine dressing with cabbage, carrot and onion in large bowl, stirring well to combine. Cover and refrigerate 24 hours or longer. Stir well before serving.

TWICE-BAKED POTATOES

4 servings as written; easily prepared for any number of servings (one potato serves 2)

Also called Stuffed Potatoes, these tasty spuds go particularly well with grilled meats or Oven-Barbecued Ribs (page 354). Feel free to jazz them up with any of the optional ingredients listed—or with anything else that sounds good to you!

2 baking potatoes, about ¾ pound each
1 tablespoon butter or margarine, plus a little additional for topping
2 to 4 tablespoons milk
½ cup shredded Colby or other cheese
3 thinly sliced green onions, optional
1 teaspoon salt

Heat oven to 400°F. Scrub potato skins well, and prick each side of each potato several times with a fork. Place directly on oven rack (do not wrap in foil) and bake until tender when pierced with a fork, about 1 hour (if you are baking the potatoes with another dish at a different temperature, simply adjust the cooking time as necessary; at 300°F, for example, potatoes take 1½ to 1¾ hours to get done). Remove potatoes from the oven to cool slightly.

When potatoes are cool enough to handle, cut each in half the long way. Scoop most of the flesh out with a spoon (a grapefruit spoon works great, if you have one), leaving a thin but intact shell about ¼ inch thick or even thinner. Add the tablespoon of butter to the scooped-out flesh, and mash well. Add milk as needed to get a smooth, creamy consistency; stir in the cheese, green onions (or any other additions as noted below) and the salt. Divide the mashed potatoes evenly between the four shells, spreading it into an even mound. Top each with a few dabs of additional butter. At this point, the potatoes can be refrigerated, covered, as long as 2 days before final baking; or, they can be re-baked immediately.

When ready for final baking, heat oven to 375°F (or reduce temperature if cooking immediately after stuffing). Place potatoes in a single layer on a baking sheet or dish, and bake until the cheese melts and the top is beginning to brown. If the potatoes are still slightly warm when you re-bake them, this will take 25 to 30 minutes; if the potatoes have been refrigerated before re-baking, re-baking time will be 40 to 45 minutes.

Tasty additions:

Stir any of these into the mashed potatoes before stuffing the shells:

- Cooked, crumbled bacon (or imitation bacon bits)
- Chopped fresh chives or other herbs
- Minced cooked broccoli or other vegetable
- Crumbled French-fried onions

For another flavor variation, use cottage cheese or sour cream in place of the milk. Another idea is to top the stuffed potatoes with shredded cheese (rather than using the additional butter) before baking. Use your imagination!

TWICE-BAKED POTATOES ON THE GRILL

When you have the oven going for something else, pre-bake some potatoes, stuff them, and refrigerate for a day or two until you've got a grilled meal planned. Then, you can do the second baking on the grill.

Follow recipe on page 366, baking the potatoes in the oven for the preliminary baking. Stuff as directed, then wrap each potato half in buttered foil. Refrigerate a day or two if desired before final baking. Place the foil-wrapped potatoes in a cooler area of the grill (not directly over the hottest coals; and a covered grill works best for this) and cook until hot, 30 to 45 minutes; move the potatoes around occasionally on the grill to encourage even heating.

CHEESY POTATO GRATIN

4 to 6 servings

This luxurious dish uses a homemade cheese sauce, which takes just a few minutes to make. The flavor of the homemade sauce is so much better than canned cheese soup or pasteurized process cheese sauce that the extra step is worth it.

2 pounds baking potatoes (about 3 or 4 medium russets)
2 tablespoons butter or stick margarine
2 tablespoons flour
1 cup milk (reduced-fat works fine)
½ teaspoon salt
Several dashes of Tabasco sauce, optional
¾ cup shredded cheddar or other firm cheese (about 3 ounces)
¼ cup grated Parmesan or Romano cheese

Spray a 2-quart baking dish with nonstick spray, or butter lightly; set aside. Scrub potatoes and cook in a large pot of boiling water until just tender. Drain and set aside.

Heat oven to 350°F. In heavy-bottomed medium saucepan, melt butter over medium heat. Sprinkle flour gradually into the saucepan, stirring constantly with a whisk or fork. Cook, stirring constantly, until mixture turns light golden in color; this will take about 2 minutes. Add the milk, salt and Tabasco sauce, stirring constantly to prevent lumps; cook until mixture thickens and bubbles. Add shredded cheese slowly, stirring constantly, and cook until cheese melts. Remove from heat.

Peel potatoes (or leave unpeeled if you prefer) and slice ¼ inch thick. Arrange half the potatoes in the prepared baking dish; top with half the cheese sauce. Add remaining potatoes and cheese sauce. Sprinkle top with Parmesan cheese. Bake until bubbly and nicely browned, 25 to 35 minutes.

JANSSON'S TEMPTATION (POTATOES WITH CREAM AND ANCHOVIES)

4 to 6 servings

I don't know who Jansson is, but I can understand why he was tempted by this creamy, salty casserole. In Sweden, this is often served as a smörgåsbord dish, especially at holiday time; it is also a favorite late-night party snack.

¼ cup butter or margarine (half of a stick), divided
2½ to 3 pounds baking potatoes (about 5 or 6 medium russets)
2 medium onions, cut into halves from top to bottom and thinly sliced
1 can (3½ ounces) anchovy fillets, preferably Scandinavian
1 cup heavy cream
White pepper to taste
Fresh parsley sprigs for garnish, optional

Heat oven to 400°F; have a large pot of cold water ready. Generously butter a wide, shallow 2-quart casserole with about a teaspoon of the butter; set aside. Peel the potatoes and cut them into strips that are ¼ inch square and about 2 inches long; drop the strips into the cold water as you cut them.

In large skillet, sauté the onions in 2 tablespoons of the butter until just tender; remove from heat. Drain the juice from the anchovies and combine with the cream; chop the anchovies into ¼-inch pieces. Drain the potato strips and pat dry. Layer one-third of the potatoes in the casserole; top with one-half the onions and one-half the anchovies. Sprinkle lightly with white pepper. Repeat the layers, using half of the remaining potatoes and all remaining onions and anchovies; dust again with pepper. Arrange the remaining potatoes on top. Pour the cream mixture over the top; dot with the remaining butter. Bake until potatoes are tender, the top is golden brown and most of the liquid is absorbed, 45 to 55 minutes. Serve warm; garnish with fresh parsley sprigs.

Scalloped Hashbrowns

Servings as listed below

Ingredient	Small: 4 to 5 servings	Large: 6 to 8 servings
Diced onion	¾ cup	1¼ cups
Butter, margarine or vegetable oil	2 tablespoons	3 tablespoons
Flour	2 tablespoons	3 tablespoons
Half-and-half or evaporated skim milk	¾ cup	1¼ cups
Sour cream (light sour cream works fine)	1 cup (8 oz.)	2 cups (16 oz.)
Frozen shredded potatoes, thawed*	3¼ cups	5½ cups
Shredded Colby or other cheese	1¼ cups	2 cups

*A 2-pound bag of frozen shredded potatoes is about 5½ cups. You may also use fresh potatoes; shred as thickly as possible, so the shreds are not too watery.

Baking dish sizes: For small dish, use an 8- or 9-inch-square baking dish or a wide, flat 2-quart casserole. For large dish, use 13x9-inch baking dish or a wide, flat 4-quart casserole.

Heat oven to 350°F (325°F for glass baking dish). In medium skillet, cook onions in butter over medium heat until just tender, stirring occasionally. Add the flour, stirring constantly to prevent lumps, and cook, stirring constantly, about 1 minute. Stir in the half-and-half and cook, stirring constantly, until slightly thickened. Remove from heat and stir in sour cream.

Spray baking dish with nonstick cooking spray. Distribute half the potatoes in dish. Sprinkle generously with salt and pepper, then top with half the cheese and half the sauce. Repeat layers, ending with sauce; smooth sauce on top. Bake until golden brown and bubbly, 35 to 45 minutes.

Make-ahead note: You may layer all ingredients in the casserole, then cover and refrigerate as long as several hours. Uncover before baking, and add about 15 minutes to the baking time.

MY GRANDFATHER'S SPAGHETTI WITH GARLIC AND HOT PEPPERS

4 to 6 servings

My grandfather was born in the Abruzzi region of Italy (basically, across the mountains from Rome). This quick-and-easy pasta dish, which is called Spaghetti con Aglio, Olio e Pepperoncini *in Italian) is traditional to that region of Italy. It's one of my all-time favorite cabin meals … a plate of* aglio-olio, *some vegetables and a loaf of bread, and I am happy. But it also makes a fine side dish with grilled burgers or chicken. By the way, the proper pronunciation is "ALL-yo, OHL-yo eh pepper-on-CHEE-nee."*

One-half to a whole head of garlic
2 or 3 dried hot peppers, or ¼ to ½ teaspoon crushed dried hot red pepper flakes
⅔ cup olive oil, plus a little extra if needed
½ teaspoon salt
1 pound spaghetti (uncooked; you may use linguini if you prefer)
Freshly grated Parmesan or Romano cheese for serving

Peel the garlic cloves. Chop the garlic finely; a food processor makes quick work of this, but you can also do it by hand, as my grandfather did. Pull off and discard the stem ends of the dried hot peppers, and gently roll the peppers to dislodge the seeds; discard the seeds. Add the oil, chopped garlic and salt to a small skillet. Crumble the peppers into the skillet; wear rubber gloves if you are sensitive to hot-pepper oil. (If you are using a food processor to chop the garlic, you may add the deseeded peppers along with the garlic and chop them together.) Heat the oil mixture over medium heat until the oil just begins to bubble; reduce heat immediately and cook a minute or two, stirring frequently. Do not let the garlic get browned, as this makes it bitter; you simply want to cook it gently. Remove the skillet from the heat; set aside.

Heat a very large pot of salted water to boiling. Add the spaghetti slowly, stirring constantly to prevent sticking. Cook, stirring very frequently at first and less often after a while, until the pasta is tender yet still has a firm bite. Drain and return the pasta to the pot. Add the oil mixture and stir well to coat; if it seems too dry, add a little more oil. Serve with grated Parmesan cheese on the side.

MACARONI AND CHEESE CASSEROLE

6 servings

When you want something different from the stuff in the blue box, try this custard-style macaroni and cheese. It's not as creamy as some macaroni and cheese dishes.

8 ounces macaroni or small shell pasta (uncooked; about 2 cups)
1 tablespoon butter
3 cups grated sharp cheddar cheese, divided
1 egg
1 teaspoon dry mustard powder
1¾ teaspoons celery salt or plain salt
1½ cups whole milk
¼ teaspoon Tabasco sauce

Heat oven to 350°F. Spray 3-quart casserole or baking dish with nonstick spray, or coat with a little butter or oil; set aside. Cook macaroni in boiling salted water until just tender. Drain and let stand in the strainer for a minute or two. Transfer to prepared casserole; add the butter and stir until the butter melts. Stir in 2 cups of the cheese. In mixing bowl, whisk together egg, dry mustard and celery salt. Add milk and Tabasco sauce. Pour mixture over macaroni in casserole; stir gently. Top with remaining 1 cup cheese. Cover and bake 30 minutes. Remove cover and bake 20 minutes longer, or until bubbly.

BEER-HERB QUICK BREAD

1 loaf

Slightly sweet, this bread has a mild flavor that works well with most soups, salads or meat dishes. Slices make fantastic toast the day after baking; keep it refrigerated after the first day and slice it as you're ready to toast it.

2½ cups flour
3 tablespoons sugar
1 tablespoon baking powder
1 tablespoon chopped fresh parsley, or 1 teaspoon dried
1 tablespoon snipped fresh chives, or 1 teaspoon dried
1 teaspoon minced fresh marjoram leaves, or ½ teaspoon dried
1 can or bottle (12 ounces) beer; try a darker beer for more flavor
1 egg
2 tablespoons butter, melted

Heat oven to 350°F. Spray a standard loaf pan (9½x5x3 inches) with nonstick spray, or butter lightly; set aside. In mixing bowl, combine flour, sugar and baking powder; mix well with a fork (if you have a flour sifter, simply sift the ingredients together into the bowl). Add the parsley, chives and marjoram, and stir until the herbs are coated with flour. In measuring cup or small bowl, combine beer, egg and melted butter; beat with a fork. Add the beer mixture to the flour mixture and stir just until blended. Pour the mixture into the prepared loaf pan and smooth the top slightly. Bake 40 to 50 minutes, or until the top is lightly browned and a toothpick inserted into the center comes out clean. Cool completely before slicing.

Desserts and Sweets

QUICK POPPY SEED BREAD

1 loaf

If your sweet tooth suddenly needs something, you can run to the local convenience store in even the smallest town and get the ingredients for this easy bread. You can probably even find foil loaf pans, which work just fine.

3 eggs
½ cup cold water
¼ cup vegetable oil
1 tablespoons poppy seeds
1 small package (one-layer size, about 9 ounces) yellow cake mix
1 package (3.4 ounces) instant lemon pudding mix
Butter-Rum Glaze (facing page), optional

Heat oven to 350°F. Spray a standard loaf pan (9½x5x3 inches) with nonstick spray, or butter lightly. If you have a little flour, sprinkle a tablespoon into the pan and shake it around to coat, then dump out excess flour; otherwise, use just a little of the cake mix in the same way, dumping the excess into a large mixing bowl.

In large mixing bowl, beat together eggs, water and oil with an electric mixer, whisk, or fork; stir in poppy seeds. Add cake mix and pudding mix, then beat 3 minutes with electric mixer or about 4 minutes with whisk or mixing spoon; the batter should be smooth and creamy. Pour into prepared pan. Bake until a toothpick inserted in the center of the bread comes out clean, 45 to 55 minutes. Cool 15 minutes on a wire rack before turning bread out. If using Butter-Rum Glaze, prick the top of the cooled bread with a fork and drizzle the warm glaze evenly over the loaf. As the glaze cools, spoon the excess that pools around the bottom of the loaf back on top.

BUTTER-RUM GLAZE

¼ cup butter (half of a stick)
¼ cup Bacardi Limón rum or plain rum
3 tablespoons sugar

In heavy-bottomed small saucepan, heat butter and rum over medium-low heat until butter melts. Stir in sugar. Increase heat to medium and the mixture until it becomes foamy, stirring constantly. Continue to cook and stir constantly to a count of 100 ("one-thousand-one, one-thousand-two ..."). Remove from heat and allow the foam to die down before using to glaze the bread. Safety note: Although unlikely, it's possible that the rum will ignite, especially during the first part of cooking when the alcohol is burning off. Pay attention, use a long-handled spoon for stirring, and keep long hair or anything flammable out of the way.

PINEAPPLE UPSIDE-DOWN CUPCAKES

6 or 7 cupcakes

A fun new twist on an old favorite! Kids love these individual upside-down cakes and will also enjoy helping in the kitchen when they're being made. A popover pan is ideal for this because the cups are deeper than a standard cupcake pan; the cake mix makes a bit more batter than fits comfortably into 6 regular cupcake cups. If you have an 8-cup cupcake pan, use that and make 7 of these; fill the eighth cup half-full with water to prevent scorching. If all you have is a 6-cup cupcake pan, don't use quite all the batter; spoon the rest into a greased custard cup and bake as a plain cupcake.

3 tablespoons butter or margarine, melted
3 tablespoons cup packed brown sugar
3 maraschino cherries, halved
Half of an 8-ounce can pineapple chunks packed in juice
2 tablespoons chopped pecan pieces, optional
1 small box (9 ounces) yellow cake mix
1 egg

Heat oven to 350°F. Spray an 8-cup cupcake pan, or a 6-cup popover pan, with nonstick spray. Divide the melted butter evenly between the cups; each will get about 1½ teaspoons. Sprinkle about 1½ teaspoons brown sugar over the bottom of each cup. Place a cherry, cut-side up, in the center of each cup. Drain pineapple chunks, reserving 2 tablespoons juice; cut pineapple chunks in half. Divide pineapple evenly among the cups. Sprinkle about 1 teaspoon chopped pecans into each cup.

In mixing bowl, combine cake mix, egg, reserved pineapple juice and 2 tablespoons water. Beat well with hand mixer, or beat by hand for 300 strokes. Pour mixture evenly into cups as noted above. Bake 23 to 28 minutes, or until cake springs back when touched lightly. Cool the pan on a wire rack 3 or 4 minutes. Loosen the edges of each cupcake with a table knife. Place a small baking sheet* on top of the pan and invert, holding the pan and baking sheet together carefully. Let stand about 2 minutes before carefully lifting the pan off.

*If you don't have a small baking sheet, any large, flat pan or platter will work. In a pinch, you could even cover a piece of corrugated cardboard with foil; spray lightly with nonstick spray before using to prevent the cupcakes from sticking.

Saltine Toffee Cookies

40 cookies

My grandmother gave me this recipe when I was a kid, and it's been a favorite of mine ever since. The saltines have just enough salt to cut some of the richness of the toffee ingredients, and these ingredients are available everywhere.

1 box saltine crackers (you won't need the whole box)
½ pound butter or stick margarine (2 sticks)
1 cup packed brown sugar
1½ cups semisweet chocolate chips (three-quarters of a 12-ounce bag)
1 cup finely chopped pecans or cashews

Heat oven to 350°F. Line a cookie sheet with foil. Arrange the crackers snugly in a single layer, filling the sheet completely; this will probably take about 40 crackers. In a saucepan, melt the butter over medium-low heat (or melt in the microwave at MEDIUM/50% power). Add the brown sugar and stir until well mixed. Pour the butter mixture evenly over the crackers, spreading as necessary. Bake 8 to 10 minutes, or until the butter is bubbly. Remove the sheet from the oven and sprinkle the chocolate chips evenly over the crackers. When the chips have softened (in about 2 minutes), spread them over the crackers with a knife. Sprinkle immediately with nuts. Let the cookies cool 5 to 10 minutes, then use a spatula to cut between the individual crackers and transfer them to a plate in a single layer. The cookies need to be warm when you remove them from the pan; if they cool too much, they won't come away from the foil. To solve this problem, place the pan back into the warm oven for a minute or two, then promptly remove the cookies.

Rice Krispie Bars with Variations

24 pieces

Originally called Marshmallow Treats, these crispy bars have been pleasing kids—and grownups, for that matter—for decades. The original recipe follows, along with some variations you might like to try.

¼ cup stick margarine or butter (half of a stick), plus a tablespoon for buttering 9x13-inch dish
1 bag (10.5 ounces) regular-sized or mini marshmallows
5 cups Kellogg's Rice Krispies cereal

Butter a 9x13-inch baking dish generously; set aside. In 3-quart saucepan, melt margarine over low heat. Add marshmallows and cook, stirring constantly, until marshmallows are completely melted and mixture is smooth. Remove from heat and add cereal; stir until well coated. Press evenly into buttered dish, patting with a buttered spatula. Cool completely, and cut into 2-inch squares.

Marshmallow Creme Krispie Bars: Substitute a 1-pint jar (2 cups) marshmallow creme for marshmallows. Add to melted margarine, stirring until well blended. Cook 5 minutes longer, stirring constantly. Proceed as directed.

Peanut Butter Krispie Bars: Add ¼ cup smooth peanut butter to marshmallow mixture after removing the mixture from the heat; stir until well mixed. Proceed as directed.

Jumble Krispie Bars: Add ⅔ cup salted cocktail peanuts and ⅔ cup M&M candies to the marshmallow mixture along with the cereal. Proceed as directed.

Loopy Marshmallow Bars: Substitute 6 cups Froot Loops or Cheerios for the Rice Krispies. Proceed as directed.

Caramel Krispie Bars: Use two 10.5-ounce packages mini marshmallows. Increase margarine to ¾ cup (plus 1 tablespoon for greasing dish). Increase cereal to 8 cups. You'll also need a 14-ounce package caramel candies and a 14-ounce can sweetened condensed milk. To make, heat ¼ cup margarine, the caramels and sweetened condensed milk in a medium saucepan over medium heat until the caramels melt, stirring constantly; keep warm. Melt remaining ½ cup margarine in 3-quart saucepan and add 1½ bags mini marshmallows; cook as directed above. Pat two-thirds of the cereal mixture into the prepared pan; top with remaining mini marshmallows. Pour caramel mixture over marshmallows, then top with remaining cereal mixture. Cool completely, and cut into squares.

Beverages and Miscellaneous

BRANDY SLUSH

About 1 gallon slush; enough for about 20 servings

You'll need a big place in the freezer for this slush, which has to freeze 24 hours before it's ready to use. In Minnesota, we sometimes make this for winter holiday parties, and just put the pail of mix in a protected snowbank to chill.

9 cups cold water
2 cups sugar
4 Lipton's or other tea bags
3 cups brandy
1 can (12 ounces) frozen lemonade concentrate
1 can (12 ounces) frozen orange juice concentrate
Ginger ale for serving

In large saucepan, combine 7 cups cold water and the 2 cups sugar. Heat to boiling and cook, stirring frequently, until the sugar dissolves. Set aside to cool. In a small pan, heat remaining 2 cups water to boiling. Add tea bags and immediately remove from heat. Steep 5 minutes, then remove and discard tea bags. Set tea aside to cool. When both sugar water and tea have cooled completely, combine with all remaining ingredients except ginger ale in a clean 1-gallon ice cream bucket (or other lidded container). Stir to mix well. Place in freezer and freeze at least 24 hours, stirring occasionally. To serve, fill a glass three-quarters full with slush, then top off with ginger ale.

TROPICAL SLUSH

About 1 gallon slush; enough for about 20 servings

This is similar to the slush on page 379, but has a tropical flair.

1 quart apricot nectar
1 quart pineapple juice
1 can (12 ounces) frozen lemonade concentrate
1 can (12 ounces) frozen orange juice concentrate
1 pint (2 cups) apricot brandy
2 cups gin or vodka
Lemon-lime soda for serving

Combine all ingredients except lemon-lime soda in a clean 1-gallon ice cream bucket (or other lidded container). Stir to mix well. Place in freezer and freeze at least 24 hours, stirring occasionally. To serve, fill a glass three-quarters full with slush, then top off with lemon-lime soda.

HOT BUTTERED RUM

Per serving

When you've been out skiing or enjoying other outdoor winter activities, nothing eases weary bones like a mug of hot buttered rum. This simple version uses pantry staples … that is, if rum is a staple for you!

1 jigger rum (dark rum is very good)
1 teaspoon packed brown sugar or honey, optional
¾ cup boiling water
¼ to ½ teaspoon butter
A thin slice of lemon

Pour rum into a heatproof mug; add brown sugar and stir until blended. Add boiling water and stir well. Float the butter and a lemon slice on top, and serve.

MEXICAN COFFEE

6 or 7 servings

Cinnamon-spiked coffee smells great as it brews. Be sure to use dark-roast coffee grounds; the coffee needs to be very full-flavored for this because it gets diluted with the other ingredients.

1 cup dark-roast coffee grounds
2 teaspoons cinnamon
6 cups cold water
1¼ cups whole milk or half-and-half
4 squares bittersweet baking chocolate, or ½ cup powdered cocoa such as Hershey's
⅓ cup sugar
Whipped cream, and nutmeg for garnish

Place coffee and cinnamon in filter basket of drip coffee maker; fill coffee maker with 6 cups cold water. Brew as usual. Meanwhile, combine the milk, chocolate squares and sugar in a saucepan and heat over low heat, stirring frequently, until the chocolate melts and the sugar dissolves (if using powdered cocoa, stir the mixture very vigorously with a whisk or fork to blend before placing on the heat). Combine the milk mixture with the brewed coffee, and pour into individual serving mugs. Top each with a dollop of whipped cream; sprinkle with nutmeg.

MEXICAN COFFEE WITH A KICK

Follow recipe above, using half-and-half but reducing to 1 cup and using only 2 squares chocolate (or ¼ cup powdered cocoa). Heat half-and-half, chocolate and sugar as directed. When combining the half-and-half mixture with the brewed coffee, add ¼ cup Kahlúa or other chocolate liqueur.

Kids in the Kitchen

There are lots of fun things kids can do in the kitchen on a cold, nasty day. Following are five boredom-busting "recipes."

Cinnamon Ornaments

12 to 18 ornaments, depending on size

I first saw this recipe, which I have modified only slightly, in an ad for—what else—Schilling cinnamon! It's great fun for kids to make this on a cold winter evening, and the ornaments will stay fragrant for a very long time. After the holiday season, wrap the ornaments in foil and store in plastic containers to keep them from crumbling.

¾ cup applesauce, plus a tablespoon or two more if needed
1 bottle (4.12 ounces) Schilling/McCormick cinnamon
Decorative ribbon for hanging

Heat oven to lowest setting possible. Mix applesauce and cinnamon to form a stiff dough; if it is too crumbly, add additional applesauce, a teaspoon at a time, until the dough holds its shape when pressed together with your hands. Roll out to ¼ inch thickness and cut with cookie cutters; re-roll as many times as you need to. Use a straw, chopstick or small knife to make a hole in the top of the ornament (this is easiest to do before you remove the cookie cutter from the ornament; the cookie cutter prevents unsightly bulging when you poke the hole into the ornament).

Use a spatula to lift the ornaments onto a cake-cooling rack that has been set on a baking sheet. Place in oven; prop oven door open with a ball of foil or an empty can, and bake at lowest setting until ornaments are hard and dry, 3 to 5 hours. String ribbon through holes for hanging (I like to use about 20 inches of curling ribbon, and tie a knot so there is about 6 inches of excess ribbon on both ends above the knot; then, I curl the ribbon so the curls will festoon over the ornament when it is hung).

Dehydrator option: A food dehydrator makes quick work of drying these ornaments. Place cut-out ornaments on dehydrator trays, and dry at LOW setting until ornaments are hard and dry; this will take from 1 to 3 hours, depending on your dehydrator.

Air-dry option: Place cut-out shapes on cake-cooling rack and air-dry 1 to 2 days, or until thoroughly dry. Don't try to air-dry these if it's extremely humid; they may spoil before they dry.

Play-dough

- 2 cups flour
- ½ cup salt
- 2 tablespoons cream of tartar (in the baking or spice aisle)
- 2 cups water
- 1 tablespoon vegetable oil
- Food coloring

In a large bowl, stir together the flour, salt and cream of tartar, mixing very well. In a large pot, heat the water to boiling; stir in the oil and food coloring. Add the flour mixture, stirring constantly, and cook over medium heat until the mixture forms a ball. Remove from heat and let cool. Transfer the ball of dough to the countertop and knead for a few minutes. Store in an airtight container.

Finger paint

- 1 cup laundry starch
- 5 cups boiling water
- ½ cup Ivory Snow flakes
- Food coloring

In a large bowl, mix the laundry starch with enough cold water to form a smooth paste. Add the starch mixture to the boiling water and cook, stirring frequently, until it is thick and glossy. Remove from heat and stir in the soap flakes. Divide the mixture into 3 or 4 smaller batches, and add food coloring to each batch. Store in airtight containers for up to a week.

Pomander Balls

These make nice holiday gifts and are one of those homemade gifts that people actually enjoy!

For each pomander:

1 box whole cloves
1 whole apple, orange, lemon or lime
Thin decorative ribbon (about 1 yard)
1 whole cinnamon stick, optional

Push the cloves into the fruit, keeping them as close together as possible but leaving 4 clear strips, one on each side of the fruit, for a ribbon to go around. If the rind of the citrus fruit is too difficult to puncture, have an older child (or yourself) puncture starter holes with an ice or nut pick, but be careful! When the fruit is covered with cloves, dry the clear strips with a cotton swab and tie the ribbon around the fruit. Tie the cinnamon stick at the top of the fruit, and make a loop for hanging.

STRING BALLOONS

Liquid laundry starch
Colored embroidery thread or light string
Balloons

Line the table with a lot of newspaper, as this is messy! Place the laundry starch in a bowl, and spool the embroidery thread or string into the starch; let it sit, stirring occasionally, for a few minutes so the string is completely saturated. Blow up and tie off a balloon. Now let each kid wrap the wet string around a balloon in a crisscross fashion until the balloon is lacy-looking. Let the balloon dry completely, which could take a day or so; then, pop the balloon and pull the deflated rubber out through one of the gaps between the strings. Hang the finished string balloon from the ceiling.

INDEX

A

B

C

D

H

I

J

K

L

M

N

O

P

Q

R

S